OXFORD STUDIES IN POSTCOLONIAL LITERATURES

The *Oxford Studies in Postcolonial Literatures* aim to offer stimulating and accessible introductions to definitive topics and key genres and regions within the rapidly diversifying field of postcolonial literary studies in English.

Under the general editorship of Professor Elleke Boehmer, the *Studies* in each case elucidate and explicate the informing contexts of postcolonial texts, and plot the historical and cultural co-ordinates of writers and of the leading movements, institutions, and cultural debates situated within those contexts. Individual volumes reflect in particular on the shaping effect both of international theory and of local politics on postcolonial traditions often viewed as uniformly cross-cultural, and also on the influence of postcolonial writing on the protocols of international theory. Throughout, the focus is on how texts formally engage with the legacies of imperial and anti-imperial history.

OXFORD STUDIES IN POSTCOLONIAL LITERATURES
IN ENGLISH

GENERAL EDITOR: ELLEKE BOEHMER

THE INDIAN ENGLISH NOVEL

Nation, History, and Narration

Priyamvada Gopal

OXFORD
UNIVERSITY PRESS

OXFORD

UNIVERSITY PRESS

Great Clarendon Street, Oxford OX2 6DP

Oxford University Press is a department of the University of Oxford.
It furthers the University's objective of excellence in research, scholarship,
and education by publishing worldwide in

Oxford New York

Auckland Cape Town Dar es Salaam Hong Kong Karachi
Kuala Lumpur Madrid Melbourne Mexico City Nairobi
New Delhi Shanghai Taipei Toronto

With offices in

Argentina Austria Brazil Chile Czech Republic France Greece
Guatemala Hungary Italy Japan Poland Portugal Singapore
South Korea Switzerland Thailand Turkey Ukraine Vietnam

Oxford is a registered trade mark of Oxford University Press
in the UK and in certain other countries

Published in the United States
by Oxford University Press Inc., New York

© Priyamvada Gopal 2009

The moral rights of the author have been asserted
Database right Oxford University Press (maker)

First published 2009

British Library Cataloguing in Publication Data

Data available

Library of Congress Cataloging in Publication Data

Data available

Typeset by
SPI Publisher Services, Pondicherry, India
Printed in Great Britain
on acid-free paper by
the MPG Books Group in the UK

ISBN 978–0–19–954437–0 (Pbk.)
978–0–19–954438–7 (Hbk.)

1 3 5 7 9 10 8 6 4 2

ACKNOWLEDGEMENTS

With gratitude to: Elleke Boehmer, for helpful suggestions and great generosity; the editors at OUP for letting me try their patience; Meenakshi Mukherjee, for paving the way through her scholarship; the University of Cambridge and Churchill College for a term's leave; Chris Warnes for collegiality and picking up the slack; Michael Perfect for research assistance; Benita Parry for getting on my case; Anny King for spaghetti and company; my family and friends for their love and support; my barista friends for caffeine and good cheer; Hailey O'Harrow and Sam Dean for troubleshooting; Susan Daruvala and Sundeep Dougal for invaluable references; Sylvie Jaffrey for excellent copy editing; and finally, my remarkable students on whom these chapters were first tried out. They were the best interlocutors I could have asked for.

CONTENTS

Timeline   ix
Maps   xxi

Introduction: Ideas of India   1

1 Making English India   11

Writing nation and history   13
Anglicizing India: project and response   15
Bilingual self-fashioning   17
Two early historical novels   20

2 Ethnography, Gender, and Nation   25

The first anglophone novel: *Rajmohan's Wife*   28
Sacred nationhood: *Anandamath*   31
Woman, nation, and idolatry: *The Home and the World*   34
Women and self-representation: *Kamala and Saguna*   39

3 'Mahatma-Magic': Gandhi and Literary India   43

Mythmaking: *Kanthapura*   46
The machine: Mulk Raj Anand's *Untouchable*   50
All Gandhi's men: *Waiting for the Mahatma*   54
Spiritual leadership and self-knowledge: *The Guide*   57
The perils of performance: *He Who Rides a Tiger*   61
Colonial legend to postcolonial touchstone:
    Gandhi in Nayantara Sahgal's novels   63
Great Indian soul and *The Great Indian Novel*   67

4 Writing Partition   69

Witnessing the past: *Train to Pakistan*   70
Gender and the romance of nation: *The Heart Divided*   72
Violence and the Other: *Ice-Candy-Man* and *Noor*   75
Fragmented nations, divided histories: *Shame*   78

Othering the self: *The Shadow Lines*   81
Writing the counterfactual: *Looking Through Glass*   82
Reconstructing historiography: *In an Antique Land*   86

5 Midnight's Legacies: Two Epic Novels of Nation   90

Intertexts: Hatterr and Trotter   92
A thousand and one possibilities: *Midnight's Children*   94
Middle-class self-fashioning: *A Suitable Boy*   105

6 Bombay and the Novel   116

Real and imagined citizens: *Such a Long Journey*   119
The story-factory: *A Fine Balance*   121
Millenarian dreams: *The Death of Vishnu*   125
Whose home? *Baumgartner's Bombay*   126
The urban and the pastoral: *Tara Lane*   129
In praise of the bastard: *The Moor's Last Sigh*   130
Meditations on neighbours: *Ravan and Eddie*   135

7 Family Matters: Domesticity and Gender in the Novel   139

Narrating change: *Sunlight on a Broken Column*   140
Outside history: *Twilight in Delhi*   144
Pushing the perimeter: *The Walled City*   145
The woman I am now: *Difficult Daughters*   148
Tragic transformations: *Family Matters*   149
'Irrelevant, middle class'? Shashi Deshpande
    and Anita Desai   151
Of 'Small Things'   155

8 Imagining 'Origins': The Literature of Migration   160

The making of a diaspora   161
The Caribbean: *A House for Mr Biswas*   162
England: *The Satanic Verses*   165
Britain: *The Buddha of Suburbia*   170
Kenya: *The In-Between World of Vikram Lall*   172
United States: *Jasmine*   174

Conclusion: The Contemporary Scene   177

Notes   188
Bibliography   193
Index   205

INDIAN TIMELINE

Year	Historical event	Key anglophone novels and related works
1757	Battle of Plassey which gives the victorious British East India Company control of the Diwani of Bengal by 1765. The Bengali poet Nabin Chandra Sen proclaims 'a night of eternal gloom for India'.	
1760–84	Years of plunder and war with various rulers ensue, giving the Company control of large portions of the land over time. Vast sums are drained from Bengal, 'not to know peace again until it had been bled white', as some contemporary British historians put it.	
1784	The India Act brings the East India Company under Crown control.	
1793	Permanent Settlement fixes land revenue and creates landlordism, depriving cultivators of customary rights.	
1800	Establishment of Fort William College, and Serampore Mission and Press.	
1813	Charter Act ends Company, monopoly on trade with India, and Crown control of territorial acquisitions. Debates begin on educational policy in India.	

(Contd.)

INDIAN TIMELINE

Year	Historical event	Key anglophone novels and related works
1815	Establishment of Bombay Education Society for English education.	
1817	Hindu College established in Calcutta to provide an English education to upper-caste Hindu elites.	Rammohan Roy, *A Defence of Hindoo Theism*.
1828	Brahmo Samaj founded.	Henry Derozio, *The Fakeer of Jungheera* (long poem).
		Calcutta Literary Gazette started by Derozio.
1829	Sati prohibited.	
1833		
1835	Macaulay, Minute on Indian Education and Bentinck, Education Act. English is made language of instruction in government schools and colleges.	K. C. Dutt, *A Journal of Forty Eight Hours of the Year 1945*.
1845		S. C. Dutt, *The Republic of Orissa: A Page from the Annals of the Twentieth Century*.
1849	Bethune School for Girls founded in Calcutta.	
1855	Santal uprising and brutal suppression with 25,000 killed.	
1857	First War of Independence, known by the British as the 'Sepoy Mutiny'. Establishment of Universities of Madras, Calcutta, and Bombay.	
1858	India Act transfers power from East India Company to Crown. Last Mughal emperor, Bahadur Shah Zafar, deported to Rangoon.	*Indian Field* magazine founded.

1859		Revolt of indigo growers against planter exploitation.
1860		Dinabandhu Mitra, *Nildarpan* (Bengali, *In the Mirror of Indigo*). English translation proscribed.
1863	Founding of Mohameddan Literary Society.	
1864		Bankim Chandra Chatterjee, *Rajmohan's Wife*, serialized in *Indian Field*. Bankim, *Durgeshnandini* (Bengali).
1865	Millions die in Orissa Famine.	
1866	Indian Reform Association founded.	
1870		
1872	Revolt of 'raiyats' or tenant farmers in Pabna, Bengal.	
1874		Lal Behari Day, *Govinda Samanta or The History of a Bengali Raiyat*.
1875	Founding of Arya Samaj; Muhammedan Anglo-Oriental College established in Aligarh.	
1876	Inauguration of Bharat Sabha or Indian Association to promote nationalist awareness.	Toru Dutt, *A Sheaf Gleaned in French Fields*.
1878		Toru Dutt, *Bianca, or the Young Spanish Maiden* serialized.
1882		Bankim Chandra Chatterjee, *Anandamath* (Bengali, *The Sacred Brotherhood*).
1883		S. C. Dutt, *The Young Zamindar*.

(Contd.)

INDIAN TIMELINE

Year	Historical event	Key anglophone novels and related works
1885	Founding of the Indian National Congress (INC) in Bombay.	
1889		O. Chandu Menon, *Indulekha*, based on Disraeli's *Henrietta Temple*, published in Malayalam.
1895		Krupabai Satthianadhan, *Kamala, a story of a Hindu Life*, and *Saguna, a Story of Native Christian Life*.
1897		Fakir Mohan Senapati, *Cha Mana Ana Guntha* (Oriya, *Six Acres and a Half*), serialized.
1899	Munda uprising against British in Ranchi.	Mir Hadi Ruswa, *Umrao Jan Ada* (Urdu).
1900		R. C. Dutt, *The Ramayana and the Mahabharata: The Great Epics of Ancient India Condensed into English Verse*.
1901		Cornelia Sorabji, *Love and Life Behind the Purdah*.
1903	Delhi Durbar crowning Edward VII Emperor of India.	T. R. Pillai; *Padmini: An Indian Romance*; K. K. Sinha, *Sanjogita or The Princess of Aryavarta*. Tagore, *Chokher Bali*; A. Madhaviah, *Thillai Govindan*.
1905	Partition of Bengal along communal lines. Swadeshi movement is inaugurated.	Rokeya Sakhawat Hossain, *Sultana's Dream*.
1906	All-India Muslim League founded.	
1908		Sorabji, *Between the Twilights*.

1909	Morley Minto Reforms introduce separate electorates for Muslims in legislative councils	Tagore, *Gitanjali* (Bengali, poems); Gandhi, *Hind Swaraj* (English version).
1910	Partition of Bengal revoked.	
1911	Nobel Prize for Literature bestowed on Tagore.	
1913	Gadar Revolutionary Party established in USA.	
1914	European 'Great War'.	Rabindranath Tagore, *Ghare Bhaire* (Bengali), written and serialized between 1915 and 1916; A. Madhaviah, *Clarinda*.
1915	Gandhi returns to India; Tagore is knighted and travels to Japan and America to give lectures on 'Nationalism'.	
1917	October revolution in Russia. Gandhi starts Champaran Satyagraha to protest against indigo planter exploitation.	Sarojini Naidu, *The Broken Wing* (poems); Sarat Chandra Chatterjee, *Devdas* and *Srikanta* (Bengali) (serialized).
1919	Gandhi assumes leadership of the INC. Protests against Rowlatt Act; Jallianwala Bagh Massacre in April. Tagore gives up knighthood; Khilafat movement against dismemberment of Turkish empire unites Hindu and Muslim nationalists.	
1921	Non-Cooperation movement launched by Gandhi.	

(Contd.)

Year	Historical event	Key anglophone novels and related works
1922	Violence at Chauri Chaura police station results in Gandhi calling off Non-Cooperation.	
1923		V. Savarkar, *Hindutva* (Marathi); Premchand, *Nirmala* (Hindi).
1924		Premchand, *Rangbhumi* (Hindi/Urdu).
1925	Formation of Rashtriya Swayamsevak Sangh (RSS); Dravidian Self-Respect movement against Brahmin domination launched.	
1926		Sarat Chandra, *Pather Dabi* (Bengali, *The Right of Way*).
1927	Second Non-Cooperation movement launched.	K. S. Venkataramani, *Murugan, the Tiller*.
1930	Second Civil Disobedience movement launched by Gandhi. Famous Dandi March to break Salt Laws.	Premchand, *Gaban* (Hindi/Urdu).
1932		Publication of *Angarey* (Urdu, *Live Coals*). All copies confiscated under Section 298 of the Indian Penal Code.
1934		K.S. Venkataramani, *Kandan the Patriot*; Tagore, *Char Adhyaya* (Bengali, *Four Chapters*); Cornelia Sorabji, *India Calling*.
1935	India Act gives limited central government and autonomy to provinces.	Anand, *Untouchable*; Narayan, *Swami and Friends*.

Year	Events	Literary Works
1936	Founding conference of the All-India Progressive Writers Association (PWA)	Jawaharlal Nehru, *Autobiography*; Premchand, *Godan* (Hindi, *The Gift of a Cow*); Anand, *Coolie*.
1937	League against Fascism and War established with Tagore as President.	K. Nagarajan, *Athawar House*; R. K. Narayan, *The Bachelor of Arts*; Anand, *Two Leaves and a Bud*.
1938		Narayan, *The Dark Room*; Raja Rao, *Kanthapura*.
1939	World War II breaks out. Congress governments resign as Government declares India is at war without consultation.	Anand, *The Village* (first of war trilogy).
1942	Quit India resolution passed by the Congress under Gandhi. All-India Depressed Classes Conference presided over by Dr B. R. Ambedkar.	Narayan, *Malgudi Days* (short stories); Anand, *The Sword and the Sickle* (last in war trilogy).
1943	Bengal Famine in which over three million people die by 1944	K. A. Abbas, *Tomorrow is Ours: A Novel of the India of Today*.
1944		Iqbalunnisa Hussain, *Purdah and Polygamy: Life in an Indian Muslim Household*.
1945	World War II ends. Trial of members of the Indian National Army. Widespread protests and demonstrations to demand their release.	Santha Rama Rau, *Home to India*; Anand, *The Big Heart*; Humayun Kabir, *Men and Rivers*; Gopinath Mohanty, *Paraja* (Oriya); Ismat Chughtai, *Terhi Lakir* (Urdu, *The Crooked Line*).
1946	Widespread labour unrest and strikes. Naval ratings revolt; strikes in armed forces. Britain sends Cabinet Mission to India to negotiate terms of transfer of power. Plans for Partition announced; communal riots spread. Gandhi fasts and brings temporary halt to rioting in Noakhali.	Anand, autobiography, *Apology for Heroism*. Nehru, *The Discovery of India*; Narayan, *The English Teacher*.

(*Contd.*)

INDIAN TIMELINE

Year	Historical event	Key anglophone novels and related works
1947	Independence and Partition accompanied by widespread violence.	Bhabani Bhattacharya. *So Many Hungers.*
1948	Assassination of Mahatma Gandhi. Telengana peasant uprising led by armed communists commences.	Abbas, *I Write as I Feel* (autobiography); G. V. Desani, *All about H. Hatterr.*
1950	India becomes a Republic and adopts Constitution. Zamindari Abolition Acts initiated on a state-by-state basis.	G. V. Desani, *Hali* (play) performed in London.
1951		Zeenut Futehally, *Zohra.*
1952		Bhattacharya, *He Who Rides a Tiger.*
1953	First General Election.	Attia Hosain, *Phoenix Fled* (short stories); Anand, *Private Life of an Indian Prince.*
1954	Establishment of Sahitya Akademi or Academy of Letters with the aim of fostering literary production in all Indian languages including English.	Nayantara Sahgal, *Prison and Chocolate Cake* (autobiography); P. Renu, *Maila Anchal* (Hindi; *The Soiled Border*); Kamala Markandaya, *Nectar in a Sieve.*
1955	Hindu Marriage Act changes Hindu matrimonial law towards recognizing autonomy of women; 'Bandung' conference of Afro-Asian nations.	Narayan, *Waiting for the Mahatma*; Markandaya, *Some Inner Fury*; Abbas, *Inquilab: A Novel of the Indian Revolution. Quest*, an English literary quarterly, founded.
1956		Khushwant Singh, *Train to Pakistan*; Faiz Ahmad Faiz, poetry collection *Zindan Nama* (Urdu; *Prison Chronicles*).

Year	Event	Literary works
1958		Narayan, *The Guide*; Sahgal, *A Time to be Happy*;
1961		Attia Hossain, *Sunlight on a Broken Column*; V. S. Naipaul, *A House for Mr Biswas*.
1962	Indo-Chinese War.	
1963	Death of Nehru in May.	Anita Desai, *Cry, the Peacock*.
1965	Formation of Shiv Sena in Bombay in 1965. First India–Pakistan War.	
1966	Indira Gandhi becomes Prime Minister for the first time.	
1967	Naxalbari peasant revolt.	Narayan, *The Vendor of Sweets*.
1971–2	Civil war breaks out in Pakistan; formation of Bangladesh after India enters military conflict.	
1974	Jayaprakash Narayan (JP) calls for 'Total Revolution' against corruption and Indira Gandhi's leadership.	Kiran Nagarkar, *Saat Sakkam Trechalis* (Marathi, *Seven Sixes are Forty Three*).
1975	Court finds Indira Gandhi guilty of election malpractice. Emergency imposed in June.	Chaman Nahal, *Azadi*.
1977	Elections held and Mrs Gandhi is defeated.	Desai, *Fire on the Mountain*; Narayan, *The Painter of Signs*.
1980	Elections held again and Mrs Gandhi returns to power.	Salman Rushdie, *Midnight's Children*; Shashi Deshpande, *The Dark Holds No Terrors*; Desai, *Clear Light of Day*.
1983		Rushdie, *Shame*.

(Contd.)

INDIAN TIMELINE

Year	Historical event	Key anglophone novels and related works
1984	Indian army storms Golden Temple in Amritsar to flush out Sikh militants. Indira Gandhi assassinated; anti-Sikh pogroms take place. Mrs Gandhi's son, Rajiv Gandhi, becomes Prime Minister and initiates economic reforms towards a free-market economy. US-owned Union Carbide plant leaks poisonous gas, injures and kills several thousands in Bhopal over the years.	
1985		Sahgal, *Rich Like Us*.
1986		Amitav Ghosh, *The Circle of Reason*; Vikram Seth, *The Golden Gate*.
1988		Upamanyu Chatterjee, *English, August*; Ghosh, *The Shadow Lines*; Shashi Deshpande, *That Long Silence*; I. Allan Sealy, *The Trotter Nama*; Bapsi Sidhwa, *Ice-Candy-Man*; Rushdie, *The Satanic Verses*.
1989		M. G. Vassanji, *The Gunny Sack*; Bharati Mukherjee, *Jasmine*; Shashi Tharoor, *The Great Indian Novel*.
1990		Farrukh Dhondy, *Bombay Duck*; Rushdie, *Haroun and the Sea of Stories*.

1991	Rajiv Gandhi assassinated by Sri Lankan Tamil militants. New Prime Minister Narasimha Rao undertakes further structural reforms to the economy away from Nehruvian socialism.	Rohinton Mistry, *Such a Long Journey*; I. Allan Sealy, *Hero*.
1992	Babri Mosque torn down by Hindutva militants and hundreds killed in ensuing riots in which Mumbai is badly hit.	Amitav Ghosh, *In an Antique Land*; Gita Hariharan, *The Thousand Faces of Night*.
1993	Several co-ordinated bomb blasts in Mumbai in which many die or are injured. Believed to be masterminded by underworld dons in retaliation for the massacre of hundreds of Muslims in the 1992 riots.	Shama Futehally, *Tara Lane*; Vikram Seth, *A Suitable Boy*; Amit Chaudhuri, *Afternoon Raag*.
1994		Tharoor, *Show Business*; Rushdie, *East, West* (short stories).
1995		Nagarkar, *Ravan and Eddie*; Mukul Kesavan, *Looking Through Glass*; Vikram Chandra, *Red Earth on Pouring Rain*.
1996	United Front government.	Rohinton Mistry, *A Fine Balance*; Ghosh, *The Calcutta Chromosome*; Rushdie, *The Moor's Last Sigh*.
1997	50th anniversary of Independence.	Arundhati Roy, *The God of Small Things*; Ardashir Vakil, *Beach Boy*.
1998	BJP forms coalition government at Centre. Nuclear weapons successfully tested at Pokhran.	Chaudhuri, *Freedom Song*; Manju Kapur, *Difficult Daughters*.
1999	India-Pakistan military clash in Kargil.	Rushdie, *The Ground Beneath Her Feet*.

(Contd.)

INDIAN TIMELINE

Year	Historical event	Key anglophone novels and related works
2001		Manil Suri, *The Death of Vishnu*; Ghosh, *The Glass Palace*.
2002	Anti-Muslim pogroms in Gujarat after a train carriage carrying Hindutva activists is apparently deliberately set on fire.	Siddhartha Deb, *Point of Return*; Mistry, *Family Matters*.
2003		Futehally, *Reaching Bombay Central*; Vassanji, *The In-Between World of Vikram Lall*; David, *The Book of Esther*; Hariharan, *In Times of Siege*.
2004		Ghosh, *The Hungry Tide*.
2005		Rushdie, *Shalimar the Clown*.
2006		Kiran Desai, *The Inheritance of Loss*.
2007		Vassanji, *The Assassin's Song*; Manju Kapur, *Home*; Vikram Chandra, *Sacred Games*; Indra Sinha, *Animal's People*.
2008		Ghosh, *Sea of Poppies*.

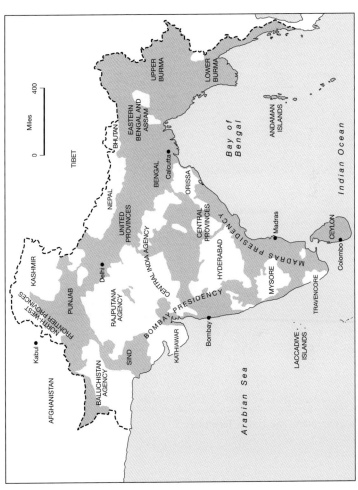

British India, 1909, from the *Imperial Gazetteer* shaded areas indicate British India and areas
administered by the Government of India
Unshaded areas indicate 'Native States and Territories'

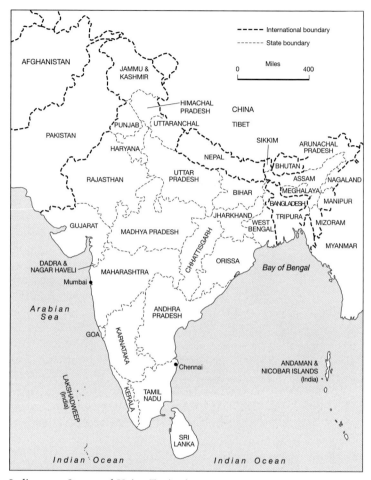

India, 2007, States and Union Territories.

Introduction: Ideas of India

Few postcolonial literary genres have been either as prominent or as contentious as the Indian novel in English. Even as several anglophone writers from decolonizing regions have achieved a global readership in recent years and even canonical status in some cases (Walcott, Naipaul, Soyinka, among others), novelists from the Indian subcontinent have dominated the international scene in unprecedented numbers. This is manifest partly in their repeated appearances on shortlists for the Booker and the Commonwealth Prize as well as increasing, indeed, guaranteed, attention from reviewers in prestigious literary institutions, including the *New York Review of Books* and the *Times Literary Supplement*. Writers such as Salman Rushdie, Vikram Seth, and Arundhati Roy are staples on postcolonial and 'world literature' syllabi. While these writers as well as others such as Anita Desai and Amitav Ghosh now have assured access to international publishing houses with considerable global reach, less-established figures also benefit from a relatively well-developed publishing industry for English-language works in India itself; Penguin India alone, for instance, publishes scores of original anglophone novels each year.

Yet, of course, this very prominence has rightly been the source of vigorous, even fractious, debate. Many critics, including some scholars of Indian writing in English, have pointed out that the representative status and institutional strength of English fiction is starkly out of proportion to its actual presence as a spoken and comprehended language on the subcontinent. Salman Rushdie's somewhat jejune remarks in a now infamous *New Yorker* article commemorating fifty years of Indian Independence only served to inflame an already polarized situation: 'the prose writing—both fiction and non-fiction—created in this period by Indian writers working in English is proving to be a stronger and more important body of work than most of what has been produced in the eighteen "recognized" languages of India.... "Indo-Anglian" literature represents perhaps the most valuable contribution India has yet made to the world of books' (1997: 50). The faultline approvingly evoked here, that dividing English from the 'so-called vernaculars', is one that has profoundly inequitable consequences in terms of both economic privilege and cultural capital. Significantly, other anglophone writers have often written about this divide eloquently. So, for instance, this ironic salutation by Vikram Seth (1999: 66):

> English! Six armed god,
> Key to a job, to power,
> Snobbery, the good life,
> This separateness, this fear.

Bilingual novelist Kiran Nagarkar (1995: 180) puts it more starkly: 'Those who have English are the haves, and those who don't, are the have nots. How could you possibly grasp the meaning and value of English if you spoke it before you were toilet-trained or had a place reserved for you in an English-medium school? English is a mantra, a maha-mantra.'[1] Should a language that is still restricted to 6 per cent of India's population, an English-educated elite, be invested with such global representational power in literary and cultural terms? What does it mean that the world reads and believes that it comprehends 'India' through Rushdie and Roy rather than Kamleshwar (Hindi), Ambai (Tamil), or Qurrutalain Hyder (Urdu)? These questions are important ones and have necessarily animated the critical discussion. Fortunately, good translations and scholarly editions of 'bhasha' or indigenous language literatures are beginning to make their appearance and are beginning to challenge sanctioned ignorance of these literary languages and traditions. Writers such as Mahasweta Devi (Bengali), U. R. Ananthamurthy (Kannada), Qurrutulain Hyder (Urdu), Fakir Mohan Senapati (Oriya), and Rabindranath Tagore (Bengali) are now at least partially accessible to those literate in English but not (as few can be) in all Indian languages, although they are still not widely distributed or well represented at a global level in bookshops and libraries.[2]

Jauntily premised as they are on ignorance of other Indian literatures, the sentiments so carelessly expressed by Rushdie are not, however, effectively countered by reverse crudities. A denunciatory tendency, often noticeable in writers and critics who themselves work primarily in English, will insist on the inauthenticity of (other people's) anglophone writing, its distance from the 'real concerns' of most Indians and its being in thrall to the critical fads and fashions of Western academia.[3] While there are undoubtedly questions of privilege and reach to be considered seriously, the fact remains that like all literary traditions, anglophone writing in India, particularly prose fiction, is a heterogeneous and capacious body of work, replete with mediocrities, masterpieces, and downright failures. As Aijaz Ahmad, one of the most articulate critics of the primacy accorded to English within literary studies generally and postcolonial studies more specifically, also acknowledges, English is now, 'for better or for worse, one of the *Indian* languages' and needs to be studied as such (1991: 282, original emphasis). Its very influence and reach, as the 'key professional language and certainly the main language of communication between the schooled sections of different linguistic regions', requires that it be situated historically and studied in its specificity as a literary and cultural phenomenon (ibid.). To not do so and accord it either unmitigated praise or scorn, ironically, allows the anglophone to perpetuate itself as a given, an unmarked global term taken for granted in a sea of lesser provincial specificity.

Not all forms of anglophone writing are, however, equally prolific or visible. While English-language poetry has had a steady if relatively muted presence, it is one that has generally been eclipsed by the vibrancy and popularity of verse and lyric traditions in other Indian languages that have an oral rather than strictly literary presence. Here, as with drama, the 'Indian scene' contrasts with regions such as the Caribbean or parts of West Africa. Anglophone dramatists too are a small tribe and rarely attain critical or popular acclaim, sidelined as they are by the dynamism of theatre and film in 'regional' languages and India's other national language, Hindi. (Hindi/Hindustani can arguably claim subcontinental reach even as its claim to singular 'national' status among Indian languages is justifiably challenged outside its home states.) Though a handful of anglophone short story collections have won critical approval, it is undoubtedly one single and specific genre—the anglophone novel—that has won for Indian writers 'working in English', the global currency celebrated by Rushdie and others. In part this is due to the prominence of the genre on the world literary map from the late nineteenth century onwards and the recognition accorded to it in mechanisms of canon formation such as the Booker, the Commonwealth, and the Guardian Fiction Prizes, and even France's Prix Goncourt. These in turn are backed by powerful commercial concerns with vast publication, translation, distribution, and film rights networks which ensure the salience of prose fiction in bookshop windows across the globe.

It is often argued that unlike the British novel or the novel in indigenous Indian languages, anglophone fiction in India has no 'tradition' to call its own, no literary-historical genealogy or movement that is inherent to its development or sense of itself. In his introduction to the now iconic special issue of *The New Yorker* on Indian fiction, Bill Buford (1997) remarks that many leading anglophone novelists from the subcontinent had never met, leave alone compared manuscripts over drinks, before being photographed for the special issue: 'they work, some of them in an adopted language, and often in isolation, even thousands of miles from their homeland' (ibid. 8).[4] Similarly, A. K. Mehrotra (2003: pp. xx, 25) has recently observed that Indian literature is 'piecemeal and ragged' and one 'whose writers have seldom acknowledged each other's presence'. While it is certainly true that the history of the anglophone novel in India is both relatively contained (developing over a span of less than 150 years) and patchy, often lacking clear genealogies or intertextual lines of influence, it is also possible to overstate the lack of literary community or indeed, shared influence. For one thing, these lines of influence did not necessarily derive along literary lines or from other anglophone writers alone; Mulk Raj Anand, for instance, was an influential member of the All-India Progressive Writers Association which sought to bring together politically minded writers from across languages and regions. Gandhi, as we shall see in a subsequent chapter, was a shared literary, philosophical, and cultural influence for Anand and many other writers of his time. The 'Bombay' novel exists in languages such as Marathi as well, a crossover embodied by the work of bilingual novelist, Kiran Nagarkar. Class and educational privilege also constitute a powerful shared context, one which has specific implications for the anglophone novel, as we shall see: 'The only *national* literary intelligentsia that exists in India today—an intelligentsia constituted as a distinct social stratum and dispersed in all parts of the country, which brings to bear on its vocation and its work a *shared* body of knowledge, *shared* presumptions and a *shared* language of mutual exchange is the one that is fairly well grounded in English' (Ahmad 1991: 278, original emphasis).

It is this very *national* (which is not the same as national*ist*, of course) dimension that bears thinking about in our attempts to situate the anglophone novel (a term this study will use in preference to the quaint 'Indo-Anglian') in India. The principal argument in this book is this: the anglophone Indian novel is part of a heterogeneous corpus in which certain dominant trends, shared concerns, and recurrent themes are, nevertheless, discernible. It is a genre that has been distinguished from its inception by a preoccupation with both *history* and *nation* as these come together to shape what political scientist, Sunil Khilnani (1997) terms, after Nehru, 'the idea of India'. Inasmuch as its very emergence was generated by the colonial encounter, the novel is an ineluctably postcolonial genre; its concern has been with that equally postcolonial entity, the nation-state. English in India, as many critics have noted, is simultaneously rootless (in the sense of lacking a specific region and cultural context) as well as pan-Indian. This is a fact that merits acknowledgement rather than unexamined celebration or reductive denunciation, and it is in this light that the anglophone fiction of India merits *situated* study. Rushdie himself notes the tendency to read contemporary writers 'in a kind of literary isolation; texts without context'; this is a tendency that can only be undone by, first, understanding the history of the genre, and secondly, as Ahmad argues, studying English in India in the multilingual frame in which it emerged, jostling for space and recognition among a myriad other linguistic and literary traditions (Rushdie 1997: 50).

The link between the novel and the 'narration' of nation is, of course, a familiar one. As Timothy Brennan (1990: 49) puts it: 'Nations, then, are imaginary constructs that depend for their existence on an apparatus of cultural fictions in which imaginative literature plays a decisive role.' While the novel is not the only such imaginative vehicle, it remains the case that the rise of nation-states and the flowering of the genre have coincided across cultural contexts (setting aside the vexed question of when the novel as a literary entity can be said to have begun). Many of the more general reasons offered for this congruence are arguably applicable to the Indian context as well: the rise of industrial and urban modernity accompanied by transformations in agrarian life, the mass production enabled by printing presses, and the concomitant rise of a literate middle class. The 'manner of its presentation', Brennan (ibid.) argues, accounts for the novel's centrality, 'objectifying the "one, yet many" of national life, and ... mimicking the structure of the nation, a clearly bordered jumble of languages and styles'. In some postcolonial contexts, Latin American nations being one example, the 'inextricability of politics from fiction in the history of nation-building' made the novel the paradigmatic site for the 'imagining' of national foundations and futures. Benedict Anderson's work on 'print culture' and nationalism has been hugely influential here, particularly his suggestion that the newspaper and the novel were the key media for ' "re-presenting" the *kind* of imagined community that is the nation' (1991: 25, original emphasis). Others, such as Neil Larsen (2001: 169), have sounded a necessary cautionary note, pointing out that claims for the nation as a fundamentally narrated entity have become 'a virtual routine of historical and postcolonial studies'. The argument in this book is not so much that the nation is a 'narrated' entity in itself as that the narration of nation gave the anglophone novel in India its earliest and most persistent thematic preoccupation, indeed, its raison d'être, as it attempted to carve out a legitimate space for itself. The conditions of its emergence—out of the colonial encounter, addressing itself to empire rather than a specific region or community—meant that the anglophone novel in the subcontinent returned repeatedly to a self-reflexive question: 'What is India(n)?' This was to become a question with chronological, metaphysical, religious, personal, political, aesthetic, historical, and geographical dimensions and in the most significant works of fiction, India emerges not just as theme or imaginative object, however, but also as a point of debate, reflection, and contestation.

More recently, this contention was illustrated by I. Allan Sealy's sense of the similarities between *Midnight's Children* and his *Trotter Nama* which, in an earlier version, also had a character born at the stroke of freedom's midnight. Sealy understands this coincidence in terms of 'two writers responding to the same historical moment. They have read the same book but the book is India. India is dictating, the country is doing the thinking. We do not write but are written' (cited in Mee 2003: 318). The anglophone novelist is, in some constitutive sense, a writer *of* India. This is not, of course, to claim that 'India' emerges as theme and preoccupation in every anglophone novel written in this region. Nor, conversely, is it to claim that novels in other Indian languages do not address similar questions. It *is* saying, however, that the evolution and morphing of the idea of India constitutes both the condition of possibility for the emergence of the anglophone novel *and* a conceptual link between some of the most significant works produced in the genre. As such, this book neither attempts to 'cover' all works that could conceivably be seen to belong to the genre nor even all those that engage with the theme of 'India'; the sheer number of relevant texts, for one thing, makes this an impossible task. What it seeks to provide are readings of symptomatic texts towards a historicized framework of study. This is also not a study of the 'South Asian' novel which would be in itself an important undertaking. The anglophone literature of Sri Lanka has a quite distinct and distinctive history that merits a book-length study of its own while the postcolonial (and post-Partition) nation-states of Pakistan and Bangladesh enjoy far greater literary output in their various indigenous languages than in English, although anglophone writers in their diasporas have recently enjoyed a degree of critical acclaim and exposure. Nepal and Bhutan were not, of course, formally part of the British empire and therefore, have a different relationship to both English and English literature. It is the nation-state of India in which the genre has found both enormous institutional and *commercial* backing (a point conspicuously absent in Rushdie's reflections) that enabled it to come into its own and flourish. Here is where it continues to engage, if variously and differently, with its earliest preoccupation, that of the idea of India itself.

The range and variety of the anglophone novel's engagement with 'India' as imaginative concern is clear from the topics around which the following chapters are organized. The first chapter sets out the colonial encounter and the consequent emergence of the 'idea of India'. It argues that it was during the making of English India that the challenge of writing both prose histories and prose fictions was taken up by writers working in the new language. The constitutive importance of gender and sexuality to early narratives of and debates on nation is addressed in the second chapter. The imaginative power exercised by one man and his unique elaborations of India and Indian-ness is the subject of the third chapter, which examines the connection between 'Mahatma-magic' and the first flowering of 'Indo-Anglian fiction' in the years leading up to Independence and thereafter. The silences generated by the 'stained dawn' of Independence and Partition have been broken only sporadically by literature on the subcontinent and, curiously, it is anglophone fiction that has provided the most sustained novelistic engagement with the horrors of the moment; these novels are the subject of the fourth chapter. The optimism and betrayals that characterized the post-Independence decades have been treated in two great epic novels of transition to nation—Rushdie's epochal *Midnight's Children* and Vikram Seth's no less magisterial *A Suitable Boy*, both of which are examined in their literary-historical contexts in Ch. 5. The betrayals of the postcolonial era, symbolized most powerfully by the Emergency imposed by Indira Gandhi in 1975–7, continue to haunt the 'Bombay novel' of Ch. 6 where the city becomes the paradigmatic site for the exploration of that which haunts the margins of the aspiring democratic nation—the disenfranchised, the minorities, the unvoiced—and so challenges its claims to inclusivity and full representation. Similarly, the domestic and the familial are the themes of Ch. 7 as these spheres—and what subaltern historian, Ranajit Guha, terms 'the small voice of history'—intersect with, transform, and are transformed by the grand narratives of nation and national history (Guha 1996). Chapter 8 considers ideas of India as homeland that powerfully engage writers of the diaspora while Ch. 9 provides, by way of conclusion, a brief overview of the contemporary scene in anglophone fiction that continues to be preoccupied with the idea of India, marked as much by fissures and faultlines as by a continued hold on the imagination.

A word on critical approach and structure: since this study attempts to offer a historical and conceptual argument about the novel, it does not attempt to be encyclopaedic. Individual chapters combine an overview of key texts and themes with short, but detailed, close readings that show how certain historical and critical concerns emerge from the text (as opposed to 'applying' those concerns a priori to texts). Short suggestions for further reading point to primary texts in English and in translation that can be fruitfully considered under a particular rubric.

Further Reading

General accounts of Indian writing in English include Mukherjee's *The Twice-Born Fiction* and *The Perishable Empire*; K. S. Iyengar's *Indian Writing in English*, Tabish Khair's *Babu Fictions*, and A. K. Mehrotra's *A History of Indian Literature in English*. Sisir Kumar Das's two edited volumes, *A History of Indian Literature*, provide a compendious and indispensable comparative overview of the region and its literature over a century and a half.

1
Making English India

When the adjective 'Indian' attaches to a literary tradition or cultural formation, it necessitates a greater degree of scrutiny than is usual in literary discourse which, for the most part, takes the national affiliations of various literatures for granted. 'Indian literature', as one critic has argued, is not itself a 'theoretically coherent category' even if, in some sense, 'every book written by an Indian, inside the country or abroad, is part of a thing called Indian Literature' (Ahmad 1991: 244). Comprising many different languages and literary traditions, this literature has emerged from within shifting cultural boundaries over the centuries. Even the study of a relatively contained, if high-profile, corpus of texts—fiction written in English—is complicated by the question of what precisely constitutes the 'Indian'. Passport, geographical location, ancestry, linguistic competence, cultural ethos, or political loyalties: none of these are in themselves self-evident common factors. India seems to be a paradigmatic example of that very modern phenomenon, an 'imagined community' whereby large numbers of people come together to constitute that political and cultural entity known as 'the nation'; though they will never meet or even hear of each other, 'in the minds of each lives the image of their communion' (Anderson 1991: 5–7). India, argues Sudipta Kaviraj (1992: 1), 'is not an object of discovery but of invention. It was historically instituted by the nationalist imagination of the nineteenth century'. Partha Chatterjee argues similarly that nationalism in India is 'derivative' of European nationalism, a 'different discourse, yet one that is dominated by another' (1993: 42). In other words, the Indian nation-state as we know it today is a fairly recent construct, a consequence of historical accidents and political transformations that took place over the nineteenth and twentieth centuries.

The relative newness of 'India', the modern nation, does not mean, however, that no other unities or conceptions of larger polities existed in the subcontinent even as, over the centuries, it has been home to a diverse range of peoples, cultures, languages, and religions. To name but two examples, as early the third century BC, the Buddhist emperor Ashoka ruled over the kingdom of 'Bharat' while the Mughals called the territory they ruled 'Hindustan', indicating, first, conquered land across the Indus river and later, a cultural realm shared by Hindus and Muslims (Bayly 1998: 38). Despite the absence of a common and consistently used term for 'the wider nationality', one historian argues, 'broader loyalties and imagined communities' beyond clan and region did exist in precolonial India, ones that would later 'play a subtle role in the construction of Indian nationalism' (ibid. 37). Although more proximate neighbours such as present-day China and Iran have long had terms (Jiandu/Xiandu, Hinduka) denoting the area from which present-day India would be carved, until the eighteenth century Europeans 'conceived of Asia as an ill-defined series of exotic and fabulously wealthy countries' among which were the 'Indies', which signified the lands east of the Indus river, 'the traditional eastward limit of the Hellenistic world' (Edney 1997: 3). Some of these conceptions of 'the Indies' included present-day Afghanistan, Indonesia, and Vietnam; all of them broadly included the region that is known in contemporary geopolitical terms as 'South Asia' which comprises the modern nation-states of Bangladesh, Bhutan, India, the Maldives, Nepal, Pakistan, and Sri Lanka. Even as 'the Indies' became the fabled destination for early modern explorers such as Vasco da Gama and Christopher Columbus, and a literary trope for the dominion of untold riches in the work of early modern writers such as Shakespeare, Marlowe, and Donne, it was not until the eighteenth century that a specific geographical and political entity named 'India' began to emerge in European encyclopaedias and maps. The first such map was made by the French cartographer, J. B. B d'Anville in 1752; his *Carte de l'Inde* included the Indian subcontinent and Indochina.

Around the same time, British India started to come into being as the mercantile East India Company's territorial holdings in the subcontinent began to grow in the wake of military victory over the Nawab of Bengal in the Battle of Plassey in 1757. With the India Act of 1784, intended to curb the powers of the East India Company, the British Crown took over political control of Bengal as well as the Bombay and Madras presidencies in the west and south respectively.

As the region became the site of a struggle for control between the declining Mughal empire, the Marathas, and the British, 'Modern India was born', with new maps reflecting Britain's interests and dominion. The subcontinent was now seen 'as an actual region in and of itself... a meaningful, if still ambiguous geographical entity' (Edney 1997: 9). From these imperial holdings, which would eventually become the site of anti-colonial and nationalist struggle, emerged the English-language or anglophone Indian novel. From its inception this genre has been deeply engaged with the idea of India, perhaps much more so than other literatures of the region. This is perhaps unsurprising given its derivation from a (then) foreign language and new genre, both of which were intimately tied to the project of British imperialism and native responses to it. The idea of a modern Indian 'nation' was, arguably, articulated in English-language fiction before literature in other languages began to engage with the idea. As a literary concern, the idea of India was also tied in to two other challenges: writing prose and writing national history.

Writing nation and history

By the beginning of the nineteenth century, as European empires began to expand and dominate the globe, the 'nation' became the privileged category for demarcating larger political entities and cultural groupings. One of the interesting paradoxes in the ways in which nations represent themselves, argues Anderson (1991: 11), is that despite their relative newness as political entities, they see themselves as possessed of great antiquity, as looming out of an 'immemorial past' which constituted national history. Nation-statehood, however, was not a status that all could aspire to. In order to be admitted to the club of nations in the early nineteenth century, it was necessary to have a History and not all cultures or civilizations were deemed to possess one. In his *Lectures on the Philosophy of World History*, the influential German philosopher, G. F. Hegel argued that World History or 'die Weltgeschichte' found its highest expression in European conceptions of Reason, Freedom, and the State. Devoid of these conceptions, China and India existed outside World History, in 'Prehistory'; they 'are lacking in the essential self-consciousness of the concept of freedom' (cited in Guha 2003: 37).

Despite its wealth of 'spiritual achievements of a truly profound quality', India, according to Hegel, 'has no history'. This kind of pronouncement on the 'unredeemable historylessness' on the vast civilizational and geographical region that was now Britain's dominion in the East was to become influential, both in colonial discourse as well as anti-colonial responses to it (Guha 2003: 52). From a colonial perspective, it justified regarding 'uncivilized' peoples as not entitled to the same rights and freedoms. This difference was also one of the guiding themes of James Mill's breathtakingly contemptuous engagement with India in his ten-volume work, *A History of British India*, which, unlike Hegel's writings, gives short shrift even to India's intellectual and cultural achievements. For Mill, India—synonymous with the Hindu people—is a false claimant to nationhood because its claims to antiquity and historical record are patently fabricated. Conceptions of time in its written records are marked by a 'wildness and inconsistency [that] evidently place them beyond the sober limits of truth and history'. There is no point in reading the Hindu legends allegorically (for their poetic and figurative truths) because they 'present a maze of unnatural fictions, in which a series of real events can by no artifice be traced' (1997: i. 115). In the final instance, he pronounces: 'These people, indeed, *are perfectly destitute of historical records*' (ibid. 116, emphasis mine). Mill, like Hegel, believed that it was only prose that could express the reality of experience; prose 'stands both for a condition of language and a condition of being' (Guha 2003: 16). The 'fabrications' of the Hindus are in poetic form, and poetry, as 'the language of the passions' (Mill 1997: ii. 33) cannot be the vehicle for historical truth. In an extended consideration of 'the literature of the Hindus', Mill is scathing about their 'habit of expressing everything in verse' which, in turn, is rife with '[i]nflation: metaphors perpetual, and these the most violent and strained, often the most unnatural and ridiculous; obscurity; tautology; repetition; verbosity; confusion; incoherence' (ibid. 34, 36). The legends and epics of the Hindus, praised by the likes of Sir William Jones are, Mill counters, the 'offspring of a wild and ungoverned imagination' which 'mark the state of a rude and credulous people, whom the marvellous delights' (ibid. i. 115).

Mill's dismissal of Jones's admiration for Hindu Sanskritic tradition is indicative of a struggle, the outcome of which would define the intellectual and literary contours of colonial India: the argument between the 'Orientalists' and the 'Anglicists' over the education of

Britain's new colonial subjects. The first phase of British rule in India, from the late eighteenth century onwards, was broadly Orientalist in its educational policy, combining 'the initiation of the West to the vast literary treasures of the East [and] the reintroduction of the natives to their own cultural heritage, represented ... as being buried under the debris of foreign conquests and depredations' (Viswanathan 1989: 28). Scholars like Sir William Jones and Nathaniel Halhed learned languages such as Sanskrit and Persian and undertook research into the classical literary traditions of the subcontinent. All this was, of course, also central to the fledgling colonial state's acquisition of knowledge and information about those whom it governed, the combination which Bernard Cohn (2002: 16) has pithily described as 'the command of language' and 'the language of command'. By the early nineteenth century, however, a counter movement called Anglicism—which advocated English and European education—was on the rise. When the East India Company was dogged by financial scandals, Anglicists claimed that Orientalism was responsible for driving British officials to degeneration and corruption (presumed to be the natural state of the Orient), and that it was necessary to introduce Indians to European learning to remedy this state of affairs. Though Orientalists continued to dominate official policy for a while, partly because of the belief that the natives were not ready for a European education, over time, historical exigencies—particularly the prospect of long-term British rule and the opening up of the region to missionaries—swung the pendulum in the Anglicist direction. In her *Masks of Conquest*, Gauri Viswanathan has argued that while the English parliament wished to see a Europeanized improvement in the morals and manners of natives, partly to suit its administrative needs, it was nervous about interfering in their religious beliefs through missionary activity. The teaching of English literature, she argues, was seen as a way to disseminate English values without coming into direct conflict with native religious beliefs.

Anglicizing India: project and response

It was, however, only in 1835 that Anglicism was to proclaim its own definitive victory in the form of Thomas Babington Macaulay's notorious 'Minute on Indian Education', a paean to English language and literature:

The claims of our own language it is hardly necessary to recapitulate. It stands pre-eminent even among the languages of the west. It abounds with works of imagination not inferior to the noblest which Greece has bequeathed to us; with models of every species of eloquence; with historical compositions, which, considered merely as narratives, have seldom been surpassed, and which, considered as vehicles of ethical and political instruction, have never been equalled; with just and lively representations of human life and human nature; with the most profound speculations on metaphysics, morals, government, jurisprudence, and trade; with full and correct information respecting every experimental science which tends to preserve the health, to increase the comfort, or to expand the intellect of man. Whoever knows that language has ready access to all the vast intellectual wealth, which all the wisest nations of the earth have created and hoarded in the course of ninety generations. It may safely be said, that the literature now extant in that language is of far greater value than all the literature which three hundred years ago was extant in all the languages of the world together.   (1995: 428)

In the 'Minute', Macaulay—clearly drawing on Mill's work—attacks Orientalist education as 'useless' and 'unmeaning' and asserts that the languages of India 'contain neither literary nor scientific information' (ibid. 430). It is only through the introduction of English with its 'intrinsic superiority' that any improvement in this state of affairs can be brought about. Macaulay's argument won the day and was shortly followed by Lord Bentinck's English Education Act of 1835 which formalized the teaching of English literature and science to natives. The goal of this programme of cultural eugenics was, in Macaulay's now famous words, the formation of 'a class who may be interpreters between us and the millions whom we govern; a class of persons, Indian in blood and colour, but English in taste, in opinions, in morals, and in intellect'.

What of the natives, this vaunted class of interpreters themselves? As critical responses to Edward Said's *Orientalism* pointed out, the subjects of colonialism and colonial discourse were not passive canvases for civilizational missions. The history of colonialism is also, of course, the history of colonial subjects' engagement with and resistance to it. The famous uprising of 1857—which generated a myriad sensationalist English novels—was, despite its undoubtedly large scale, no exception: 'armed revolt was endemic in all parts of early colonial India'(Bayly 1998: 170). At the same time 'collaboration' was also an element of colonial rule as native subjects engaged with the new power structures in their own self-interest. They occupied lower-level administrative posts, participated in commercial ventures and enrolled themselves in educational institutions. Colonial policy on education shifted and changed in relation to the response of its subjects who had ideas of their own on how they could benefit from new educational initiatives, including English education.

Bilingual self-fashioning

The rise of prose and prose fiction in nineteenth-century India is intimately connected to the growth of a bilingual native middle-class, specifically a Hindu middle-class intelligentsia in Bengal, the first region to come under formal British rule. The city of Calcutta, which generated this English-educated intelligentsia, was the centre of commerce as well as the seat of colonial government. The Permanent Settlement imposed by the British Crown in 1793 had created a class of wealthy absentee proprietors of land who lived in the city where they pursued commercial activities as well as literary and intellectual interests. The less wealthy worked as teachers and as lower-level functionaries for the East India Company. This new urban elite came to be known as the 'bhadralok' or 'respectable people'. It was at the instance of sections of this social group that the Hindu College of Calcutta (known as the 'Oxford of the East') was established in 1817, 'an institution of English/western learning that would at the same time be capable of upholding the orthodox Hindu hierarchies' (Bagchi 2004: 147–8). Jasodhara Bagchi suggests that the Hindu College epitomized the integration of Anglicism and Orientalism, the powerful mixture that enabled the Bengali bhadralok to fashion themselves into modern Hindus, Bengalis, and, over time, into Indians.

It was on this terrain—controversially termed 'the Bengal Renaissance'—that powerful literary and cultural conceptions of India as an ancient and great nation in its own right would emerge. The idea of a 'Renaissance' was itself based on the Orientalist idea that 'Asian civilizations were truly healthy and vigorous in ancient times but had somehow degenerated' and that it would be possible to bring them back to life and health (Kopf 1969: 97). One of the more problematic assumptions of this thinking, as we shall see later, was that Islamic rule was a period of medieval darkness (a Protestant concept) which had to be expunged from the idea of a reinvigorated Hindu India. For the intelligentsia of Bengal, the 'Renaissance' inaugurated a search for cultural and, eventually, national identity, a place from where they could articulate a sense of individual and collective selfhood. In this quest, thinkers and reformers such as Raja Rammohun Roy, attempted to reinterpret Hindu tradition to align it with their own understanding of the meaning of modernity and progress. This entailed a rewriting of Indian history that argued that an 'original' monotheistic Hinduism had been corrupted into polytheistic idolatry and superstition.

A significant strand of the so-called Bengal Renaissance was the Young Bengal movement which coalesced around the iconic figure of a young Hindu College lecturer by the name of Henry Vivian Derozio. A Eurasian by birth, the iconoclastic Derozio fostered an intellectual atmosphere that valorized rationalism and scepticism; his students read then-radical writers such as Tom Paine and were encouraged to 'Break down everything old and rear in its stead what is new' (cited in Mukherjee 2000: 44). He became one of India's first anglophone versifiers, one who 'brought into his writing on Indian themes a wide variety of metres, rhythms, forms and images from English poetry' (Dalmia 1992: 43). Yet, oddly, it was in this very language that he was to express what has been read as a nascent nationalism, though the oppressors referred to are Muslim tyrants: 'Oh! when our country writhes in galling chains, | when her proud masters scourge her like a dog . . . we should rush to her relief, | like some at an unhappy parent's wail' (cited in Mukherji 2003: 47).[1] Derozio's tutelage produced another famous literary figure, the poet Michael Madhusudhan Dutt, who began as an Anglicist whose passion for English almost outdid Macaulay: 'I acknowledge to you, and I need not blush to do so—that I love the language of the Anglo-Saxon. Yes—I *love* the language—the glorious language of the Anglo-Saxon. My imagination visions forth before me the language of the Anglo-Saxon in all its radiant beauty; and I feel silenced and abashed' (cited ibid. 49). But Dutt's relationship to the English language and its literature became more fraught and complicated over time, and as he sought to explore and express an Indian cultural

identity in his writing, he turned first to the mythic resources provided by works such as the *Ramayana* and *Mahabharata*, and finally,
to the Bengali language itself. Ironically for a man who began his
career as a literary anglophile, today Dutt is regarded as one of greatest
poets in the Bengali language, a reputation cemented by his epic
poem, *Meghanadabadha Kavya*, which was inspired by Milton's *Paradise Lost.*

By 1835, even before Macaulay's 'Minute' had formalized English
education in British India, a vocal and articulate bilingual intelligentsia
had created a public sphere for itself in Bengal, one where it debated and
disagreed but also cohered as a social group. Its members owned
newspapers, journals, and presses and this was one crucible of ideas
where an emergent nationalism articulated itself. As the historian
Sanjay Joshi (2001: 2) has argued, the power of the middle class in
colonial India was based less on economic power—constrained and
limited under colonialism—than on 'the abilities of its members to be
cultural entrepreneurs'. What they had, above all, was the ability to
define what it meant to be 'modern', to have a 'history', and, consequently, what it was to be 'Indian'. As we have already seen, one of the
key claims made by the likes of Mill was that 'the Hindu race' lacked
not only history but also prose. All their literature was in verse, a genre
that Mill saw as encouraging a flight from actual experience and reason.
This pervasive colonial attitude also had material consequences; in 1791,
for instance, the Native Exclusion Act debarred Indians from higher
administrative posts, relying in part on the reasoning that this was
a subject race prone to mendacity and exaggeration.

It was not long, however, before the intelligentsia in Bengal began
to produce challenges to this discourse. In 1828, for instance, a young
Hindu College scholar, Kashi Prashad Ghosh, wrote an essay attack-
ing Mill's *History* and defending Hindu chronology as meant 'for
astronomical calculations, not for historical purposes' (Kopf 1969:
264). But 'the connection between history and prose [had] come to
be taken for granted in the West' and an argument can be made that
this was the gauntlet picked up by the Bengali intelligentsia in their
quest to discover and write India as a nation with its own history
(Guha 2003: 12). Prose also represented modernity; to have a prose
history was to have made progress in time. Ranajit Guha contends
that inasmuch as the writing of prose histories and the birth of
the novel coincided in British India, both were a response to the

intellectual dominance of 'World History' and to the primacy of individual experience. It is not necessary to agree with this contention to see that the emergence of the novel in India was closely connected to experiments in prose, realism, and the writing of 'national' history. What Mill and his ilk would have seen as 'a passage from myth to history; from fantasy to reason' could be seen from the perspective of the colonized, argues Guha, 'as a shift from a particular paradigm of storytelling to another' (ibid. 54). Whether in the novel or in the new writing of history, experience and evidence are placed at the centre; in both cases, now 'it is the narrator's testimony that is under scrutiny' (ibid. 55).

And so it was that the novel emerged in nineteenth-century India with a profound interest in the writing of history and, relatedly, in articulating a sense of nationhood. This concern was particularly visible in the anglophone novel written, at the time, with a mainly European reader and interlocutor in mind. Guha (ibid. 72) is, however, somewhat too absolute, indeed melodramatically so, when he pronounces that 'the battle of paradigms was won for the West' and that 'experience' triumphed over 'wonder'. As we shall see, at no stage was such a paradigm shift either complete or decisive. Repressed elements—wonder, fantasy, poetry—would emerge through the gaps in even many stolidly realist works and, of course, over time, 'magical realism' or the bringing together of the fabulous and real, would come to be one of the most celebrated achievements of the tradition. Prose, realism, the novel—all were appropriated and reworked rather than simply imitated and absorbed.

Two early historical novels

Although, as Mukherjee (2000: 7) points out, the English-language novels of the time have more or less faded into obscurity, eclipsed by the far better-known works in languages such as Bangla, Marathi, and Malayalam, they were written 'in considerable numbers'. Even those early novelists who did not write in English were often indebted to their reading of English fiction and translations of other Indian fiction into English.[2] That anglophone fiction was, from its inception, invested in the writing of prose history is evident from early English-language texts. In May 1845, Soshee Chunder Dutt, scion of an

English-educated Calcutta literary family, published a short piece of narrative fiction entitled *The Republic of Orissa: A Page from the Annals of the 20th Century* (Dutt 1885a). This and Kylas Chunder Dutt's *A Journal of Forty-Eight Hours of the Year 1945* are the two earliest-known attempts at producing Indian fiction in English. Interestingly, both are set in the then-distant future of the twentieth century and imagine uprisings against British rule. Set in 1916, *Orissa* describes the legalizing of slavery by the British, 'permitting a system of oppression revolting to the refined ideas of the Indian public' (1885a: 347). After listing, in the manner of official documents, the injuries suffered by slaves (who are always 'Hindus by birth'), the narrator describes how, peaceful means and petitions having failed, 'the spirit of the populace was kindled...[and] everywhere was raised the cry of revolt' (ibid. 349). Despite the arguments of pro-imperialist voices against an uprising, the rebellion coalesces around the Kingaries' tribal leader, Bheekoo Barik. After a truce, during which the patriots are betrayed by the cunning British, the plot deploys the twists and turns of a love affair to arrive at a point where rebellious feelings reignite and the British are finally routed on 15 October 2001, whereupon Orissa declares itself a republic: 'A splendid spectacle is presented to the eyes of wandering millions, of a nation emerging from the chaos of ignorance and slavery, and hastening to occupy its orbit on the grand system of civilization' (ibid. 356). Here, India ('Hindustan') is exhorted to follow the example of Orissa, which has joined the order of world nations by laying claim to the idea of freedom over tyranny.

It is striking that both *Orissa* and *Journal* are fictional narratives that take the form of 'annals' or historical accounts, but ones set in the future—as though it is only in the future, when Hindustan's national spirit coheres, that a historical approach to the present will be possible. Dutt draws not only on history, but also colonial ethnography, inverting the values traditionally assigned to various groups. Thus, the 'tribals', often categorized as criminally inclined by colonial administrators, emerge as courageous, patriotic, and freedom-loving while it is 'the superstitious nations of Europe' that endorse tyranny. This sets the stage for the final triumphant reversal where we find Orissa in splendid freedom while the 'British Empire is sinking fast into that state of weakness and internal division which is the sure forerunner of the fall of kingdoms. Its formal glory is now no more. We regret for its fallen grandeur; we regret to see an imperial bird, shorn of its wings and plumage of pride, coming down precipitately from its aëry height' (ibid.). Given the time of writing as well as Dutt's own background, *Orissa* is a remarkably radical text, unrestrained in its critique of the tyrannies of empire, including 'dishonest and inefficient administration', 'gross corruption', and 'the total exclusion of the whole native population from every legitimate object of ambition, and every honourable species of employment' (ibid. 349). Satire is deployed strategically, targeting bureaucratic euphemisms and journalistic pieties. Warning against the consequences of an uprising, a loyalist newspaper editorializes: 'The Hindus are like children. They want what they cannot understand, fret because with paternal care we refuse to indulge them, and cry because we are deaf to their entreaties . . . But "why does the enactment exclude Europeans from slavery?" they ask. *Why*, dear patriots? Because ye are the conquered, we the conquerors. Are you answered?' (ibid. 351, original emphasis).

If *Orissa* is little more than an imaginative exercise, where romance is largely a plot device and the characters are notional types rather than individuals, in a later work, *Shunkur: A Tale of the Indian Mutiny of 1857*, Dutt (1885*b*) would try his hand at writing a full-fledged novel of rebellion. *Shunkur* is that rare object, a novel of the 1857 Sepoy 'Mutiny' in English written by an Indian. Although the title suggests that the novel will focus on a single protagonist, the eponymous Shunkur, we are not introduced to this character until late in the narrative. The opening chapters suggest that the key issue is that of what constitutes 'India' or 'Hindustan'. The plot hinges around the question of who will rule India once the British have been thrown out and those involved in this fraught discussion are actual historical characters such as Nana Saheb, 'the notorious hero of the Cawnpore atrocity' and Azimoolah Khan, 'who represented the Mahomedan interests in the councils of Bithoor' (ibid. 86–7). In the early sections, the novel seems to follow the familiar contours of a 'Mutiny' novel, depicting 'treacherous and cowardly' natives plotting the downfall of their British overlords (ibid. 107).

Remarkably, however, as the narrative seems to head towards the typically gory climax of 'Mutiny' novels, the narrative scrutiny shifts suddenly towards the British themselves: 'This has been and still is the position of Englishmen in India.[3] They do not feel in common with the races they have conquered; there is no sympathy on one side, and no confidence on the other' (ibid. 110). Now it is the two male fugitives, Bernard and Mackenzie, with their 'cunning and hypocrisy' and 'well-developed audacity and insolence' who are seen to betray the trust of their rural hosts. Given the prevalence of sensationalist narratives in which innocent white women are raped by marauding native men, it cannot but be deliberate that in this novel, it is a trusting Indian woman who is raped by the British men she shelters in her home. 'It has often been said', the narrative reminds its reader, as if to set the historical record straight, 'that the natives throughout the country were hostile towards their rulers during these disturbances. It has conveniently been forgotten that every man or woman that was saved was protected by the natives who were friendly to them' (ibid. 111). The racial logic shown to justify the rape is horrifying: 'There is no harm in that when the woman is a nigger, you know. It would be a different thing if she were a European' (ibid. 112).

The awkwardness of this novel's attempts to integrate fictional and historical narratives is most evident in the uncertainty with which it juxtaposes the stories of Shunkur's personal quest to avenge his wife's rape and the collective dissatisfaction that leads to the Mutiny. Shunkur's 'is a grievance of a different kind; we bear the State no grudge' (ibid. 134). For the Havildar, a fighting man, in times like these, the private necessarily takes on an allegorical dimension: 'though you are not opposed to the State, the prosecution of your private vengeance against two Englishmen can, at this moment, be regarded in no other light than as rebellion against the State' (ibid. 134). Shunkur, the peasant, remains uncomfortable about yoking his own search for revenge to a collective project: 'But we that have suffered, how can we avoid feeling for those who suffer like us?' (ibid. 136). Far from ending on a triumphal note, the last lines of the novel are resigned and lonely:

'Return to your home at Soorajpore,' said the Havildar, 'to the old mother and little boy you have left behind. Forget your connection with these bloody doings, and no one else will remember them against you.'

'The Havildar speaks well,' said Shunkur. 'There is no further motive for the life we were obliged to adopt: let us go back to our cheerless home.'

(ibid. 158)

The nominal protagonist's last words attempt to disentangle his story from that of the Mutiny as though hoping that in some future, more cheerful heaven, there will be no need to connect private stories with public histories. But for the anglophone novel, that time was far away yet.

Further Reading

Most early anglophone texts are still available only in the archives, although there are ongoing projects of republication, particularly by OUP India. Chapter 2 provides a list of early works that are available as reprints. See Fisher 1996 for a republication of The *Travels of Dean Mahomet*. Mukherjee 2000 provides a useful overview of the archive and an insightful discussion of some key texts, as do some essays in Mehrotra 2003.

2

Ethnography, Gender, and Nation

Even if the 'private' is as yet inaccessible in English, exemplary 'lives' can, nevertheless, be rendered into public narratives. Accordingly, the voice of the lowly peasant who finds himself in an awkward relationship to great historical events is what *Govinda Samanta or Bengal Peasant Life* claims to offer. Billed as an 'authentic history' of the life of a *raiyat*, or tenant farmer in Bengal, Lal Behari Day's novel proffers itself as a documentary that will educate a reader unfamiliar with is context and culture. Outlining, rather defensively, 'what the reader is to expect and what he is not to expect', Day's preface adumbrates the anxieties generated by the foray into European-style realist prose. Deploying something like Henry Fielding's famous 'Bill of Fare' metaphor, Day's first gesture—one that would have surely pleased Mill—is to distance himself from his 'great Indian predecessors' and their 'marvellous' creations that tell of:

kings with ten heads and twenty arms; of a monkey carrying the sun in his arm-pit; of demons churning the universal ocean with a mountain for a churn-staff; of beings, man above and fish below, or with the body of a man and the head of an elephant; of sages with truly profound stomachs, who drank up the waters of the ocean in one sip... The age of marvels has gone by; giants do not pay now-a-days; skepticism is the order of the day; and the veriest stripling, whose throat is still full of his mother's milk, says to his father, when a story is told him; 'Papa, is it true?' (1969: 5–6)

Day, a convert to Christianity and a minister of the church, also distinguishes his work from that of European masters such as Rabelais and Swift, insisting on a historicity that will emerge from a sober apprehension of the everyday. His 'unpretending volume' is not going to offer the pleasures of 'the sensational novels of the day': 'Romantic adventures, intricate evolutions of the plot, striking occurrences, remarkable surprises, hair-breadth escapes, scenes of horror' (ibid. 6). At the same time, the context of writing introduces particular constraints: 'I would fain introduce love-scenes; but in Bengal—and for the matter of that in all India—they do not make love in the English and honourable sense of that word.' As Mukherjee (1985: 8) has argued, in prose, love 'could only be shown in an indigenous setting where the demands of realism were absent'. As we shall see, however, it would not be long before questions of love and passion also became central to the novel in India, imbricated in complex ways with ideas about nation, identity, and belonging.

Govinda Samanta is itself the predecessor of the 'Indo-Anglian' novels of the 1930s and 1940s (discussed in Ch. 3) which, under Gandhi's influence, would attempt to give literary voice to rural India. For its time, it was innovative in content and form, drawing heavily on the disciplines of cartography, ethnography, travel writing, and even the classificatory systems of the natural sciences (detailing, for instance, the Latin botanical names of the plants that dot the Bengal countryside). The author's compendious knowledge of the Greek and English literary traditions as well as the work of Orientalists is also apparent, with epigraphs and quotations from various authors sprinkled liberally throughout the text, providing, one critic argues, 'the ideological frame through which we are asked to view the Indian village of the second half of the 19th century' (Mohanty 2005: 21).[1] A great deal of energy is devoted not only to translation of Bengali or Sanskrit terms, but also to finding philosophical and literary equivalents from gods and literary personages to domestic implements and folk genres. Day's bilingual sensibility also makes its presence felt in the rhythm of sentences and his deployment of onomatopoeia.

The '*bhroor—bhroor—bhroor*' of the hubble-bubble kept time with the '*ghnan—ghnan—ghnan*' of the *charkha*, and the two together evoked a melody which the immortals might have heard with rapture. At last Badan broke the divine harmony.

... 'Don't you think, mother, it would be a good thing to give Govin his *hate khadi*? It is a great drawback that I cannot read a *pata* (pottah) or write a *kabuliyat*; I cannot even sign my name.' (1969: 43, explications in original)

For all his confidence with the English language, Day is acutely conscious of the issue that would continue to generate a degree of anxiety in anglophone writers, famously described, decades later, by Raja Rao in the foreword to his novel, *Kanthapura*, of expressing 'in a language that is not one's own the spirit that is one's own' (2004: p. vi). Day articulates it in terms of both class and culture:

You perceive that Badan and Alanga speak better English than most uneducated English peasants; they speak almost like educated ladies and gentlemen, without any provincialisms. But how could I have avoided this defect in my history? If I had translated their talk into the Somersetshire or the Yorkshire dialect, I should have turned them into English, and not Bengali peasants.

Unlike many others writing in English at the time, Day is also insistent on using a clear and simple prose, in contrast to Young Bengal's 'literary Bombastes Furioso [and] Johnsonese run mad' which entails the 'use of English words two or three feet long' (ibid. 7) The peasant, as subject matter, generates 'a plain and unvarnished tale'.

Clearly intended though it is for the European reader, *Govinda Samanta* is no simple paean to the British presence in India or even, indeed, to English education. Contrasting the village 'pathshala' favourably with English schools and colleges in Bengal, Day suggests that an education that sacrifices 'utility to ornament' must have in it 'something vicious, something essentially wrong' (ibid. 82). In the last third of the novel Day crafts a surprisingly fierce critique of zamindari or landlordism under the Permanent Settlement of 1793, which enabled the British administration to extract revenue indirectly, thus 'in consulting its own interest . . . [consigning] virtually the entire peasantry of Bengal to the tender mercies of a most cruel and rapacious aristocracy' (ibid. 244). The villain of the piece is the venal and tyrannical zamindar, Jay Chand, who is described as not 'having had the benefit of an English education, unacquainted with Sanskrit, and possessing only a smattering of his mother tongue . . . an ignorant man' (ibid. 178). But as it gathers political speed, the narrative turns its ire on an iconic figure, the British indigo planter, already the subject of anti-colonial literature.[2] Murray in Day's novel is an extraordinarily unpleasant character, and the author is quick to forestall his being read as an exception: 'Some planters are benevolently disposed but the system which they follow being pernicious in the extreme, is sufficient to convert the gentlest of human beings into ferocious tigers' (ibid. 208) Commenting on the distortions that colonialism produces in the colonizer's psyche, Day suggests that what makes the latter susceptible to such a 'metamorphosis' is that 'their only object is to make money and then run away to merry England as fast as steam can carry them' (ibid. 208) As with the two texts discussed in the previous chapter, rebellion remains a fantasy, an event that does, however, take place in the future when Murray's 'oppression created universal disaffection among the peasantry, and produced an outbreak' (ibid. 235).

At the same time, English education can foster the right kind of 'liberal and patriotic sentiments' (ibid. 212). Day, the Christian minister, cannot help but praise the changes in social conditions that British rule has brought about, an ambiguity many educated Bengalis would experience and express. The narrative contains the obligatory lurid account of a 'sati', though one that takes place in the past, for in the present, such customs, 'thanks to the enlightened humanity of the British Government, have altogether been suppressed' (ibid. 83). Even so, Day is reluctant to allow himself to be easily appropriated by those 'civilizers' who would speak in the name of Hindu women. His, he stresses, is an emphatically rooted perspective, free of the distortions of colonial discourse: 'It is impossible not to sympathise with a Hindu widow. It is not that she is persecuted and tormented by her relatives and friends—that is *a fiction of foreign writers*, of people unacquainted with Hindu life in its actual manifestations—but the peculiar wretchedness of her condition lies in this, that the fountain of her heart, with its affections and desires, is forever dried up' (ibid. 92–3, added emphasis). A long and somewhat defensively overstated account follows, of the far from wretched life of the Hindu widow, beyond the 'supreme privation' of losing a companion to love.

The first anglophone novel: *Rajmohan's Wife*

Written with an implied European or English reader in mind, many early Indian English novels offered themselves as guided forays, not just into Indian life, but more specifically, into a domestic sphere largely hidden from the European and colonial gaze. As Mukherjee (2000: 14) points out, their titles often 'promise an unveiling of some mystery ("A Peep into", "Glimpses of", "Revelations", etc.) pertaining to a presumably homogeneous space called India... inhabited by an undifferentiated "Hindu" community'. Perceived as the space of the feminine, the domestic sphere was not just incomprehensible, but hidden tantalizingly from the scrutiny of outsiders.[3] As with *Govinda Samanta*'s foray into peasant life, novelistic excursions into the domestic worked well with the imperative to write realistically and from experience. So it is with the first known anglophone Indian novel by an Indian writer, Bankim Chandra Chatterjee's (or Chattopadhyaya's) *Rajmohan's Wife* (1996), which also undertakes to delineate the contours of village life with a particular interest in women's lives; the inevitable chapter headed 'A Visit to the Zenana' devotes itself, with no little prurience, to elaborate descriptions of women going about their noisy business, their bodies in free and sensual movement. Elsewhere, elaborate architectural descriptions of inner and outer household spaces converge with the evocation of a Gothic atmosphere as the reader is invited to 'ascend in our company through a flight of dark and narrow stairs of solid brickwork to the upper story of the andarmahal', the women's quarters.

Written in the manner of a Gothic novel and serialized in 1864 in the short-lived weekly, *Indian Field*, *Rajmohan's Wife* is both a tragic romance and a study of an unhappy marriage. It tells of the dutiful but passionate Matangini whose father marries her to the venal and jealous Rajmohan although she is in love with Madhav, who, meanwhile, marries her sister. When she discovers a plot against Madhav, in which Rajmohan is involved, Matangini risks her husband's wrath and her own life in a night-time journey to the former's house to inform him about impending danger. After a series of mishaps, including Matangini's incarceration, the British administration intervenes to foil the plot and Rajmohan commits suicide. Matangini returns to her father and dies an early death. Though described by Salman Rushdie (1997: 57) as a 'dud...a poor melodramatic thing', this early novel by Chatterjee—while no dazzling debut—is a reasonably well-paced read, a thriller of sorts, set in the context of changing fiscal and familial relations in nineteenth-century Bengal. New wealth generated by changes in property law, English education, and migration to the city had generated a new urban culture which was very different from agrarian life. Unsurprisingly, familial and gender relations were also changing in this transitional period and in this light, Bankim's use of the protagonist's relational status—as a wife—rather than her own name in the title of his novel is significant. *Rajmohan's Wife* does attempt to 'foreground the ways in which the home and the world are inextricably linked... by locating the drama within the conjugal and domestic space in relation to the external arena of property, legality, crime and the colonial administration' (Mukherjee 2005: p. vi). Meenakshi Mukherjee (1985: 8) has also suggested that in a social milieu where 'marriage was a social institution rather than an act of individual choice, there was very little scope for romantic pre-marital love of the kind depicted in the English novels being read by the educated urban Indians'. In *Rajmohan's Wife*, premarital romance, rather than being absent altogether, haunts the edges of the narrative, a ghostly presence that will explain the suffering of Matangini who must give up the man she loves in order to become 'Rajmohan's wife'.

For all its staged coyness about sensual matters, the novel returns persistently to questions of desire and, more boldly, female desire, neither of which were, of course, absent from Bengali or other Indian literary traditions, even if they had not been evoked in prose yet. The virtuous Matangini, stoic and faithful in an arranged marriage with the tyrannical Rajmohan, who is consumed by sexual jealousy, is the first to speak—in 'the passionate language of English Romantic poetry' (Mukherjee 2005: 149) of her illicit desire for her brother-in-law:

Then, as if under the influence of a maddening agony of soul, she grasped his hands in her own and bending over them her lily face so that Madhav trembled under the thrilling touch of the delicate curls that fringed her spotless brow... [T]he wild current of passion had hurried her to that region where naught but the present was visible and in which all knowledge of right and wrong is whirled and merged in the vortex of intense present felicity. (1997: 54)

While it shies away from foregrounding this romance as its theme, *Rajmohan's Wife* raises the possibility that thwarted desire—the 'brightness of the impure felicity'—will return to haunt the space of the familial. In this case, the only resolution is the inevitable exile and Victorian 'early death' of the heroine. In later works such as *Anandamath*, as we shall see, passion and desire are sublimated by the demands of nation.

Sacred nationhood: *Anandamath*

By the last decades of the nineteenth century, in the wake of wide-spread famines and economic degradation, resentment and localized criticism of British rule were transforming themselves into a more well-defined nationalism, one that sought to unite various provincial groups and organizations under a larger 'all-India' umbrella. In December 1885, these efforts were realized in the establishment of the Indian National Congress, which sought initially, in a reformist way, mainly to elicit for Indians 'a larger share in the government of their country' (Chandra 1971: 209). A sense of unity was aided by the shared experience of imperial rule; the subcontinent's economic life had become 'a single whole and interlinked the economic fate of people in different parts of the country' (ibid. 199). It was only in 1905, however, that the demand for 'swarajya' or self-government was advanced, accompanied by more militant forms of protest and self-assertion. The novel had now established itself in Bengali, Marathi, and other Indian languages and provided a site for exploring the meanings of nation, national culture, and national identity. Though novels in English continued to be written during this period, their readership was restricted and most received little or no critical attention; it was in non-fiction prose that English-language writing now began to make its mark, in the form of speeches, petitions, essays, and journalism. At the same time—the most important and well-received novelists in Indian languages from Chandu Menon (Malayalam) and Govardhanram Tripathi (Gujarati) to the Bengalis, Bankim Chandra Chatterjee and Rabindranath Tagore—were educated in English and deeply influenced by the European novel; they also continued to write essays and occasional journalism in English.

This section examines two novels, originally written in Bengali, both of which were of immense significance in the literary exploration and articulation of India and Indian nationalism. Translated into English and other languages, and widely available, they also provide instructive points of comparison with novels written in English, particularly in their engagement with gender. After *Rajmohan's Wife*, Bankim—like Michael Madhusudhan Dutt, before him—turned to Bengali or Bangla as his chosen literary language; he went on to become Bengal's most renowned novelist. Though there is nothing in the archives to explain this decision to change linguistic medium, it is probable that Bankim realized that his readership in English was limited and that his own creative powers would flourish best, as they eventually indeed did, in his mother-tongue. However, themes incipiently raised in *Rajmohan's Wife* would find their way back into his Bengali fiction. In 1882, he published *Anandamath* (literally, 'The Ananda Monastery'), translated into several English editions as *The Abbey of Bliss* and more recently as *The Sacred Brotherhood*. Where *Rajmohan's Wife* had been an attempt to write a domestic novel within a largely realist framework, *Anandamath* returns to the mode of fictional history we encountered in *Shunkur*, imagining a rebellion against tyrannical rule but at a careful historical and allegorical distance. Where in *Shunkur*, anti-colonial rebellion was conceived of as a response to specific incidents and injuries, with only a notional invocation of 'Hindusthan', Bankim's novel came up with a visual delineation of India that would become iconic:

> ... 'an enchanting image, more beautiful and glorious than Lakshmi or Sarasvati.'
> ... 'Who is she?'
> 'The Mother.'
> 'Who is this Mother?'
> The monk answered: 'She whose Children we are.'   (2006: 149)

Drawing on existing Hindu conceptions of the earth as female and as a goddess, the image of Mother India became a powerful rallying point for Indian nationalism and continues to haunt literature and popular culture in India.[4] *Anandamath* is set about a hundred years before the time of its writing during a famine in 1770 when 'Bengal had not yet fallen under British sway' and the region of Birbhum is under the venal and incompetent Muslim ruler, Mir Jafar, who is, however, backed by British forces (ibid. 140). In the forest a band of mendicants, the monastic Santans or 'Children', have foresworn conjugal and domestic life until they have freed their Mother from bondage. They include Mahendra, who joins the Santans after giving up his starving family for dead, and Jibananda who has left behind a wife, Shanti, who eventually secretly joins the order dressed as a man. After various twists and turns, the Santans lead a massive uprising against the Muslim ruler which, however, also involves a battle with British forces. By the end, Muslim rule 'is destroyed but Hindu rule has not been established ... the English remain powerful in Calcutta' (ibid. 228). It is decided that the time is not yet ripe to overthrow the English and that this must happen in the fullness of time when Hindus have revitalized themselves (ibid.).

The contrived and often melodramatic turns of plot in this novel are less interesting than its powerful delineation of militant self-assertion in the name of nation. Bankim's rebels fight in the name of a Hindu Mother-Nation 'to uproot Muslims completely because they are the enemies of our Lord'. The rallying anthem of the Santans, 'Bande Mataram' or 'Worship the Motherland', written by Bankim and inserted into the narrative by him, is still India's 'national song' and is to this day touted by Hindu nationalists as a more genuinely 'Indian' alternative to the existing national 'anthem', 'Jana Gana Mana', written by Rabindranath Tagore in a self-consciously secular spirit incorporating a diversity into a unity. As the 'bhadralok' or 'respectable' intelligentsia of Bengal began to search for their own national identity in the mirror of Englishness, they turned to a presumed indigenous 'Aryan' and Hindu heritage as the true, hoary spirit of the Indian nation, now degraded and overlaid by centuries of Islamic rule. English rule, Bankim suggests, will be the salutary catalyst for the recovery or 'Renaissance' of this true spirit. Indeed, the Santan rebellion itself, Bankim suggests in a revisionist comment towards the conclusion of his narrative, was intended to bring about the transformation of the English from traders to rulers: '—so long as the Hindu is not wise and virtuous and strong once more—English rule will remain intact... The English will rule as friends' (ibid. 229–30). While in his prolific discursive prose, Bankim often displayed a far more nuanced understanding of Hindu–Muslim relations and even an admiration for Islam, by the late 1870s, his fiction had clearly 'evolved a denunciatory mode around Muslim rule in India' (Sarkar 2001: 184). But the polemics in the novel against Muslims as 'yauvanas' or foreigners also enable it to displace and allegorize resistance to British colonialism. Despite its apparently laudatory attitude towards the British at the end, the novel is sombre about the economic implications of the British presence in India: 'All they did was collect the revenue; they took no responsibility for overseeing the lives and property of the Bengalis... People could die of starvation but the collection of revenue did not stop' (ibid. 140).

If the critique of deleterious economic changes was a powerful element in the growth of Indian nationalism, the second half of the nineteenth century was also marked by social and religious reform movements aimed at 'regenerating' religion and community. Controversies and debates emerged around these to which, predictably, the 'woman question' became central. Here too, Mill's views summed up a pervasive colonial attitude deployed retrospectively to justify imperialism as a 'civilizing' mission: 'Among rude people, the women are generally degraded; among civilized people they are exalted' (cited in Tharu and Lalita 1991: 46). Various reformist organizations such as the Brahmo Samaj and Arya Samaj then took on issues such as the living conditions of widows, child marriage, and female education. The most well-known reformer of the times was, of course, Raja Rammohan Roy (or Ray) who was a prolific translator, polemicist, and essayist in the English language. In the main, however, it was literature in indigenous languages, novels in Marathi, Bengali, Malayalam, and Gujarati, rather than English, that addressed issues of social reform. If life behind the zenana curtain or purdah was a favoured subject for early anglophone writers, bringing upper-class women out of seclusion or 'purdah' became a shared concern for Hindu and Muslim reformers towards the end of the nineteenth century. These were fraught processes, unleashing resistance from orthodox quarters, but also anxieties among male reformers themselves about the consequences, particularly for gender and sexual politics, of educating women and bringing them out of the home into the world. In Tagore's important novel, *The Home and the World*, these anxieties merge with a critique of the libidinal charge of militant nationalism and its gendered iconography.

Woman, nation, and idolatry: *The Home and the World*

Ghare Bhaire (literally 'home and outside'), was first translated by Tagore's nephew, Surendranath Tagore, as *The Home and the World*, with the author's approval. The novel takes as its subject the cult of 'Bande Mataram', which emerged in a militant form during the years of 'Swadeshi' nationalism at the turn of the century, and was given further impetus by the British attempt to undermine growing nationalism by partitioning Bengal in 1905. Swadeshi, a movement in which Tagore himself was heavily involved at its height, was premised mainly on the economic boycott of foreign goods but drew increasingly on the rhetoric and iconography of a revivalist Hindu nationalism that sought to define the nation in religious terms. When communal (Hindu–Muslim) riots broke out following the attempts of middle-class activists to compel peasants and petty traders—many of whom were Muslim—to observe the boycott, Tagore 'became the movement's most trenchant critic, calling on it to introspect on its high-handedness and Hindu biases' (Datta 2003: 4). From 1915 to early 1916, Tagore—who had just been awarded the Nobel Prize for literature—serially published *Ghare Bhaire* which, inasmuch as it critically challenged the course of 'the first popular anti-colonial movement', became his 'most controversial moment' (ibid. 1). It earned him the sobriquet of an apologist for colonialism, criticism exacerbated by his acceptance of a knighthood in 1916 which he later returned as a protest against the infamous 1919 Jallianwala Bagh Massacre.

The novel is written in what P. K. Datta calls a 'multi-confessional form', alternating the perspectives of three narrator-protagonists: Nikhil, a wealthy *zamindar* or landowner, his wife, Bimala, and his friend, Sandip, who is a militant Swadeshi activist. The story, which E. M. Forster dismissed as a 'boarding-house flirtation', deals with the impact of Sandip's arrival on Nikhil and Bimala's happy marriage. Bimala has spent much of her life in the 'andarmahal' or women's quarters (the home or 'ghar') even as Nikhil has been encouraging her to come out into the world (the outside, the space beyond the inner quarters). She finally takes a tentative step out in Sandip's honour, drawn to his fiery nationalist rhetoric and political charisma. He in turn deifies her as a living symbol of the Goddess or 'Mother India' to whom the cry 'Bande Mataram' (worship the Motherland) might be addressed. They teeter on the brink of a romantic and sexual relationship while Nikhil watches with growing pain but without intervening. Refusing to commit an act of tyranny by curbing Bimala's newly awakened desires, Nikhil also refuses to support what he perceives as the tyrannies of Swadeshi activists being visited on poor traders and tenant farmers. He finds himself increasingly estranged from both his wife and his friend as Bimala too becomes involved with Sandip's Swadeshi activism. Bimala and Sandip's relationship takes a downturn when he asks her for money to fund the cause; she procures it by stealing from the family safe. Meanwhile,

Bimala also strikes up a maternal friendship with Amulya, a young protégé of Sandip's, and eventually both of them come to see through Sandip and what is depicted as his false heroics. At the end of the novel, Amulya dies during a raid while Nikhil is seriously injured, his fate hanging in the balance.

The Home and the World is a key text for the study of anglophone Indian fiction for several reasons. It was written in Bengali and then translated into English with modifications and substantial input from the author, to an extent that allows this English translation to be considered a literary work in its own right. Tagore's own sensibilities and talents were multilingual; he wrote and lectured widely in English, into which he also translated his own works. There is a clear discursive relationship between the novel and a series of lectures on nationalism that he gave in English on a world tour during the latter half of 1916. *Home and the World* was also experimental in form, structured as a series of interwoven interior monologues (sometimes addressed to other characters), drawing also on the author's capabilities as a dramatist and poet. But above all it is Tagore's controversial and critical engagement with nationalism that makes *Home and the World* a text of continuing relevance.

[Sandip] was familiar with my husband's views on the cult of *Bande Mataram*, and began in a provoking way: 'so you do not allow that there is room for an appeal to the imagination in patriotic work?'

'It has its place, Sandip, I admit, but I do not believe in giving it the whole place. I would know my country in its frank reality, and for this I am both afraid and ashamed to make use of the hypnotic texts of patriotism.' (1999: 36)

The novel undertook the first major literary critique of the forms taken by nationalism in Bengal and elsewhere in India. Tagore was implicitly addressing not only texts such as *Anandamath* but also his own earlier incarnation as a militant Hindu nationalist, one who wrote rousing songs adopted by Swadeshi activists. Accordingly, the novel takes seriously the role of the imagination in shaping historical events, acknowledging that it is a powerful force in bringing about new modes of individual and collective existence. But it is precisely the power of the imagination to imagine communities into being—through excluding and marginalizing—that makes it a dangerous force, one that it is imperative to keep under critical scrutiny.

For all that it gives the three protagonists almost equal voice and time, there is little doubt that Tagore's sympathies are firmly with the gentle and principled Nikhil who articulates his author's own disquiet with militant nationalism. Swadeshi is figured here as essentially destructive and tyrannical and as such, derivative of the violence of colonial power itself. The difference between Sandip and Nikhil maps neatly on to a distinction between the passion and restraint, muscularity and spirituality:

Nikhil was visibly growing excited. 'I accept the truth of passion,' he said, 'only when I recognize the truth of restraint. By pressing what we want to see right into our eyes we only injure them: we do not see. So does the violence of passion, which would leave no space between the mind and its object, defeat its purpose.' (Tagore 1999: 60)

Metaphor fails at the moment that it is literalized, becoming a weapon of hypnosis rather than an agent of awakening. Coming from a poet who believed that poetry was derived from 'enchanted seeing' and who was renowned for his own dexterity with figurative language, this is a powerful insight. It is also a position that Tagore the philosopher articulates in his lectures on nationalism, given in Japan and the USA: 'Even though from childhood I had been taught that idolatry of the Nation is almost better than reverence for God and humanity... it is my conviction that my countrymen will truly gain their India by fighting against the education which teaches them that a country is greater than the ideals of humanity' (Tagore 1994: 83). Fetishizing cultural particularity was, Tagore appeared to realize, a response to the colonial disdain for India's 'lack' of History and nation-state, as articulated by the likes of Hegel. This led to a fatal divorce in Indian nationalism between imagination and reality: 'The East, in fact, is attempting to take unto itself a history, which is not the outcome of its own living' (ibid. 83).

The critique of imagined communities as represented by the Hindu nationalism of Sandip is, at its core, a condemnation of the exclusions such communities inevitably enforce. In *Home and the World*, it is not only Muslims who are vulnerable to exclusion or containment but also the poor who cannot afford to embrace Swadeshi unconditionally. They are represented here by Panchu, the tenant farmer, whose merchandise is destroyed by zealous activists for his failure to adhere to the boycott they impose. Through Nikhil, who refuses to force his tenants to adhere to the boycott of foreign goods, Tagore pronounces aphoristically: 'To tyrannize for the country is to tyrannize over the country' (1999: 109). As though to pre-empt the charge that he and his creator are apologists for colonialism, Nikhil is figured as a pioneering but unostentatious champion of Indian goods, one committed to change without force. Tagore is clear that the needs of the individual cannot be sacrificed to those of the nation-as-collective. Sandip and Nikhil represent opposing conceptions of masculinity, the former modelling himself on a 'muscular' and appropriative Western ideal and the latter a 'spiritual', Eastern way of being a man, which asks: 'But is strength a mere display of muscularity? Must strength have no scruples in treading the weak underfoot?' (ibid. 41). Muscular masculinity as embodied by Sandip and militant nationalism as 'derivative discourse' from the West are essentially grasping and greedy ('fleshly') in their particularism, whereas Nikhil represents a true, indigenous alternative that is, at the same time, universal in its humanism. If Sandip's nationalism ultimately requires a worship of the 'self' as the highest embodiment of the particular, Nikhil's humanism holds that there is a contradiction in 'the worship of God by hating other countries in which He is equally manifest'; he refuses accordingly to 'permit the evil which is within me to be exaggerated into an image of my country' (ibid. 38).

Though Tagore's critique of militant nationalism is complex, insightful, and radical, the text's 'ideological structure', as Michael Sprinker (2003: 113) has pointed out, 'is far from stable; its conclusions highly troubled'. The ending of the novel is disturbed and ambiguous: we are left with the image (made iconic in the opening shot of Satyajit Ray's film version of the novel) of a guilt-stricken Bimala who is brought news of Amulya's death and Nikhil's possibly fatal wound. Though Bimala is the site for an interpretative contest between two men over the meaning of nation, Tanika Sarkar (2003: 29) argues that the fact that 'the woman here speaks for herself alongside the two men who talk about her' constitutes a radical literary departure; a self-representing female was 'a startlingly new character on the Bengali literary landscape'. At the same time, the novel is an exploration of crises of masculinity that are then enacted against the figure of the desirable and desiring woman. It is she, not Sandip, who embodies Swadeshi nationalism and does so in markedly sexual terms: 'My sight and my mind, my hopes and my desires, became red with the passion of this new age' (ibid. 26). Tagore's incisive critique of the power of the 'Mother' as a nationalist icon also emerges as concern about unleashing female desire:

In that future I saw my country, a woman like myself, standing expectant. She has been drawn forth from her home corner by the sudden call of some Unknown. She has had no time to pause or ponder, or to light herself a torch as she rushes forward into the darkness ahead . . . There is no call to her of her children in their hunger, no home to be lighted of an evening, no household work to be done. So, she hies to her tryst . . . She has left home, forgotten domestic duties; she has nothing but an unfathomable yearning which hurries her on . . .   (Tagore 1999: 93–4)

The critique of imagination run amok merges with an unambiguous patriarchal anxiety about the consequences of bringing women out of the home into the world. As the novel is all too aware, freedom 'granted' does not stay the course desired by the giver although Nikhil apparently reconciles himself to this: 'I had come to understand that never would I be free until I could set free' (ibid. 134). Even so, as Michael Sprinker (2003: 115) points out, 'the ideology of liberation [Nikhil] embraces here and throughout the text is no Kantian kingdom of ends where all are equally empowered to realise their freedom; it is rather the paternalist idea of the enlightened and wise patriarch extending freedom to others.' Ultimately, Bimala does shoulder the blame for the 'delusion' and 'untruth' of militant nationalism: 'We must tear away the disguise of her who weaves our net of enchantment at home, and know her for what she is' (Tagore 1999: 41, 110).

Women and self-representation: *Kamala* and *Saguna*

At the same time, as Tanika Sarkar (2003: 29) argues, Tagore's novel points to the emergence of the 'self-representing woman' on the Bengali literary landscapes. By the late nineteenth century, however, with the growth of women's education and related social reforms, women in Bengal and elsewhere in India had, in fact, begun to write and publish, and to represent their lives and experiences in literature. Unsurprisingly, a great deal of this writing was in the form of memoirs and autobiographical accounts of which there were an 'extraordinary number' (Tharu and Lalita 1991: 160). The writing of *Amar Jiban* (*My Life*, 1876), the earliest known autobiography by a woman in India, itself tells a striking tale; it was written by Rassundari Debi, a once illiterate Bengali housewife, who taught herself to 'read and write in secret by scratching the letters of the alphabet onto a corner of the blackened kitchen wall' (Tharu and Lalita 1991: 190).[5] For reasons to do with the language of women's education in the nineteenth century (in their mother tongue rather than English, which was seen as a language to be used outside the home) as well as the subject matter—the sphere of the domestic rather than matters of history and politics—anglophone writing by women in nineteenth- and early twentieth-century India is relatively limited. Moreover, where it exists, it tends to be in the form of short stories, essays, and sketches rather than longer fiction; many of these writings are also very much in the ethnographic mode, as with Oxford-educated lawyer, Cornelia Sorabji's explicitly titled *Love and Life Behind the Purdah* (2003; first pub. 1901) as well as *India Calling*, an account of her life spent working with wealthy and aristocratic widows in purdah. Another author of some significance is Pandita Ramabai, the high-profile convert to Christianity, who wrote prolifically on issues of women and social reform; her *My Testimony* and *The High Caste Hindu Woman* remain important milestones in women's writing. Perhaps the most lively anglophone fictional work of the period is Rokeya Sakhawat Hossain's remarkable 'witty utopian fantasy' of gender-role inversion, 'Sultana's Dream', where it is men who live in seclusion while women run the state in distinctly different ways. Worth a mention also are two novels by the anglicized and devoutly Christian Toru Dutt, better known as a poet, both of which are, interestingly, set outside India with European women for protagonists: *Bianca, or the Young Spanish Maiden* and *Le Journal de Mademoiselle d'Arvers*, the latter written in French.

The two most well-known anglophone novels written by a woman from this time—Krupabai Satthianadhan's *Kamala* and *Saguna*—are, like Dutt's works, devoutly Christian, and like Ramabai's writings, both heavily informed by personal experience and driven by a social reform agenda. Born in 1862, Satthianadhan, the daughter of Hindu converts to Christianity, had studied to become a doctor before ill-health forced her to give up her studies. Her literary output is unambiguously addressed to a Western and Christian audience with her own perspective constructed as that of 'An Indian Lady', a nom de plume she sometimes used. Serialized in the Madras Christian College Magazine, *Saguna* is clearly influenced by the Romantic poetry that Satthianadhan was passionate about, particularly in its detailed evocations of nature and landscapes with 'pointed rocks, hidden caves, deep caverns, foaming, rushing torrents, bold, barren, breezy uplands and dark wooden lairs' (1998*b*: 23). Saguna's story, like her author's, is that of a Satthianadhan's daughter of converts; it also incorporates an account of Satthianadhan's mother's life as a young Hindu girl, a child bride of a man who then gives up the religion of his family to the accompaniment of social opprobrium. Despite its commitment to the civilizing Christian project of rescuing 'the upper-caste Hindu woman who they felt was enslaved by repressive institutionalized Hindu ideologies', the novel is also attuned to some of the emotional contradictions of native convert life (Lokuge 1998*b*: 4). If the convert sometimes feels like 'a foreigner. . . in some strange land', the colonial homeland is no alternative: 'The sentimental stuff about the *gloaming* and the *mooning* did not annoy me so much as the expression "home". . . . It was such an affectation, and I thought I would give him a bit of my mind' (Satthianadhan 1998*b*: 146–7). Although insistent that England is the repository of liberal values and women's equality, the protagonist also experiences a degree of racial condescension and hypocrisy in her life among colonial Christians that leave her somewhat alienated: 'there seemed to be an artificiality in the life which I had shared to which, brought up as I was in almost primitive simplicity, I never became quite reconciled' (ibid. 118). Saguna is attractive as a heroine, not for the ways in which she espouses Christianity and English values, but for her obvious independence of spirit and asperity of tongue.

Both *Kamala* and *Saguna* exhibit a tension between a literary engagement with the lives of specific, quite vividly drawn, female characters and heavy editorializing on the more generic 'daughters of India whose lot is considered as not needing any improvement by many of my countrymen who are highly cultured and who are supposed to have benefited by western civilization' (ibid. 37). What the novel form makes possible, as critics such as Mukherjee have noted, is not only representations of assertive female protagonists, but also of transformations in the relationships between men and women. While *Saguna* ultimately rejects marriage as 'the goal of woman's ambition', *Kamala*, subtitled 'The Story of a Hindu Life', is more forceful in its condemnation of child marriage as well as Hindu conjugal relations (which disallow the Victorian companionate marriage) within the joint family system, opining: 'The relations between a husband and a wife in an orthodox Hindu home are, as a general rule, much constrained. The two have not the same liberty of speech and action that is accorded to them usually in European countries' (Satthianadhan 1998*a*: 62). Despite its critique of the treatment of Hindu widows, the novel stops short of imagining the possibility of a new life for the widowed Kamala, contenting itself with a thundering denunciation of Hindu life: 'It is the land of freedom I want you to come to. Have you not felt the trammels of custom and tradition? Have you not felt the weight of ignorance wearing you down, superstition folding its arms around you and holding you in its bewildering, terrifying grasp? . . . We shall create a world of our own and none dare interrupt our joys' (ibid. 155). It would be a few decades yet before the anglophone novel would engage with ideas of land, freedom, and social change that were not shaped so strongly by European and Christian ideologies of self and society. It would do so compelled by the vision of one charismatic figure and in the process, experience its first major efflorescence.

Further Reading

Bankim Chandra Chatterjee, *The Bankimchandra Omnibus*; Sarat Chandra Chattopadhyaya, *Saratchandra, Srikanta,* and *The Final Question*; Eunice de Souza and Lindsay Pereira (eds.), *Women's Voices: Selections from Nineteenth and Early Twentieth Century Indian Writing in English*; Eunice de Souza (ed.), *Purdah: An Anthology*; Toru Dutt, *Collected Prose and Poetry* and *The Diary of Mademoiselle D'Arvers*; Rokeya Sakhawat Hossain, '*Sultana's Dream*' and '*Padmarag*': *Two Feminist Utopias*; A. Madhaviah, *Muthumeenakshi*; O. Chandu Menon, *Indulekha*; Cornelia Sorabji, *Love and Life Behind the Purdah* and *India Calling*; Rabindranath Tagore, *Four Chapters* (*Char Adhyaya*).

3

'Mahatma-Magic': Gandhi and Literary India

On 30 January 1948, less than six months after he had proclaimed India free in a now famous 'midnight' speech, Jawaharlal Nehru, the independent nation's first prime minister, addressed the new nation again, this time in sorrow:

Friends and comrades, the light has gone out of our lives and there is darkness everywhere. Bapu, as we called him, the Father of the Nation, is no more... The light has gone out, I said, and yet I was wrong. For the light that shone in this country was no ordinary light. The light that has illumined this country for these many, many years will illumine this country for many more years and, a thousand years later, that light will still be seen in this country and it will give solace to innumerable hearts. (1983: 106–7)

A few hours earlier, Mahatma Gandhi had fallen to the ground at one of his prayer meetings, fatally shot by Nathuram Godse, an activist of the Hindu extremist group, the Rashtriya Swayamsevak Sangh (RSS), which blamed him for the Partition of India.

Considered unparalleled even in an era populated by political figures of great stature, in the half-century preceding his death, Mohandas Karamchand Gandhi (1869–1948) had reigned as a cultural, political, and spiritual icon. Born in Porbandar, Gujarat, Gandhi grew up in an upper-caste Hindu family, trained as a lawyer in England and began his practice in South Africa. Here, famously, he was politicized by his encounters with the vicious racism of apartheid and initiated his long career as a radical political activist, founding the Natal Indian Congress to fight racial oppression. After more than twenty years in South Africa where he also experimented with simple communal living at the Phoenix and Tolstoy farms, Gandhi returned to India in 1915 and swiftly became the leading figure in the Indian nationalist movement. In the decades that followed, in works such as *Hind Swaraj* and the autobiographical *The Story of my Experiments with Truth*, and through his journal, *Young India*, Gandhi theorized passive resistance, civil disobedience, non-cooperation, and most famously, ahimsa, or non-violence, as political strategies. He also wrote extensively, often brilliantly, in both English and Gujarati, on questions of civilization, modernity, nationalism, self-rule, freedom, religion, social reform, caste, and gender. Gandhi was quite possibly the first thinker in the Independence movement not only to bring together theory and action in so hugely influential a manner, but also to reach across a wide regional, cultural, and linguistic span to turn the freedom movement into a genuinely 'all-India' phenomenon with mass participation.

Gandhi's influence on literature generally and the anglophone novel more particularly is best understood in terms of the pivotal role he played in decisively bringing together diverse communities under the rubric of the 'India' possessed, according to him, of a civilizational and spiritual unity that long preceded 'English' rule. The historian, Percival Spear, observes that Gandhi's great work was to bring together masses and elite classes in the freedom struggle; thereby 'the Mahatma gave a nation to the country' (1965: 200). More recently, the political theorist, Partha Chatterjee, has argued that 'Gandhism provided for the first time in Indian politics an ideological basis for including the *whole people* within the political nation (1993: 110, original emphasis). This necessitated bringing the peasantry as a whole into the movement and addressing social divisions, in particular what Gandhi deemed the 'deadly sin' of 'untouchability', whereby entire groups of people were cast beyond the pale of society altogether. Spear (1965: 199) also comments on Gandhi's unique methods of bringing people together in common cause:

He dramatized his ideas by a constant stream of articles, speeches and declarations, and above all, by his own example. Gandhi, in the peasant's loin cloth and shawl, sitting at the spinning wheel, writing notes on his weekly day of silence, sitting lost in contemplation or lying exhausted during a fast, were all ways of getting his image across to a largely illiterate population. They were not Brahminic, priestly ways, but ways which made an immediate appeal to the ordinary man.

Gandhi's own prolific prose output combined with his capacity to 'dramatize himself' and his ideas with 'an unerring instinct' made him a extremely compelling figure for both folklore and writers; he became the subject of oral and written literature. The spinning-wheel, the long walk to make salt on the beach at Dandi, the fasts for self-purification and penance, the sometimes ostentatious simplicity (with the iconic image of the small bespectacled man in the loincloth walking the corridors of power to negotiate with powerful British administrators)—all made for powerful iconography and appealed, it turned out, not only to ordinary people, but to those whose work was essentially imaginative.

It was inevitable then that the literature of the time would respond, not only to the heightened sense of nationalism that dominated the decades from 1905 to Independence, but also to the presence of a figure of such legendary proportions with a penchant for both narrative and performance.[1] Gandhi's own literary output provided a ready-made resource for writers who felt impelled—more so per-haps at this time than any preceding era—to engage with the social and political issues facing the nation that was coming into being. In key works such as *Hind Swaraj* or 'Indian Self-Rule', Gandhi (1997: 13) wrote about the need to 'understand the popular feeling and give expression to it ... to arouse among the people certain desirable sentiments; and ... fearlessly expose popular defects'. For many writers, this became a literary manifesto of sorts. Though he became a lightning rod for the anti-colonial freedom movement itself, Gandhi's emphatic insist-ence that freedom ultimately had to come from within resonated with literary attempts to explore the nature of the self. Colonialism provided an opportunity, in this view, to cleanse and regenerate Indian self and society.

Gandhi's stated view that the English language was not beneficial to the regeneration of Indian civilization did not prevent the anglo-phone novel of the 1930s and 1940s from evincing a recurrent interest in him and his influence. Though he argues that 'the foundation laid by Macaulay has enslaved us' and that 'we, the English-knowing men' have furthered that slavery, Gandhi himself used English fre-quently and conceded that some strategic knowledge of the language was acceptable (ibid. 103). The anglophone novel in India not only engaged productively with Gandhi and his thought but is widely agreed to have experienced its first major flowering during the

1930s and 1940s, the epoch of Gandhi and Gandhism. Novelists of different political and philosophical inclinations, ranging from the self-consciously apolitical R. K. Narayan to the socialists, Mulk Raj Anand to Raja Rao, Bhabani Bhattacharya, K. Nagarajan, and K. S. Venkataramani wrote interesting and often powerful works thematizing the impact of Gandhi, the man and the myth, on the consciousness of the India that was taking shape around them. Even where Gandhi or Gandhism were not the explicit subject matter, there was a noticeable shift to village settings and agrarian life, in keeping with Gandhi's repeated reminder that India was a fundamentally agrarian society based in villages.

Mythmaking: *Kanthapura*

Rendering this India in the English language was, however, no easy project. In the Foreword to his novel, *Kanthapura*, the author Raja Rao seemed to speak for a generation of anglophone Indian writers when he famously asserted that the challenge was to 'convey in a language that is not one's own the spirit that is one's own' (2004: p. vi). Going on, however, to claim that English was 'not really an alien language', Rao describes the writer's challenge as one of infusing 'the tempo of Indian life . . . into our English expression'. Adopting indigenous techniques of storytelling in English-language narrative would be one way of achieving this goal. In *Kanthapura*, his best-known novel, Rao attempts this by structuring the novel as a grandmother's tale within which are embedded other stories and their narrators. This cleverly capacious structure also contains within itself a 'harikatha' or a 'story of Vishnu' in which Gandhi takes on mythological proportions as an avatar of the deity himself. Rendering Hindu legend into mildly archaic English gives it biblical resonances:

There was born in a family in Gujerat a son such as the world had never beheld . . . and hardly was he in the cradle than he began to lisp the language of wisdom. You remember how Krishna, when he was but a babe of four, had begun to fight against demons and had killed the serpent Kali. So too our Mohandas began to fight against the enemies of our country. . . . Fight, says he, but harm no soul. Love all, says he, Hindu, Mahomedan, Christian or Pariah, for all are equal before God.   (Rao 2004: 12)

The folding of secular time into the timelessness of the mythological evokes a temporality that the poet and critic, A. K. Ramanujan (1989: 145), terms 'Indian Village Time', figured as 'indefinite, continuous anywhere between a few decades ago and the medieval centuries'. In terms of the Gregorian calendar, the action of the novel takes place at some point in the 1930s just prior to the iconic Salt Satyagraha when Gandhi and his followers walked 240 miles to the sea at Dandi to break the Salt Laws imposed by the British administration. In his choice of mythic over historical time, Rao conceivably pays homage to Gandhi's (1997: 56) own disavowal of the English 'habit of writing history' and those very European conceptions of chronology and historical progress that Hegel and Mill upheld as civilizational achievements. For Gandhi (ibid.: 90): 'History is really a record of every interruption of the even working of the force of love or of the soul . . . Soul force, being natural, is not noted in history.'

Set in a small fictitious village in the southern state of Karnataka, *Kanthapura* is an account of a community's fraught experiments with Gandhian truths and the project of self-transformation enjoined by Gandhi. The village was Gandhi's exemplary social unit, the site where 'soul-force' could find regenerative expression away from the corrupting regimes of technology and modernity. At the same time, these communities had to reform themselves from within and repair those traditions that had become self-defeating and 'diseased'. In some ways, Gandhi's most significant contribution to the discourse of Indian independence lay in his insistence that *swaraj* or 'self-rule' would be meaningless, even inimical, without a fundamental transformation of character; there would be no point in replacing English tyrants and degenerates with brown-skinned ones: 'My patriotism does not teach me that I am to allow people to be crushed under the heel of Indian princes, if only the English retire' (ibid. 76–7). The cornerstones of his own programme of cultural regeneration were non-violence, personal and communal prayer, the elimination of discrimination against 'Untouchables' within the Hindu caste system, and the spinning of handloom cloth, symbolizing economic self-sufficiency. In the village of Kanthapura, these are contentious: 'What is this Gandhi business? Nothing but weaving coarse, handmade cloth, not fit for a mop, and bellowing out bhajans and bhajans, and mixing with the pariahs?' (Rao 2004: 28). Unsurprisingly, within the novel's faithfully Gandhian framework, it is the sceptics who ally themselves with the tyrannical white owner of the Skeffington Coffee Estate and the police officer, Bade Khan, who attempt to break the back of 'Gandhi vagabondage'. The sole Muslim character in the novel, Khan is depicted in unremittingly negative terms, bordering on caricature, somewhat surprisingly given Gandhi's own fostering of multi-faith tolerance. It is less surprising in terms of Rao's own commitment to a conception of India that drew heavily on the resources of a High Sanskritic and Brahminical Hindusim; the terms 'Indian' and 'Hindu' are interchangeable for him in describing his philosophical interests. Tabish Khair (2001: 204) points out that while 'Rao did give speech to subalterned Indian realities in the colonial and international context, he did so largely by recourse to Sanskritized (at times even high Brahminical) definitions and traditions', which in turn marginalized those outside those traditions.

Nevertheless, *Kanthapura* remains a successful literary attempt to imagine—from the perspective of a Hindu elite—the impact that Gandhi as Mahatma might have had on individuals and on the collective psyche of a small rural village. Given his own disapproval of urban life, it is ironic that Gandhi's representative in Kanthapura, Moorthy, is described approvingly by the narrator as a man who 'had been to the city and . . . knew of things we did not know' (Rao 2004: 9). The contentious relationship between city and village is itself also thematized in the novel where, ironically enough, Gandhian ideology—especially in its call to reject strictures against caste pollution—is seen by some to be the word from the city, to be either lionized or repudiated as such. The novel is peopled with characters who seem somewhat quaintly rustic and 'simple' from an urban perspective, susceptible to the workings of what one contemporaneous writer, observing Gandhi's impact on the Indian peasantry, described as 'the mythopoeic imagination of the childlike peasant' (cited in Amin 1988: 5). Even so, Rao is adept at evoking the idiosyncrasies of place and personality. Despite the occasional awkwardness of attempts to translate Kannada epithets into English ('Waterfall Venkamma', 'Nose-Scratching Nanjamma', 'Beadle Timmiah') or to find English equivalents for place names ('Temple Square', 'Devil's Ravine Bridge', 'Chennaya's Pond'), Rao's use of English to evoke the spirit of a South Indian place is largely successful. The 'instinctive bilingual[ism]' to which he refers in his Foreword emerges in the syntax and rhythms of the narrative that, at its best, is resonant with the 'rush and tumble' of orature.

The religiosity of the framework through which Gandhi and his message were often interpreted is a running thread through *Kanthapura*, allowing for a convergence of Rao's own interest in spiritual matters and the ways in which Gandhi self-consciously deployed a religious idiom to transmit his message. Though he was emphatic that he did not mean a specific religion but rather the 'religion which underlies all religions', Gandhi's idioms drew on Sanskritic Hindu concepts such as 'Ram-Rajya' (the utopian rule of Rama). He also advocated 'purifiying' Hindu religious practices such as fasting, vegetarianism, and the singing of bhajans or devotional songs. In an analysis of rumours and myths surrounding the figure of the Mahatma in North India, the historian Shahid Amin (1988: 317) has shown how, among peasants and the lower-castes, these were 'being read in a familiar way, that is according to the conventions of reading the episodes in a sacred text but with the religiosity overdetermined by an incipient political consciousness'. He argues that Gandhi became a kind of polysemic text, enabling marginalized groups in society to undertake 'distinctly independent intepretations' of his message. Often, Gandhian injunctions were broadened or reworked to include liberatory actions and subversive programmes not necessarily sanctioned by him—such as refusing to pay high rents or to work for exploitative landlords, or giving up hereditary callings, on the basis that Gandhiji's *Swaraj* was imminent. Similar rumours circulate in Kanthapura: 'Like Harischandra before he finished his vow, the gods will come down and dissolve his vow, and the Britishers will leave India, and we shall pay less taxes, and there will be no policemen' (Rao 2004: 124–5). *Kanthapura*, while it suggests that Gandhism had to overcome various degrees of resistance and criticism, does not, however, envision its subjects as autonomous actors. Moorthy, described as 'our Gandhi', becomes what Amin (1988: 6) calls an 'authorized local [interpreter]' of [Gandhi's] will' to whom the latter's charisma is transferred. Religion in this text, unlike in the historical actualities described by Amin, serves to solicit devotional adherence to Gandhi: 'It is not for nothing the Mahatma is a Mahatma and he would not be Mahatma if the gods were not with him' (Rao 2004: 125).

The machine: Mulk Raj Anand's *Untouchable*

Another writer to come under Gandhi's spell was the socialist, Mulk
Raj Anand, one of the founder members of the All-India Progressive
Writers Association (PWA). As were many other writers of the time,
in India and elsewhere, Anand was clear that literature could not
afford to segregate itself from the most pressing social and political
issues of the day. As a young student in London, he came in contact
with writers connected to the fabled Bloomsbury Group and found
himself drawn to the intense literary and intellectual atmosphere of
their salons. At the same time, he was disturbed by what he saw as an
'undeclared ban on political talk' and failure to criticize the British
imperial project. During a visit back to India, he visited Gandhi at
Sabarmati Ashram and showed him a draft of a novel he had written;
Gandhi reportedly gave him feedback and he rewrote the novel,
taking the great man's advice to heart. The advisory 'talisman' included cutting down the manuscript by over a hundred pages and
making his protagonist less like a Bloomsbury intellectual.

Untouchable traces the events of one day in the life of a young
sweeper, Bakha, who by virtue of his birth and hereditary profession
belongs to that most despised and oppressed caste in Hindu society
known as the 'Untouchables' (or 'Harijans' in Gandhian terminology,
and today, as Dalit); in the absence of modern sewage systems, their
job includes the removal of human ordure. A figure whose labours
are integral to maintaining hygiene, the 'untouchable' is distinguished precisely by his invisibility and ritually enforced physical
segregation from other members of society. Gandhi, who was not
opposed to the caste system as such, had come to see 'Untouchability'
as a 'blot' on religion, a practice not sanctioned by Hindu scriptures.
Drawing on childhood memories, he wrote a story, 'Uka', based on
the life of a sweeper in his parental home, a boy he was forbidden
to touch. Possibly inspired by this text, *Untouchable*'s own journey to
publication remains an instructive tale for any literary history of the
anglophone novel in India. The novel was rejected by no less than
eight publishing houses before E. M. Forster intervened; it was on his
recommendation that the left-wing publishing house, Lawrence &
Wishart, agreed to publish it with a preface by the legendary English
author. Forster praises the novel for its bold foray into a theme
traditionally shunned by literature, 'this business of the human

body relieving itself' (2001: p. v). As Forster points out, the novel is 'simply planned but it has form'. In the fictional space of about twelve hours, Anand attempts to imagine in minute detail, the quotidian actions and interactions that comprise Bakha's unvarying existence. Two events shape the day and give it structure: Bakha's accidental 'touching' of an upper-caste man in the morning and the visit of Gandhi to the town in the evening.

The opening lines seem to echo the famous introductory lines of *A Passage to India* but instead of a landscape with enigmatic promise, we are given one that defies romantic rendition: 'The outcaste's colony was a group of mud-walled houses that clustered together in two rows, under the shadow both of the town and cantonment, but outside their boundaries and separate from them. There lived the scavengers, the leather workers, the washermen, the barbers, the water-carriers, the grass-cutters and other outcastes from Hindu society' (Anand 2001: 1). Out of these habitations emerges Bakha, 'a young man of eighteen, strong and able-bodied', with a penchant for second-hand European clothing. A thoughtful and sensitive individual, he is possessed 'with a sort of dignity that', according to his creator, 'does not belong to an ordinary scavenger' (ibid. 8). Cast in the mould of Forster's punkah puller who has 'the strength and beauty that sometimes comes to flower in Indians of low birth', Bakha has the makings of a compelling character whose experience of both routine humiliation and unexpected kindness leads him to interrogate his condition and imagine the possibility of changing it (Forster 1979: 220). The drudgery of a routine spent moving from 'one doorless latrine to another, cleaning, brushing, pouring phenoil' is relieved by the joy he takes in wearing a cast-off coat given to him by a soldier and playing a boisterous game of hockey with a new stick given to him by another kindly employer (Anand 2001: 8). It is a rhythm that on this day is broken suddenly as Bakha, lost in the pleasures of eating a small packet of sweet jalebis and looking at the sights around him, forgets to keep to the side of the road and ritually announce his presence. Accidentally, his body touches that of an upper-caste man. A furore ensues and culminates in 'sharp, clear slap through the air' which falls on Bakha's stunned countenance: his 'turban fell off and the jalebis in the paper bag in his hand were scattered in the dust' (ibid. 41). For the first time, however, as he walks off with tears in his eyes, Bakha finds himself wondering why things must be as they are: 'Why was I so humble? I could have struck him!' (ibid. 42–3). The incident jolts him into a new awareness of his body in relation to other bodies and objects, sending a frisson of tension and even anger through all his subsequent encounters that day. It is only when he hears Gandhi's speech at the end of the day, however, that these inchoate feelings of discontent seem to be given voice and transformative direction.

For all its unique qualities and powerful depictions of a life lived with the kind of routine humiliation that is all the more horrifying for its ordinariness, the novel sits uneasily in the space between ethnography and fiction. What Forster (2001: p. vii) describes as Anand's 'vagueness—that curse of the generalizing mind' manifests itself in the broad brushstrokes and heavy-handed editorializing where negative capability and nuanced minutiae are called for. Often, moments of real insight and nuance are undercut by a prosiness that Anand seems to feel is demanded by social realism. The novel's delineation of Bakha is weakened by a schematic vision of social change that combines an oddly elitist understanding of the 'untouchable' as inherently servile with an equally abstract sense that a spark of resentment can be nurtured directly into cogent analysis: 'Like a ray of light shooting through the darkness, the recognition of his position, the significance of his lot dawned upon him . . . Everything that had happened to him traced its course up to this light' (Anand 2001: 43). Given that by the 1930s, Untouchables or Dalits were themselves organizing and agitating under the leadership of such figures as B. R. Ambedkar, Anand's conception of them as submissive and torpid, awaiting 'upliftment' by benevolent agents of reform such as Gandhi, should be interrogated. Referring repeatedly to Bakha and his community as 'them' or 'these people', the omniscient narrative voice both distances itself from and appropriates the sole right and ability to represent their condition.[2] For all his unstinting condemnation of mainstream Hindus' exploitative caste practices, Anand shares with Gandhi unexamined assumptions about Untouchables and their purported abandonment of 'the original Hindu instinct for cleanliness' (ibid. 76). Indeed, Bakha is deemed a fit protagonist for this novel less because he represents his community than for the ways in which he is different and seen as a 'bit superior to his job . . . with a sort of dignity that does not belong to the ordinary scavenger, who is as a rule uncouth and unclean' (ibid. 8).

Yet, as the last pages of the novel suggest, Anand was not unaware of the problems of this kind of paternalism. At first, as in *Kanthapura*, Gandhi takes on the proportions of a legend around whose divine form stories and rumours circulate: '[The peasant] had heard from time to time during the last fourteen years how a saint has arisen as great as Guru Nanak, the incarnation of Krishna-ji Maharaj, of whom the Ferungi Sarkar (English Government) was very afraid. His wife had told him of the miracles which this saint was perform-ing' (ibid. 129–30). As the Mahatma speaks of the paradox of trying to win freedom from the British while 'we have ourselves . . . trampled underfoot millions of human being without feeling the slightest remorse for our iniquity', we witness Bakha's thrill at being the subject of public discourse (ibid. 136). But interestingly, this sense of excitement is tempered by moments of boredom and resentment. Though compelled by Gandhi's 'genius that could, by a single dra-matic act, rally multicoloured, multi-tongued India to himself', Bakha is also 'irked' by the sombre religiosity of the atmosphere (ibid. 134). Crucially, he is upset by Gandhi's call to Untouchables to 'purify their lives' by giving up 'evil habits' such as meat and liquor, observing rather perspicaciously: 'But now, now the Mahatma is blaming us . . . That is not fair!' (ibid. 139) Rather than allow Bakha's justifiable scepticism to speak for itself, Anand introduces in the concluding pages of the narrative, a schematic debate between two educated gentlemen, one of whom—the left-leaning poet, Iqbal Nath Sharsar, can be read as an alter ego for the author. Like Anand and many of his fellow-travellers in the PWA, Sharsar advocates an openness to new ideas without a wholesale rejection of tradition. Though respectful of Gandhi's ideas, Sharsar deviates firmly from the Gandhian anti-technological path in suggesting that the answer to the Untouchability question is the machine, in this case, the flush toilet, 'the machine which clears dung without anyone having to handle it' (ibid. 146).

This solution, presented with a long speech and a flourish, is simultaneously bathetic and subversive, given that the novel was written under Gandhi's tutelage. For Gandhi (1997: 107), machinery was part of the problem, 'the chief symbol of modern civilization; it represents a great sin'. Heralding the need to progress and embrace the new, Sharsar's solution also represents a departure from Gandhi's cyclical conceptualization of Indian time. Anand voices, through Sharsar, the far from Gandhian claim that India has always been both realist and progressive, rooted in the materiality of life. It is the West, he argues, that stresses spiritualism in order to 'to give a philosophical background to their exploitation of India' (Anand 2001: 143). The emphasis on the 'here and the now' also subverts Gandhi's call for Indian civilization to return to the timelessness of the religious. For Anand, India's embrace of the machine is consistent with its 'genius to accept all things' (ibid. 143); for Gandhi (1997: 67), 'India remains immovable and that is her glory... [She] has nothing to learn from anybody else.' In the end, as the poet and his friend disappear over the horizon, Bakha is left with his tentative awareness of the possibility of change in the wake of Gandhi, 'by far the greatest liberating force of our age', albeit one with 'his limits, of course' (Anand 2001: 142).

All Gandhi's men: *Waiting for the Mahatma*

Where *Untouchable* poses questions of Gandhian discourse in quite specific relation to the question of caste and social transformation, it is, curiously, a writer generally regarded as apolitical, 'a man of letters pure and simple' (Iyengar 1985: 358), who has produced the most provocative literary interrogation of the impact of Gandhi on ordinary people. Like much of his fiction, R. K. Narayan's seventh novel, *Waiting for the Mahatma*, is set in the fictional town of Malgudi, which like Hardy's Wessex or Faulkner's Yoknapatawpha country he rendered instantly recognizable. It is to the familiar banks of the river Sarayu that Gandhi comes to address the citizens of Malgudi after which event a young man will find his life taking on a whole new direction. Published in 1954, six years after Gandhi's death, *Waiting* is the story of Sriram, a somewhat shiftless and dull-witted young man who develops an 'at first sight' passion for Bharati who is part of Gandhi's entourage. Hoping to win her affections and to stay close to her, he too enlists as a volunteer in Gandhi's non-violent army and gets caught up in the vicissitudes of the nationalist movement in the context of World War II and Gandhi's 1942 call for the British to

'Quit India'. Along the way, he unwittingly strays off the Gandhian path of non-violence, gets involved with the more militant Indian National Army without realizing it, and is then jailed for some time before being released at Independence. With Gandhi's blessing, he is then reunited with Bharati.

The critic Lakshmi Holmstrom (1983: 59) has described *Waiting* as 'not wholly a success', while K. S. Iyengar (1985: 373) contends that when dealing with politics, Narayan's art 'betrays unsureness and perplexity'. But arguably it is precisely the combination of Narayan's keen eye for detail, his comic sensibility, and the unusually political subject matter which makes the novel provocative. The juxtaposition of the small town of Malgudi and its denizens with the grand narrative of Gandhi and nationalism in the telling of Sriram's story makes for a piquancy that is far more effective than the staged debate we hear at the end of *Untouchable*. As Sriram attempts to paint a large 'Quit India' graffito on the walls of a village near Malgudi, he is asked by the villagers how long it must be kept there:

'Till it takes effect.'
'What does it say, sir?'
'It is "Quit"—meaning that the British must leave our country.'
'What will happen, sir, if they leave? Who will rule the country?'
'We will rule it ourselves.'
'Will Mahatmaji become our Emperor, sir?'
'Why not?' he said, shaping the letters, with his back turned to them.
(Narayan 1999: 103–4)

Without directly interrogating Gandhi—a figure treated here with familiar admiration and sympathy—*Waiting*'s interest is in the ironic gap between the high-minded religiosity of Gandhian thought and the necessarily mundane interests that motivate ordinary people. As Gandhi gives a speech on the banks of the Sarayu, his appeal to greater values in the fight for freedom is interspersed with Sriram's decidedly more self-interested thoughts: ' "But be sure that you have in your heart love and not bitterness." Sriram told himself, looking at the vision beside the microphone, "Definitely its not bitterness. I love her" ' (ibid. 32). At the same time, Sriram is capable of an unwitting perspicacity, as he marvels at the legendary Gandhian simplicity with its own exclusionary codes: 'There was a class of society where luxuries gave one a status, and now here was the opposite. The more one asserted one cared for no luxury, the more one showed an inclination for hardship and discomfort, the greater was one's chance of being admitted into the fold' (ibid. 73).

More serious, Narayan suggests, is the possibility that Gandhism—despite its explicit commitment to ahimsa, or non-violence—might have an oppressive side. Any discourse that sees itself as the only right way contains within itself the seeds of authoritarianism. In the hands of simple-minded votaries such as Sriram, who have no clear sense of what they are doing, it can become 'machine-like' in its application: 'Wherever he went he wrote "Quit India". And it was followed by loyalists amending it with: "Don't" or an "I" before "Quit" ' (ibid. 109). Sriram's aspirations to didactic patriotism are constantly and humorously undercut by the intrusions of the mundane, including helpful suggestions that his clothes, made dirty by the ground on which he lies, can be washed clean by the local dhobi who can 'remove any stain' (ibid. 121).

None of which is to say that Narayan dismisses either political activism or Sriram's muddled efforts to find meaning in his life through Bharati (her name itself signifying Bharat or India) and the freedom struggle. Though it rarely relinquishes its bantering tone, the novel does take the question of personal transformation seriously as its protagonist attempts to evolve from Malgudi delinquent to Gandhi-man and, eventually, dedicated citizen of independent India. In one sense, the structural challenge for the novel itself, as its action expands tentatively outwards from Malgudi to cover other parts of India is to juxtapose the local, the familiar, and the intimate with the imagined vastness of nation. At a philosophical level, it poses the question: what happens when our commitments must expand—sometimes overnight, as in this case—from the local and the proximate to encompass the places we have never been to and people we have never seen? As Benedict Anderson (1991: 6) has famously suggested, the nation 'is imagined because the members of even the smallest nation will never know most of their fellow-members, meet them, or even hear of them, yet in the minds of each lives the image of their communion'. The vast, new spaces of free India can only be traversed with a degree of trepidation by the brand-new 'Indian'. Sriram's comfortable ignorance of a world beyond Malgudi occasions some uncharacteristic editorializing from Narayan when his protagonist arrives at a village, having seen one only in Tamil films. 'Sriram could hardly believe he was within twenty miles of Malgudi and civilization... [His] idea of a village was nowhere to be seen' (Narayan 1999: 87, 89). If a small-town boy from South India feels so bewildered twenty miles from his home, what does it mean to be an Indian and to lay claim to so vast a geographical and cultural expanse? Who, in fact, is an Indian?

This is the question implicitly posed by the novel as Sriram's knowledge of the world is put into question and his rhetorical certainties thrown into disarray. In his encounter with a British planter, Mathieson, Sriram again finds himself at a loss for words. The indefatigably polite white man promises that he will not rub off the 'Quit India' sign that Sriram has painted on his estate walls.

> 'But won't you be leaving this country, quitting, I mean?' asked Sriram.
> 'I don't think so. Do you wish to quit this country?'
> 'Why should I? I was born here,' said Sriram indignantly.
> 'I was unfortunately not born here, but I have been here very much longer than you. How old are you?... You see, it is just possible I am as attached to this country as you are.'
> 'But I am an Indian,' Sriram persisted.
> 'So am I,' said the other.   (ibid. 114)

Though Mathieson is clearly wedded to his own particular brand of liberal imperialism, seeing himself as the benevolent capitalist who 'is of some use to the people of this country' by employing them, through him Narayan interrogates claims for national belonging that are merely racial or civilizational. A similarly jocular scepticism greets such post-Independence mantras as 'we are an infant nation': 'The word was very convincing, it had a homely and agreeable sound, nobody need worry what it meant or why it was mentioned' (ibid. 227).

Spiritual leadership and self-knowledge: *The Guide*

As he undertakes his ongoing transformations in the name of nation, Sriram is often struck by the literariness of his situation: 'He felt that he was a character out of an epic, and on his activities depended future history' (ibid. 168). In his next novel, *The Guide*, Narayan would extend his engagement with the idea of self-fashioning, pushing his protagonist's experiments with the process to its comic and tragic limits. Though neither Gandhi nor the project of nation are discussed in any detail, the novel's philosophical and imaginative explorations are, nevertheless, shaped by encounters with Gandhism and its legacies, in particular, the notion that worldly ambition should be abandoned in favour of 'illimitable' religious aspiration and a related transformation of the self. In *Hind Swaraj*, Gandhi's hypothetical interlocutor, 'The Reader', responds to this idea with the concern that such talk encourages 'religious charlatanism': 'Many a cheat talking in a similar vein has led the people astray' (Gandhi 1997: 43). Gandhi replies that 'humbug' is far more endemic to the secular culture of modern civilization than to religion, the only means to regenerate the spirit of Indian civilization. This debate shapes the central conflict in *The Guide*, with its titular allusion to spiritual stewardship or 'trusteeship', a conception of leadership much favoured by Gandhi.

'Humbug' and 'charlatanism' are integral to the novel's thematic and imaginative concerns. The question is posed, once again, of how the ordinary Indian confronts the imperative to 'behave like the Mahatma' spiritually even as he comes to grips with the material realities of life in independent India. What transpires in the gap between aspiration and practice when ordinary people follow the writer Venkataramani's assertion: 'Men like Gandhiji, instead of being a world phenomenon to be worshipped like the sun, must be grown on every hedge like blackberries' (cited in Das 1995: 75). The novel tells the story of Raju, who begins his career in Malgudi as 'Railway Raju', a much sought-after tourist guide to the town and its environs. Tourism itself appears to be on the rise as the denizens of the new nation familiarize themselves with the contours of their now free land, criss-crossed by that fabled colonial legacy, the railways. 'Railway Raju' is to be found on the platform of Malgudi station, where he runs a shop that he gradually abandons in favour of his trade in inventing both itineraries and facts for travellers of diverse proclivities. On one such occasion, he meets an archaeologist—whom he nicknames Marco Polo—and his wife, Rosie. Raju seduces Rosie and after Marco leaves her, becomes Rosie's companion and impresario, helping her to achieve celebrity status as a dancer. After a series of mishaps and the breakdown of the relationship, Raju is arrested for fraud and jailed. Upon his release, he finds himself wandering the countryside and through a series of comic misapprehensions, is taken for a spiritual 'Master' come to 'guide' the villagers to their spiritual destiny. With some reluctance, he allows himself to slip into the role with consequences that eventually turn comedy into possible tragedy.

The Guide deploys a distinctive non-linear, even cinematic, structure, alternating Raju's account of his life as a holy man with his recollections of or 'flashbacks' to his distinctly more profane experiences with Rosie; the narration also switches variably from first to third person.[3] The narrative is well advanced when we discover that the context of narration for much of the tale is a panicked Raju's attempts to unmask himself as a fraud when he is called upon to undertake a fast so that the village will be saved from famine. Unconstrained by explicit references to the actual historical figure of Gandhi, *Guide* is freer and more experimental than the novel that preceded it. Read as an enquiry into, or even an allegory of, Everycitizen's experiment with self-fashioning in the Gandhian mould, the novel takes on truly profound dimensions. That we are, in fact, meant to refer back to Gandhi and Gandhism as we observe Raju's disastrous final experiment with performing greatness is made amply clear: 'And then one of them said: "This Mangala is a blessed country to have a man like the Swami in our midst. No bad thing will come to us as long as he is with us. He is like Mahatma. When Mahatma Gandhi went without food, how many things happened in India! This is a man like that"' (Narayan 2004: 102). Without criticizing Gandhian discourse frontally, Narayan's narrative points to the perilous literalism that the former is susceptible to when translated into the quotidian and the vernacular. Moral authority, as Shahid Amin's enquiry into 'Gandhi as Mahatma' suggests, is subsumed by the discourse of religiosity but at the cost of obscuring the links between human action and material consequence. The ensuing abdication of agency, individual and collective, is both ridiculous and alarming: '[The Mahatma] has left in you a disciple to save us' (ibid. 106–7).

The absurdity of attempting to emulate the Mahatma through the performance of holiness finds its apotheosis in the interview Raju gives to an American television journalist during his accidental fast. Though the irony is aimed at the performance of spiritual leadership by this all-too-ordinary individual now trapped in his own fabrications, a hint of gentle scepticism towards Gandhian methods for the masses also emerges:

> 'Can fasting abolish all wars and bring about world peace'?
> 'Yes.'
> 'Do you champion fasting for everyone?'
> 'Yes.'
> 'Will you tell us something about your early life?'
> 'What do you want me to say?'
> 'Er—for instance, have you always been a Yogi?'
> 'Yes; more or less.' (ibid. 243–4)

The arrival of an American journalist in search of an 'Indian story' underscores the extent to which the novel explores 'Indian-ness' itself as a narrative that both enables and constrains. It is a point brought out with some force in Rosie's ultimately unhappy evolution, under Raju's controlling guidance, into an icon of 'Indian culture'. Like the Bharatanatyam she dances, Rosie has to be made 'respectable' enough in upper-caste Hindu terms to embody the new nation's 'ancient Indian traditions'. The 'old Railway Raju' is also reborn as 'a man with a mission', holding 'forth on the revival of art in India' (ibid. 176). Narayan is clearly critical of the implications of self-fashioning in the mirror of abstract ideas of India and Indian culture. Though no feminist, Narayan also problematizes the ways in which men such as Marco and Raju attempt to subdue Rosie's own will, 'which had its own sustaining vitality and which she herself had underestimated all along' (ibid. 223). By the time Raju confronts the task of self-realization, he discovers that narratives take on a life of their own; abdicating his pedestal by confessing to fraudulence is not easy: 'He had created a giant with his puny self, a throne of authority with that slab of stone' (ibid. 109). All he can do now is to inhabit his own narrative with sincerity by undoing the gap between truth and fiction. We are still left with making sense of the gesture: is it undertaken for community and country? As expiation for his misdeeds? For the American television cameras eager to capture Indian spirituality? In the absence of the guide-as-narrator, the interpretative burden is now ours. Though, in the final instance, there is a literal Gandhian 'satyagraha' or 'an offering of truth', it is left to us to decide what is offered and for whom.

The perils of performance: *He Who Rides a Tiger*

Gandhi persisted in the popular and the literary imagination as a figure of near divine proportions. In Bhabhani Bhattacharya's early, somewhat programmatic, novel of the catastrophic Bengal Famine of 1942–3, he is figured a saviour for 'simple' peasants and redemptive inspiration to the city folk who live in a degree of moral turpitude. The figure of 'Devata' (literally, 'deity'), the grandfather turned village worker, stands in for the Mahatma himself. Like his mentor, Devata advocates the village idyll: 'I am proud of my people. They are not bright and knowing and—civilized!—like you city-breds; but they are a good people' (Bhattacharya 1947: 24). Though the novel is thick with descriptions of rural life, its quotidian joys as well as the particular horrors of the Famine that killed nearly three million impoverished people, its anxieties and preoccupations are specifically those of the educated, English-speaking, city-dwelling Indian. Bhattacharya situates the dilemmas faced by the protagonist, Rahoul, a Cambridge-trained scientist, in the context of the Quit India movement and the nationalist conundrum of whether to support the Allied war effort: 'India in bondage asked to fight for world freedom.' When we first encounter Rahoul he is on the brink of politicization but, unlike his sternly upright Gandhian grandfather, filled with doubts and uncertainties. It takes some experience of village life and bearing witness to the immiserating effects of the Famine to bring him to greater political conviction.

Despite its powerful evocation of the furies of the Famine and the vast gap that separates rural and urban India, *So Many Hungers* is ultimately a somewhat hagiographic Gandhian tract ending with a rousing call to join the Quit India movement. The uncertain Rahoul is transformed into 'a ripple in the risen tide of millions for whom prisons enough could never be devised, nor shackles forged' (ibid. 205). Bhattacharya's second novel, *He Who Rides a Tiger* (1954), offers a more complex exploration of social transformation in the context of the freedom struggle. How, beyond rousing calls to action, will transformation in a deeply hierarchical society actually take place? Despite its ultimate, somewhat contrived, fidelity to Gandhian nationalism and an oddly schematic resolution, this novel raises some troubled questions about nationalism, spirituality, and reform. Like *Guide*, it does so through the figure of the trickster/charlatan and by examining the role of language in shaping both oppression and resistance. The novel tells the story of Kalo, a low-caste villager, who, along with his daughter, Lekha, is forced into penury and petty criminality during the Famine. Having migrated to the city, Kalo is frustrated in his attempts to make an honest living and repelled by the trade in women's bodies in which he briefly participates. He decides to hit back by defrauding the establishment that exploits him. Pretending to be a Brahmin holy man, Kalo flouts pollution laws with a mixture of fear and glee. He becomes the powerful and admired custodian of a new temple, built with vast donations even as millions starve on the streets of Calcutta. Utterly convincing in and convinced by his performance, he forgets his original aim of taking revenge on caste hierarchies and becomes a member of its top echelons. Finally, however, a series of events revolving around his daughter, Lekha, who becomes increasingly unhappy with the situation, results in Kalo's decision to unmask himself dramatically and return to the fold of the ordinary masses who are now united against oppression—but this time, under the Quit India movement's umbrella.

Tiger makes powerfully visible the ways in which oppression was not a dyadic affair, with colonizer pitted against colonized. Indeed, anti-colonial agitation is a fairly distant activity for much of the novel, which focuses instead on the iniquities of caste oppression made more horrific by the depredations of the Famine. The mass starvation had multiple causes, including colonial mismanagement of food supplies, hoarding by local profiteers, and caste-based systems of entitlement and deprivation (ibid. 15). As such, for many writers, it 'became emblematic . . . of the intersection of imperialist, capitalist, feudal, caste-based and patriarchal violence' (Gopal 2001: 62). The nation that was coming into being already by 1942 was egalitarian in its proclamations, but its ideals were not necessarily being realized on the ground of actual social relations. The Famine of 1942–3 made these inequalities more starkly visible with special efforts mounted to spare upper castes the worst of it. In the face of this complexity, Kalo's 'terrible fraud' is a means of exploring the nature of social transformation and whether it can, in fact, be effected by speech acts or performance. Kalo's appropriation of symbolic resources has great subversive potential and, like a secret Caliban, he is able to use caste discrimination against his erstwhile oppressors, now being polluted and defrauded without their knowledge. However, as happened sometimes with actual caste protest movements, such as that undertaken by the Namasudras of Bengal, the appropriation of upper-caste symbols and practices could also have the effect of co-opting some of them into the status quo; this is what ultimately happens to Kalo, who actually begins to uphold the myth of Brahmin superiority, 'making it his strength' (Bhattacharya 1954: 112). The novel's depiction of this contradiction underlying the subversive use of trickery is compelling; less so is the final, rather contrived resolution, whereby Kalo, under the aegis of Biten, the 'real' Brahmin, throws his lot in with the nationalist movement (and implicitly, Gandhi's spiritual and political leadership) to become 'a legend of freedom'. Bhattacharya seems to share Gandhi's own misgivings about independent subaltern action, including temple-entry by those who were debarred from 'polluting' sacred ground.

Colonial legend to postcolonial touchstone: Gandhi in Nayantara Sahgal's novels

Gandhi's appeal to the literary imagination did not wane after Independence and his death in 1948. In the work of Nayantara Sahgal, one of the best-known anglophone writers of the post-Independence era, many characters are preoccupied with the question of what it means to be an Indian. Gandhi, unsurprisingly, provides the touchstone against which this project is defined. Sahgal's first novel, *A Time to be Happy* (1958), is a novel of transition that examines the minutiae of changes in personal relationships, political attitudes, and psychological dispositions, first as the Quit India movement comes to a head and later after British rule gives way to Independence. As with the several novels that were to follow, Sahgal's characters themselves belong to the English-educated milieu from which many of the new nation's nationalist and ruling elite—the bureaucrats, politicians, industrialists, landowners—were drawn. Sahgal is an insightful observer of the foibles, pretensions, and contradictions as well as real material anxieties and moral dilemmas that marked the lives of those who inhabited this narrow, but immensely influential, social stratum. Narrated by an unnamed Gandhian worker, *A Time to be Happy* is about a crisis of postcolonial identity for this class, particularly its writers and intellectuals:

You know, Mr McIvor, it is a strange feeling to be midway between two worlds, not completely belonging to either. I don't belong entirely to India. I can't. My education, my upbringing, and my sense of values have all combined to make me un-Indian. What do I have in common with most of my countrymen? And, of course there can be no question of my belonging to any other country. I could not feel at home anywhere else. (Sahgal 1958: 151)

The anxieties of being 'nearly English' and feeling 'like a stranger among my own people', are, arguably, particular to the anglophone novel, preoccupations shared by both author and characters: 'I've studied English history and literature. I've read the English poets. It's all more real to me than the life I live every day' (ibid. 235). If the Gandhian character wonders at his ability to share convivialities at the club with the English box-wallah, his creator ruminates on what it means to write an anti-colonial novel in the language of the colonizer. If one justification is that India is distinguished by a 'magic assimilative quality' and welcomes all who come to her, it is also true that the English are outsiders with a difference: 'But it would be simpler, far simpler, if these conquerors would, like the others, pause to breathe the message of this air, to grieve at the tragedy of this scene and rejoice in its splendour' (ibid. 191). Madan voices a classically Gandhian idea when he suggests the English should 'take all they want of [India]' but 'ennoble her in return'. Yet, Gandhism itself is vulnerable to becoming a form of stylized performance as embodied by one character's fashionable 'village-consciousness' (ibid. 262).

If in the period leading up to Independence 'Gandhi' functioned as the horizon of idealism, at once desirable and unattainable, the transition to independence brought a subtle shift in this now posthumous role. As the cracks between anti-colonial ideals and postcolonial realities became more visible, 'Gandhi' began to signify a legacy under threat and ideals honoured more in the breach than observance, a touchstone for 'nationalitarians' who, in Neil Lazarus's (1990: 11) terms, criticize 'nationalists for conflating independence with freedom' and for not undertaking the radical social and economic restructuring that would mean real freedom. In *Rich Like Us* (1985), perhaps her best work to date, Sahgal's narrative weaves its way between two historical moments to assess the road taken by India in the three decades following Independence. The first is Gandhi's totemic call to the British to 'Quit India' in 1942 and the second, the declaration of a national Emergency in 1975 by Prime Minister Indira Gandhi (Nehru's daughter and no relation to the Mahatma, she rose to power after Nehru's death in 1964). The latter was a time when the 'world's largest democracy was looking like nothing so much as one of the two bit dictatorships we had loftily looked down upon' (Khilnani 1997: 31). As will be seen in the following chapters, for many writers and intellectuals the Emergency came to signify the final betrayal of the legacy of the freedom struggle, its idea of India and of those like Gandhi who symbolized it. (During the Emergency, politically active Gandhians such as Jayaprakash Narayan or 'JP', mentioned in Sahgal's novel, were specifically targeted by Mrs Gandhi and her henchmen.)

Narrated by Sonali, a civil servant who loses her job after refusing to abet a corrupt deal in which Mrs Gandhi's son is implicated, the novel is part family story and part political thriller. It is also an anti-colonial text dedicated, nevertheless, to 'the Indo-British Experience and what its sharers have learned from each other'. As such, it is also the story of the warm-hearted Rose, a working-class Englishwoman who comes to India as the second wife of a bigamous Hindu businessman, Ram, and becomes deeply involved in the lives of both adopted family and homeland. In the India of the Emergency where power and money reign interchangeably and ruthlessly, Gandhi is betrayed not in explicit repudiation but through the perversion of those who would claim his legacy for their own ends. These include 'pro-poor' commercial scams for the wealthy, population control measures where the poor are forcibly sterilized, and 'beautification' projects in which slum-dwellers lose their homes:

You had to start somewhere, he expounded wittily, and Madam's son had, vasectomizing the lower classes, blowing up tenements, and scattering slum dwellers to beautify Delhi, setting up youth camps with drop-outs in command, loafers and ruffians who would otherwise have been no more than loafers and ruffians. With his ill-wishers out of the way, a patriotic hand-spun, hand-woven car, every nut and bold of it made in India, would soon be on the road.   (Sahgal 1985: 91–2)

In contrast, Gandhi's desire to forge a radically different, non-Eurocentric path for India is the source of some nostalgia for Sonali:

Wasn't it time after all these centuries to produce a thought of our own and wasn't that what Gandhi had done, pack off an empire with an antique idea instead of an atom bomb? And half naked in his middle-class middle-caste skin he'd taken human rights a hundred years ahead in two decades without a glimmer of class war... The man had used his brains, and what we needed now was a like inventiveness to suit our own conditions.   (ibid. 113)

In many ways it is Rose, with her refreshingly untrammelled honesty and refusal to be bamboozled by wealth or glamour, who represents a continuity with that legacy, just as Gandhism had made a place for her in India as a fellow human being rather than a foreigner. Her own lifelong outsider position in relation to both the British and Indian middle classes is shown to bestow her with both critical insight and an ability to love and cherish strangers. It is a privilege, along with an almost casual willingness to tell the truth, that will ultimately have tragic consequences but allow her to have 'transcended those things, blood, race and distance' (ibid. 259).

Though the Emergency represents a definite betrayal, Sahgal is not entirely starry-eyed about the moment of freedom at midnight, when in her uncle Jawaharlal Nehru's words, India awoke 'to life and freedom'. The apparently clean slate of that moment is one wiped free of historical residues: 'We were Not Guilty of Hiroshima, Nagasaki, or sending Jews in cattle cars to gas ovens. We could afford to remind ourselves of a past others were trying to forget, and we joined ours seamlessly to the present' (ibid. 165). A gentle interrogation of notions of primordial national innocence is muted but audible. But it is also quickly recuperated into the more familiar nationalitarian story of idyll and betrayal. Sonali reflects on her times as one when 'the saga of peaceful change I had been serving from behind my desk had become a saga of another kind, with citizens broken on the wheel for remembering their rights' (ibid. 258). For Sahgal, both Gandhism and Nehruvian socialism have the virtue of emphasizing peaceful change: 'It was a time when irresistible forces and immovable objects curtsied politely to each other and stepped aside to let enormous changes take place without a sound' (ibid. 165). It is arguable whether the scale of changes were always that large and even Sahgal, via Sonali's mother, poses a humorous question about

Nehru's version of a 'socialistic' society: 'I don't understand this "tic,"' said my mother. Either we are socialist, I don't know why we are, or we aren't, but what is this "tic"?' (ibid. 166). Becoming 'Indian', the great project of the postcolonial era, isn't always quite as radical as it purports to be; like Indian glass, 'the bumps straightened out and everything else under the sun became Indian too, including millionaires' (ibid. 166). As patriotic 'Republic Days', with their shows of Made in India military might, come and go, the saluting beggar remains a beggar, 'but our managers, politicians and bureaucrats like me got into our cars and hurried away to our next engagement unlike the Buddha who took a thornier path after the sights he saw outside him, and after him no one until Gandhi' (ibid. 167).

Great Indian soul and *The Great Indian Novel*

The betrayals of the Emergency and the attacks on Gandhians such as JP also figure in the climactic last chapters of Shashi Tharoor's *The Great Indian Novel* which, as an epigraph states, is a play on the Mahabharata (literally, Great India), an epic that is transformed almost seamlessly into this anglophone novel of modern India. Gandhi, 'Father of the Nation' looms large in the allegorical form of Gangaji/Bhishma, the original epic's great patriarch or 'pitamaha'. In a witty rendition of the Mahabharata that is (often somewhat laboriously) faithful to both epic and history, Tharoor's treatment of Gandhi and his methods is both irreverent and admiring:

He is a star—hairless, bony, enema-taking, toilet-cleaning Ganga, with his terrible vow of celibacy, and his habit of arranging other people's marriages—is a star! (1989: 52)

Shall I tell of the strange weapon of disobedience, which Ganga, with all his experience of insisting on obedience, developed into an arm of moral war against the foreigner? Shall I speak, Ganapathi, and shall you write of the victory of non-violence over the organized violence of the state; the triumph of bare feet over hobnailed boots ...? (ibid. 46)

Postcolonial India is one where this legacy has been honoured in its vitiation: 'He might as well have been a character from the Mahabharata, so completely had they consigned him to the mists and myths of legend' (ibid. 47). In the final instance it is undermined, not only by The Siege (the novel's allegory of the Emergency) but also by the apathy into which the people—whom Ganga/Gandhi had once made to 'feel that they had a stake in the struggle for freedom' and the nation—have fallen (ibid. 371). Ganga/Gandhi, of course, had already died a sad man in the wake of Partition and its violence, dying in the narrator's dream, on a symbolic bed of arrows 'the bed which was all that a torn and jagged nation could offer its foremost saint to rest on' (ibid. 233). As the next chapter shows, the darkness that set in on the 'stained dawn' of Independence would cast a very long pall on the subcontinent.

Further Reading

U. R. Anantha Murthy, *Samskara*; Premchand, *Godaan* (*The Gift of a Cow*) and *Karmabhumi* (*The Field of Action*).

4

Writing Partition

In June 1946, one year before formal Independence from British rule, plans were announced to partition colonial India along religious lines into what would become the sovereign nation-states of India and Pakistan. The division would mainly affect Punjab in the north-west and Bengal in the east, both of which regions had large Muslim populations. Partition was the (for many people, unexpected) culmination of several years of political manoeuvring or a 'triangular game plan' of the Indian National Congress, the Muslim League, and the colonial government (Mushirul Hasan cited in Francisco 2000: 381). The hardening of divisions between Hindus and Muslims was itself a product of the colonial policy of *divide et impera*, or 'divide and rule'. In the months that followed, the subcontinent witnessed a bloodbath on a hitherto unimaginable scale as riots and pogroms spread across the affected areas. As over ten million ordinary people—Sikhs, Hindus, and Muslims—were dislocated from their homes and became refugees, at least a million were killed in retaliatory violence undertaken by members of all three communities while thousands of women were abducted, raped, and in many instances, forced to commit suicide to preserve the 'honour' of their communities. Suddenly, religious identity seemed to take precedence over all other ways of being and relating to each other, 'an enforced regression of national politics to a brutal, primitive level' (Rai 2000: 364). National 'belonging' became a sharply polarized and contested matter with life-and-death consequences. The violence that accompanied Partition often echoes in postcolonial India, in what are called the 'communal riots' or inter-community violence. As Urvashi Butalia remarks, contemporary communal violence often invokes the trope of Partition: ' "it was like partition again", "we thought we had seen the worst of it during partition, yet …" ' (Butalia 2000: 178).

In the face of this horror, the unspeakable cruelties visited by neighbours and friends upon each other, writers retreated into what seemed to be a stunned silence, as though unable to bear witness to the unimaginable. Eventually, the intrepid Urdu writer and humanist, Saadat Hasan Manto, emerged from a stupor of disorientation, exiled to Karachi from his beloved Bombay, to pen a handful of very short stories including the justly famed *Siyah Hashiye* (2003), which can be translated as 'Black Margins' or, better still, as the 'Black Marginalia'. For marginalia they are: in the first instance, only the laconic vignette, the troubled aphorism, the glancing allusion to fear, seemed appropriate in addressing that gigantic and infamously homicidal void. As Alok Rai (2000: 368) remarks, in early post-Partition writing, the 'anguished failure to understand, to stare unblinking into the glowing inferno, itself becomes a negative way of representing that which is truly horrific'. It would be twenty-odd years before longer narrative forms in any language of the subcontinent would address the topic of the 'stained dawn' commemorated in Faiz Ahmad Faiz's (2000: 123) famous poem on the occasion of Independence. Even so, given the enormous significance of that moment, to this day only an oddly small number of longer prose fictions in Hindi, Punjabi, Bengali, Urdu, or other Indian languages have taken it on in any substantive or sustained way. This may be because novels, epic novels in particular, necessitate an analytical engagement with history, causality, and possibility. Where the Partition is concerned, the novel on the subcontinent is only now beginning to find a way to do this and a place of collectedness from which to do it.[1]

Witnessing the past: *Train to Pakistan*

Due perhaps to its relative distance from other Indian languages as well as its circumscribed readership, the novel in English seems to have been able to undertake a more sustained engagement with the ugliness and pain of that moment in a historical frame. Of these, the few novels that came out in the late 1960s and early 1970s, such as Chaman Nahal's (2001) *Azadi* or, more famously, Khushwant Singh's (1961) *Train to Pakistan*, mainly undertook the task of naming and describing that fratricidal violence. As such, they tended to be

prolonged exclamations of horror combined with sentimental evocations of love and fellow feeling. At times, however, their graphic
descriptions and prurience seem to exploit rather than interrogate
'the pornography of violence'. The anthropologist, Valentine Daniel
(1996: 4), observes: 'Accounts of violence ... are vulnerable to taking
on a prurient form. How does an anthropologist write an ethnography—or to borrow a more apt term from Jean Paul Dumont—an
anthropology of violence without its becoming a pornography of
violence?'

Train tells the story of a sleepy Punjabi village, Mano Majra, and its
enforced awakening to the political reality of Partition. As ten million
human beings were forced to flee across the borders in either direction, it became impossible to stay insulated from the violence. The
eponymous train to Pakistan had become one of the most horrific
icons of reciprocal brutalities: trains packed with refugees headed
across the newly minted borders were stopped and their passengers
butchered before they were allowed on their way, arriving with the
macabre cargoes on the other side. Mano Majra, as a village by a
railway track, is 'very conscious of trains', its unvarying diurnal
rhythms regulated by their stopping or passing 'until the summer
of 1947' (Singh 1961: 4–5). Now, 'ghost trains went past at odd hours
between midnight and dawn, disturbing the dreams of Mano Majra'
(ibid. 77). One day, a train stops mysteriously in the sidings and
several hours later the flames of a mass cremation leap into the night
sky, confirming the villagers' ghastly suspicions: 'The village was
stilled in a deathly silence. No one asked anyone else what the odor
was. They all knew. They had known it all along' (ibid. 84).

The novel is at its most interesting when it tries to account for
the ways in which neighbours are goaded to become 'Others' and
murderers. Inciting the mild-mannered peasants of Mano Majra to
violence proves to be a daunting task for the outsiders and organized
criminals who come in to undertake it: 'Could they ask their Muslims
to go? Quite emphatically not! Loyalty to a fellow villager was above
all other considerations' (ibid. 124). What the ordinary folks of Mano
Majra cannot grasp is precisely the history-altering dimensions of
what has taken place: 'They went from house to house—talking,
crying, swearing love and friendship, assuring each other that this
would soon be over. Life, they said, would be as it has always been'
(ibid. 132). Unfortunately, not only will history overtake them, it

will require of them that they participate in its brutalities as representatives of homogenized communities rather than individuals. In the crucible of hatred, not even the self-professed atheist, Iqbal, has the choice of seceding from community. Through Iqbal, the communist activist, who is generally a figure of derision for his author, Singh allows himself one long diatribe: 'India is constipated with a lot of humbug. . . . We are of the mysterious East. No proof, just faith. No reason; just faith' (ibid. 171). In this India, Singh suggests, only death will redeem the Nehruvian nation's vaunted tryst with destiny. But, in the final instance, so does the love of the village petty criminal, a Sikh, for the daughter of the village imam.

Gender and the romance of nation: *The Heart Divided*

Such transgressive intercommunity romance emerges as a persistent theme in writing about the Partition and its divisive legacy. In Singh's hands, it is something of a blunt instrument, allowing him to depict amorous activity at the start of the novel and symbolize, somewhat schematically, the redemptive triumph of true love. A more nuanced and complex account of the emotional cost of Partition and the challenges of creating a secular, multi-faith society is to be found in a work by a woman writer, the first anglophone novel to engage with the subject. Written during the 1940s, *The Heart Divided* is that rare specimen, a contemporaneous account of the politically and emotionally fraught two decades that culminated in the partition of the subcontinent and the formation of the Islamic Republic of Pakistan. It was published posthumously after its author, a well-known women's rights activist and Muslim League member, Mumtaz Shah Nawaz, died tragically in a plane crash. The semi-autobiographical text offers a poignant and often compelling account of the personal and political transformations that take place in the lives of two young Muslim women from an upper-class family, Zohra and Sughra, as the subcontinent lurches towards independence. In his foreword to a recent edition, the eminent scholar Krishna Kumar suggests that the novel's importance lies in the ways in which it is able to address gaps in present-day Indian and Pakistani narrative histories of that period, especially a silence around what took place in the

1930s as the idea and reality of Pakistan started to germinate and grow. For Kumar (2003: p. vi), the novel makes the simple point that 'the division of India had already taken place . . . in the heart, i.e., in the universe of emotions and relations'. This reading somewhat inverts and simplifies the novel's project, which is not only to calibrate the complexities and emotional cost of division but also to ponder the meanings of 'unity' and 'division' themselves. The title of the novel also points to the manifold complexities of dividing the 'nation' which is assumed, in the first instance, to be an organic whole but is, in fact, a complex construct with its own contradictions.

Though it ends on a note of resolve, even triumph, with the lovers headed 'Towards Pakistan!' (heralded by 'the crescent moon with its accompanying star sailing in a sea of pale green'), the novel generally maintains a critical distance from nationalist pieties. Significantly, this critical edge is a gendered one deriving mainly from the female protagonists' constant awareness of how they, as women, are positioned differently in relation to the project of nation-formation which is controlled by the men in their lives and patriarchy more generally.[2] Though weakened by its rather mannered prose in some places as well as a tendency to provide ethnographic accounts of Muslim women's lives, rather like the early domestic fiction discussed in Ch. 2, the novel is effective in its use of the afsana, or romance (a genre widely available to Urdu-literate women), as a critical lens through which the stories of individual and collective can be told. With its emphasis on love and loss, the romance can be deployed to scan the delicate interface of personal and political, individual and collective as the upheavals of the 1930s and 1940s made and unmade lives and communities. The tragic transgressive romance at the heart of the novel is that between Mohini, a young upper-caste Hindu woman active in the freedom struggle and Habib, scion of a landowning Muslim family, with his own commitments to a free and inclusive India. The melodrama of this romance, which ends eventually with the death of Mohini through tuberculosis, provides material for reflections on the paradoxes of identity and community whereby the union of two lovers threatens to divide rather than bring together the two communities: 'You two would only bring dishonour and ridicule upon both households and thus tear them apart for ever' (Shah Nawaz 2004: 188).

The romance that will not unite but set asunder two communities with irrevocable force illustrates vividly the paradoxes of anti-colonial nationalism in the Indian context. If, on the one hand, it exhorts unity against the colonizer, a unity that will underpin the future nation, its dualist 'us and them' logic also then sharpens internal divisions of community and identity. Nationalism asserted against the British also generates self-assertion by other communities, whether in the form of Muslim disquiet about Hindu majority rule or Tamil resistance to the imposition of Hindi. This hardening of cultural particularism was one of Tagore's anxieties about the harmful effects of nationalism. Community, in this instance, undermines humanity, a frustration voiced by Zohra: 'Is there not a greater law than the law of communities? The law of humanity that denies any barrier between man and man... [A]re you going to build your nationalism upon the flimsy foundation of communal barriers?' (ibid. 186–7). But as Tagore had suggested, nationalism itself necessarily erects communal barriers and cultural boundaries in order to assert sovereignty. Nations, of course, need historical narratives to account for and tell of their emergence. One of the real achievements of *Heart* is the way in which it lays out a multiplicity of such histories, through the stories of different characters. But as it nears its own ending in Partition, the novel effects an uneasy closure, suggesting, against its own grain, that Hindus and Muslims have different histories and thus constitute separate national communities. Where intercommunity romance symbolized the novel's engagement with secularism and anti-colonial nationalism, the last chapters of the novel emphasize a turn away from both transgression and romance and a return to domesticity. Smoothing over its own questions and anxieties about the idea of Pakistan, it arrives at the conclusion that Partition is inevitable (ibid. 346). Zohra, 'saw the fading of her dream, the dream of Hindu–Muslim unity in an India free and whole. But she also saw... the dawn of a new ideal' (ibid. 390). As she accepts that 'the cry of Pakistan is an expression of the freedom-urge of the Muslim people', left unanswered is the question of whether political organizations such as the Muslim League could be said to have represented ordinary Muslims (ibid. 401).

Violence and the Other: *Ice-Candy-Man* and *Noor*

Two postcolonial novels by women writers from Pakistan make useful points of comparison here. *Ice-Candy-Man* by Bapsi Sidhwa (1988) and *Noor* by Sorayya Khan (2004) are, like *Heart*, concerned with the experience of Partition and nation-formation for women and for young people, neither of whom were centrally involved with the political processes leading up to it. Sidhwa's famous novel, now made into a film, *1947: Earth*, is charmingly written as a child's-eye account of the bewilderingly sudden transformations in daily life and social relations that take place when Partition is formalized. The device of a handicapped Parsi child narrator ('Lame Lenny') allows Sidhwa to craft a self-consciously marginalized and innocent perspective on the horrors of the time, although a knowing authorial voice intrudes far too often. Set in Lahore in the 1940s, *Ice-Candy-Man* manages to tell a compelling story of a life where the joys and jollities of an idyllic childhood carry on uneasily next to a the chilling cruelties of the time. This combination is epitomized by the eponymous seller of sweet ices, a Muslim whose love for Lenny's Hindu ayah leads him, terrifyingly, to participate in her abduction, rape, and eventual prostitution.

For all that it is a tale told with a comic sensibility and witty characterization, *Ice-Candy-Man*, like *Train to Pakistan*, is largely a literary 'eyewitness account', an attempt to chronicle the happenings of the time albeit, interestingly, from the perspective of non-actors—children and the Parsi community. The latter self-consciously 'adopt a discreet and politically naive profile . . . We have to be extra careful or we'll be neither here not there' (ibid. 16). As such, like *Train*, this novel is vulnerable to a certain prurience with regard to violence, particularly sexual violence. Iconic images of the Partition are catalogued reiteratively: railway carriages full of corpses, burning houses, the 'intolerable shrieks and wails' of women being raped, 'hairy vengeful demons, wielding bloodied swords', a 'tangled pile of unrecognizable bodies', and gunny sacks filled with chopped-off breasts which for 'a grisly instant' remind Lenny of 'Mother's detached breasts: soft, pendulous, their beige nipples spreading' (ibid. 149). Indeed, the separate section called 'Ranna's Story', told by another child narrator, one who unlike Lenny has suffered directly from the violence, feels distinctly gratuitous, as though graphic reportage is needed to compensate for the subtleties of the Lenny's story: 'He knew it was wrong of the Sikhs to be in the mosque with the village women. He could not explain why: except that he still slept in his parents' room. "Stop whimpering, you bitch, or I'll bugger you again!" a man said irritably. Other men laughed. There was much movement. Stifled exclamations and moans' (Sidhwa 1988: 203). Written forty years after the events, Sidhwa's novel is a powerful rendition of the experience of Partition for a sheltered upper-class child and reminds us that not all children were afforded the luxury of innocence. But for all its representational force, *Ice-Candy-Man*'s depictions of violence offer the reader little towards understanding its nature and its reach in those terrible times.

A more nuanced engagement with the legacy of violence and its lasting impact on individuals, families, and communities is to be found in Sorayya Khan's compelling first novel, *Noor*, which, like *Ice-Candy-Man*, is concerned with the relationship of memory, as a private act to the larger frame of public and official histories. Unlike Sidhwa's novel, however, *Noor* scrutinizes the act of remembering itself and all that it entails—trauma, loss, elisions, the rewriting of what took place, the undoing of lies told to oneself and to others and the return of the repressed which both hurts and heals. Its powerful depictions of violence recalled serve less to 're-present' horror and brutality than to engage with the trauma of bearing witness—and to suggest that forgetting is not an option. The context of this telling is not the Partition of 1947 but a second and subsequent division of this territory:

On 25 March, 1971, civil war between East Pakistan and West Pakistan began. On 3 December 1971, India entered the war on the side of East Pakistan. West Pakistan surrendered on 16 December 1971. Bangladesh, formerly East Pakistan, won its independence.
Between 300,000 and three million people died.   (Khan 2004: epigraph)

In citing widely varying estimates of the death toll in the novel's epigraph, Khan suggests that numerical statistics are less important than the terrible reality and reach of violence itself, both for perpetrator and victim. Indeed, violence makes victims of all who are affected by it, as Saadat Hasan Manto (2003) suggested in his famous story, 'Cold Meat', where a would-be rapist is rendered impotent. Though the larger context of social and political violence frames the narrative, *Noor* is very definitely a family story concerned with love, conflict, loss, and recovery. The titular character is a child born with an unnamed developmental condition, and like Sufiya Zinobia in Rushdie's (1989) *Shame* or Beloved in Toni Morrison's eponymous novel (1987), she is a figure with magical, even supernatural, capabilities, 'connected to some other world in a way that no one else was' (Khan 2004: 122). Gifted with the ability to paint the many things that remain unspoken and unnamed by the adults in the family, Noor enables her wounded elders to tell the stories that will no longer brook being hidden.

It is not a simply redemptive or cathartic process:

> 'You killed someone?'
> She said it directly. She didn't falter.
> '. . . What did you think I was doing?' he asked, his hands in the air waving the empty sugar bowl.
> 'Who?'
> 'Who?' Ali answered incredulously. 'Is that what you think war is? Excuse me, before I shoot you, what's your name? So I can tell my mother when she asks?' (ibid. 147)

But it is not only characters like Ali who have gone to war, seen and done the unspeakable, who carry within them the painful burden of the unspoken. Sajida carries within herself the trauma of the baby brother wrenched from her arms during the great cyclone of 1970 which orphans her just before the civil war. Her husband, Hussein, cannot accept the reality of Noor's condition and for years on end, will not even acknowledge his daughter's presence. Even Naanijan, the beloved grandmother, carries within herself guilty memories of an abusive husband who releases her by dying unexpectedly. All of them must come to the recognition that their private pain is necessarily connected to that of others. Out of this recognition emerges not only the possibility of a shared healing, but also a more profound truth about violence: even when we imagine that it is 'others' we are maiming, raping, or killing, they may, in fact be 'our own', literally and metaphorically. Ali, the East Pakistani soldier who picks Sajida up from the roadside in West Pakistan and makes her his daughter realizes in horror that he 'might once have lifted his rifle and blindly aimed in a torrent of rain and rising waves of heated fog—and shot her dead' (ibid. 219). Perhaps, at the end of the day, the truth of violence is this: for all that we proliferate partitions— 'Indians', '*Bengalis*, dark and stupid', 'not really Muslims'—there are, in fact, no 'others' who might not also just as easily be 'our own' (ibid. 183).

Fragmented nations, divided histories: *Shame*

In Salman Rushdie's *Midnight's Children* (discussed in Ch. 5), India is figured as a land of myriad possibilities but also as a collective myth that 'would periodically need the sanctification and renewal which can only be provided by rituals of blood' (1991: 112). Rushdie also proclaims a silence in response to Partition, albeit an ostentatious and allusive one: 'I shall not describe the mass blood-letting in progress on the frontiers of the divided Punjab (where the partitioned nations are washing themselves in one another's blood)... I shall avert my eyes from the violence in Bengal and the long pacifying walk of Mahatma Gandhi' (ibid. 112). *Shame*, which came out a few years after *Children*, can be read as a companion text to the latter, with the focus shifting to the making of postcolonial Pakistan. This inevitably entails an engagement with the territorial division between the 'stone-godly' and the 'one-godly' and the ensuing formation of a nation comprising 'two chunks of land a thousand miles apart. A country so improbable that it could almost exist' (Rushdie 1989: 62). Drawing on the resources of European fairytales and Asian folktales—'don't imagine stories of this type always take place long-long ago'—*Shame* is explicitly allegorical: 'The country in this story is not Pakistan, not quite. There are two countries, real and fictional, occupying the same space, or almost the same space' (ibid. 6, 24). The authorial voice frequently intervenes to make biographical connections, editorial observations, and, as in *Children*, literary-critical claims. The title of the novel refers at once to the emotion of 'sharam' itself and the pathologically blushing, unwanted girl child, Sufiya Zinobia, who comes to embody shame and, eventually, the murderous consequences of repressing it. Her husband, Omar Khayyam, the novel's 'peripheral hero', is her opposite, forbidden by his three mothers to feel shame even before he learns what it is. Like their union, Pakistan as 'Peccavistan' is, for Rushdie, itself an amalgam of shame and shamelessness.

During Partition, as Bilquis Hyder, Sufiya's future mother, flees from an explosion that strips away her clothes and eyebrows, she finds herself shamed by her naked body. For Rushdie (1989: 64), this is emblematic of the literal and symbolic havoc wreaked by the dislocations of Partition, for 'it is the fate of migrants to be stripped of history, to stand naked amidst the scorn of strangers upon whom they see the rich clothing, the brocades of continuity, the eyebrows of belonging'. Though Rushdie claims to prefer the mode of the 'modern fairytale', which eschews direct reference to actual historical events ('Realism can break a writer's heart'), the narrator also makes a suggestive allusion to the great unspoken: the humiliation and shame suffered during the Partition by women of all communities who bore the brunt of sexual violence: 'In that generation many women, ordinary decent respectable ladies of the type to whom nothing ever happens, to whom nothing is supposed to happen except marriage children death, had this sort of strange story to tell. It was a rich time for stories if you lived to tell your tale' (ibid. 72, 66). Feminist scholars of Partition have shown us that sexual violence against women was its 'most predictable aspect' with women's bodies treated 'as territory to be conquered, claimed or marked' (Menon and Bhasin 1998: 41, 43).

Despite his well-known antipathy to Pakistan—'a failure of the dreaming mind'—Rushdie as narrator also finds himself in an odd kind of empathy with a country born out of secession, comparing its status with his own condition as a migrant: 'What is the best thing about migrant peoples and seceded nations? I think it is their hopefulness' (1989: 91–2). Though drawn to the postmodern joys of floating 'upwards from history, from memory, from Time', Rushdie sees this release as double-edged. Since the new nation of Pakistan must give itself a new history, the past must be rewritten as a palimpsest that 'obscures what lies beneath' (ibid. 91). Those accustomed to 'living in a land older than time ... being told to think of themselves, as well as the country itself, as new' (ibid. 85). Ironically, in Pakistan, the job of rewriting history is undertaken by those who flee from Indian Punjab into the new land as migrants or *mohajirs*. Again, Rushdie acknowledges his affinities, this time as artist, with those who seek to rewrite history:

It is the true desire of every artist to impose his or her vision on the world . . . I too, like all migrants, am a fantasist. I build imaginary countries and try to impose them on the ones that exist. I, too, face the problem of history: what to retain, what to dump, how to hold on to what memory insists on relinquishing, how to deal with change. (ibid. 92)

Yet, as though to forestall readings of the novel as depictions of 'the physical and psychic landscapes of the East', Rushdie reminds us that the ghosts that inspired his story 'inhabit a country that is entirely unghostly; no spectral 'Peccavistan,' Proper London' (ibid. 125). In a short essay in the novel's third section, evoking his inaugural claim that his story is not only about Pakistan, Rushdie writes movingly of three London incidents that provided inspiration for his literary excursus into 'shame': the murder of a daughter by an Asian father shamed by her relationship with a white boy; the racist beating by white boys of a young Asian girl too ashamed to speak about it; and finally, a boy found in a parking lot, apparently burned to death by igniting of 'his own accord'. Shame, which breathes 'its favourite air' in Pakistan, nevertheless, finds homes across cultures and spaces, across the geography of human emotions: 'Between shame and shamelessness lies the axis upon which we turn; meteorological conditions at both these poles are of the most extreme, ferocious type' (ibid. 124).

The conjunction of shame and violence may have a universal human resonance but it found particularly painful form in the violence visited by neighbours upon one another, a recurrent theme in the literature of Partition. As the Urdu writer Saadat Hasan Manto showed so powerfully in stories such as 'Cold Meat', violence upon putative 'Others' often rebounds on the self. Similarly, it is suggested, Sufiya Zinobia 'is willing the damage to herself . . . a suicidal rebellion' (ibid. 155). Like the scavengers praised by Gandhi for keeping an ungrateful society clean, the girl who was meant to be a boy mops up the collective shame of a society that can then proceed with shamelessness, the business of ignoring what has happened and allowing it to happen over and over again: 'so into the ether goes the unfelt shame of the world. Whence, I submit, it is siphoned off by the misfortunate few, janitors of the unseen, their souls the buckets into which squeegees drip what-was-spilled' (ibid. 132). Though Rushdie has been criticized for the putative misogyny underlying the character of Sufiya Zinobia, she can also be read as a profoundly compelling invocation of the gendered nature of the shame and violence of Partition where women were subjected to violence 'in a way that they *became* the respective countries, indelibly imprinted by the Other' (Menon and Bhasin 1998: 43, original emphasis). Rushdie's larger point is sternly moralist: shame, wherever repressed, will return in the form of a terrifying and destructive force. Sufiya Zinobia may have been then, ultimately, 'the collective fantasy of a stifled people, a dream born of their rage' (ibid. 291).

Othering the self: *The Shadow Lines*

Partition is the power, then, to make the familiar unfamiliar, even uncanny. It is the drawing not just of any borders, but like the allegorical upside-down house in Amitav Ghosh's *The Shadow Lines*, borders that divide the self and so have profound psychic consequences: 'It is this that sets apart the thousand million people who inhabit the subcontinent from the rest of the world—not language, not food, not music—it is the special quality of loneliness that grows out of the fear of the war between oneself and one's image in the mirror' (1988: 204). This sense of contingency, ironically, undermines the power of the boundaries over which so much blood has been spilled. As the senile grand-uncle informs the relatives who have come to 'rescue' him from East Pakistan in 1964: 'Once you start moving you never stop...That's what I told my sons when they took the train. I said: I don't believe in this India-Shindia. It's all very well, you are going away now, but suppose when you get there they decide to draw another line somewhere? What will you do then?' (ibid. 215). This is, of course, precisely what happens to Pakistan a few years later when it undergoes yet another division into two nations, generating Bengali Bangladesh. Partitions happen over and over again: once difference is privileged as the basis for nationhood, there open up endless possibilities for fissure.

The novel's title refers to the curious nature of borders, the imagined yet all-too-real lines that so puzzle Mayadebi, the narrator's grandmother, as she flies back to her old home in East Bengal, now Bangladesh:

When my father laughed and said, why, did she really think the border was a long black line with green on one side and scarlet on the other, like it was in a school atlas, she was not so much offended as puzzled.

    ... But if there aren't any trenches or anything, how are people to know? I mean what's the difference then? And if there's no difference both sides will be the same; it'll be just like it used to be before, when we used to catch a train in Dhaka and get off in Calcutta the next day without anybody stopping us.   (ibid. 151)

Even if all nations are 'imagined communities', those that have been created out of a series of Partitions emerge from a process that distorts reality: 'What was it all for then—the partition and all the killing and everything—if there isn't something in between?' For Mayadebi, there is a stark contrast between the horrific physicality of the killings and the abstractness of the nations that emerge out of this blood-letting. Clearly influenced by *Midnight's Children*, Ghosh's novel is a family story profoundly aware of the ways in which the smaller stories of families and individuals are shaped by the larger stories of nations. The experience of Partition has created a particular subcontinental sensibility, 'a fear that comes of the knowledge that normalcy is utterly contingent, that the spaces that surround one, the streets that one inhabits, can become suddenly and without warning, as hostile as a desert in a flash flood' (ibid. 204).

Writing the counterfactual: *Looking Through Glass*

But what if Partition hadn't happened? What possibilities were violently interrupted by the events of 1946–7 and the two hundred years of colonial rule that preceded and, arguably, culminated in it? At its best, the imaginative work done by the novel challenges the teleologies of Partition, the assumption that what happened historically was inevitable. To do this is also to interrogate the fundamentally colonial idea that communities have to be homogeneous in order to survive and that national boundaries should be determined by religious communities. In the wake of Partition, argues the critic Aijaz Ahmad (1991: 119), Indians and Pakistanis were forced to reflect on 'our own willingness to break up our civilisational unity, to kill our neighbours, to forgo that civic ethos, that moral bond with each other, without which human community is impossible'. Fifty years or so after 1947, as writers and cultural practitioners reflected on the legacy of that moment, they also contended with the crisis of secularism in an India that had witnessed the fearsome rise of militant Hindu chauvinism or 'Hindutva' with its ugly symbolic triumph in 1993 as militant activists reduced an ancient mosque to rubble in the historic town of Ayodhya. This crisis raises the question of what precisely the unity and ethos referred to by Ahmad might have once consisted of. Did the many regions, languages, and communities that came under the banner of India indeed once have the civilizational resources from which a plural and heterogeneous nation-state could be forged or was that a delusion to begin with? What were those intellectual currents, ways of thinking about selves and others, cultural practices, economic systems, social institutions, and spatial arrangements either entirely destroyed or distorted by the violent interruptions of European colonialism and what followed? Was the secularism of the post-independence nation-state also 'derivative discourse', alien to Indian soil, like its opponents on the Hindu right claim, or could its genealogies be traced back to something other than the European model of the separation of church and state?

Mukul Kesavan's *Looking Through Glass*, for instance, poses a deceptively simple counterfactual question: what might have happened if in 1942, Gandhi had not famously called on the British to 'Quit India'? He did so suddenly although he had initially been waiting for Muslim organizations to overcome their distrust of the Indian National Congress and come on board before issuing the ultimatum. In Kesavan's novel, which draws to some extent on the magical realist resources put into play by *Midnight's Children*, the day after the resolution is announced, several Muslims who are loyal to the Congress vanish into thin air:

Like a bunch of yogis fired by the power of the mind, they concentrated on the Hindu–Muslim problem and made it vanish. Along with the problem, said Masroor, we vanished as well.

Not every Muslim—just those...who had risked ostracism within the community by opposing the League's demand for a Muslim homeland because they were committed to one secular nation.   (Kesavan 1996: 246)

The disappearance of secular Muslims from sight is a powerful metaphor for the contradictions of Indian nationalism, which was formally secular and plural but was, in fact, powerfully determined by the imperatives and iconography of Hindus, the majority community. In this context, Gandhi's unilateral declaration was interpreted as a move to make Muslims disappear from the political agenda. What is typically seen, as Ayesha Jalal has pointed out, as minority separatism is often the other side of the coin of exclusionary majoritarianism. Though this is not a widely publicized fact, the suggestion that Indian Muslims should secede to their own territory was articulated by a Hindu chauvinist, V. D. Savarkar, eight years before the Muslim league articulated its own demand for Pakistan.

The novel form allows Kesavan a degree of flexibility with which to explore the myriad historical possibilities that were eliminated as certain factions and trajectories won out over others in the years leading up to Independence and Partition. Crystal Bartolovich (2006), drawing on Walter Benjamin, describes such imaginative moves as 'critical' (as opposed to 'conservative') counterfactuals whereby the status quo is questioned through the positing of different, more radically transformative, historical possibilities. The classic plot device that enables this imaginative excursus is the time travel undertaken accidentally by the unnamed first-person narrator who, as he tries to take a photograph, hurtles down from a railway bridge in the 1990s into a river in 1942 where he is rescued by Masroor, one of the central characters in the narrative. Peopled by quirky characters such as Haasan, the apostate Brahmin and humanist, and the outspoken journal editor Ammi, who writes columns under different women's pseudonyms, the novel undertakes several detours through diverse incidents and locales from the making of a pornographic film with a reluctant heroine in Banaras and waiting on Jinnah's table in Simla to a 'reformatory for repentant prostitutes' run by the narrator's grandmother who, of course, does not recognize her future grandson when he brings her a new recruit. Interestingly, the transgressive romantic relationship at the heart of this novel is not that between a Hindu and a Muslim but one between two young women, Asharfi and the 'fallen' Parwana.

Despite its generally comic mode, often bordering on high camp, the novel is seriously engaged with the ways in which the history of the 1930s and 1940s in India was itself a struggle over history. Gandhi and the INC's failure to allay Muslim fears that they will be forced to live in an essentially Hindu nation is interpreted by some Muslims as an attempt to wrest history away from them: 'It first bleaches us with its secularism till we are transparent and then walks through us... in the name of the Masses and History and Freedom' (Kesavan 1996: 188–9). Families also try to write their histories in the mould of nations and religions. When his son converts to Islam, the patriarch of the Ganjoo family interprets this as 'the end of the world, or, at least the end of history. He, Kalidass... whose ancestor, Kalhana, was the first to write India into history... had in the wink of an eye acquired a Semite son who knelt to the west, never bathed and washed his bum with a beak-spout kettle' (ibid. 27). If this means that the family epic, Destiny of the Ganjoos, 'would never be completed', the novel's Jinnah, on the other hand, is determined not let Nehru successfully hijack the Independence as his exclusive patrimony: 'Nehru believes he has History on his side... Because the Congress is Mother India's only son' (ibid. 311). Out of that deadlock and eventual division of the patrimony between the two men and the parties they represent, the Partition takes place: the inevitability of Independence is transformed into the inevitability of Partition.

But were there, in fact, other possibilities for postcolonial collectivities, ways of living together, that lost out to this inevitability that was put in place in 1942? For the disillusioned and once-disappeared Masroor, neither a formally secular Hindu India nor a Muslim 'land of the pure' have much appeal:

If the idea of his country purged by struggle and glued by nationalism didn't make his heart leap, the thought of a separate Muslim state distilled into two-hundred proof purity didn't set his pulse raising. What he really wanted was a sporadically republican, inconsistently democratic version of the Austro-Hungarian Empire; a jerry-built coalition of statelets, joined by local self-interests and trade, deaf to large ideas and blind to crusading visions. That's what he wanted.   (ibid. 253)

We see Masroor and other characters drifting to the Muslim League, 'not out of a great deal of conviction, but with the modest aim of consolidating his grip on reality' (ibid. 252). For young idealists like him, the forms of nation that were being offered up by 1942 represent the narrowing of visions rather than the opening up of options. This results, of course, in the straitjacketing of identity in ways that puzzle and confound—and go against the lived complexity of actual existence. In one of the most poignantly comic episodes in the book, Ammi, the beloved and feisty matriarch of the family, alarmed at the thought of having to move to Pakistan, decides to float her own party and contest elections. The party is called Anjuman-Bara-i-Tahaffuz-i-Haal or The Society for the Defence of the Present. Her first interview with an uncomprehending reporter who cannot understand why she isn't fighting on an Islamic party platform is worth quoting in some detail.

> . . . why did you as a Muslim lady set up a Muslim party when you already have the . . . umm . . . Muslim League?
> What Muslim party? said Ammi shortly. She had run out of patience with the press.
> The . . . unn . . . , he said uncertainly, then peered at his diary notes, the Anjuman-ul-Hi . . . fazat Islam . . . ?
> Ammi snorted.
> You've got Islam on the brain, she said scathingly. The Anjuman-Bara-i-Tahaffuz-i-Haal is what my party is called.
> Exactly, agreed the reporter, brushing details aside to return to the big question. So why did you, a Muslim lady, establish another Muslim party? (ibid. 326)

In a milieu preoccupied with imaginings of future states of grace, Ammi's simple proposal to form the Defence of the Present, the 'haal', is both ridiculous and sublime, but certainly radical in its refusal of singular narrative teleologies of either community or nation. Her manifesto is a series of negatives, including, for 'five years after the English leave, there be no republic constituted, no text books written, no laws made, no boundaries erased and no frontiers drawn . . . till we sort out what we want to keep, from what they left behind' (ibid. 333).

What might have been if Ammi had had her way?

Reconstructing historiography: *In an Antique Land*

While *The Shadow Lines* is considered Ghosh's Partition novel, a different and later text by the same author undertakes a more powerful engagement with the afterlife of Partition, one that affects the subcontinent politically, culturally, and psychically. At once memoir, fiction, travelogue history, and anthropology, *In an Antique Land* opens out the idea and fact of Partition to encompass not just the drawing of imaginary lines through the subcontinent and Palestine, but also the segregation of knowledges, histories, religious practices, and languages into separate units and, therefore, into distinct cultures, civilizations, and nations. There is, Ghosh suggests, a material and ideological connection between the classification of books in European libraries and ideas such as the 'clash of civilizations' or 'the two-nation theory' that underlay Partition. The singular and monolithic destinies narrated by nations, in the mirror of empire, obscure their own heterogeneity as well as the diverse history of cultural encounters not mediated by European colonialism. It is in this regard that the Indian ocean trade, from the twelfth to the fourteenth centuries is paradigmatic, providing a framework for interaction between Indian and African cultures before the historical and epistemic break enacted by colonialism. It provides Ghosh, the young anthropologist, with a precedent for his own sojourn as an Indian in Egypt. But the heated argument he has with the Imam over which country has better bombs and tanks is also evidence of defeat—'the dissolution of centuries of dialogue that had linked us... the irreversible triumph of the language that had usurped all others in which people once discussed their differences' (Ghosh 2000: 236). These 'two superseded civilizations', he observes wryly, are thoroughly mediated by ways of thinking inherited from the colonial encounter as they emphasize difference and separateness—the philosophical basis of partitioning cultures and lands—rather than shared ground.

If a certain optimism of will and imagination drives Ghosh's reconstruction of a benign and peaceful trading culture where private ownership of a trading zone or controlling the entire ocean were unheard of, and where the borders between cultures were less sharp than they are now, it is also driven by a careful use of the intellect and meticulous readings of the archives (ibid. 287). Without overstating the extent to which European mercantile colonialism constituted a break with the past of the region, it can be argued that partitioning lands and cultures into monolithic 'nations' was an idea and practice which emerged specifically out of the strategies and then the debris of European colonialism. Partitioning presumes a clear correlation between faith, culture, territory, and nation, and this idea has triumphed over more heterodox identities and cultural practices although it has not eliminated them entirely. Ghosh painstakingly shows how the emptying in the nineteenth century of Jewish Genizas whose archival contents are then brought to the museums and libraries of the West, results in a situation where not a 'scrap of paper' remained to remind Egypt of her Jewish history: 'It was as though the borders that were to divide Palestine several decades later has already been drawn.' What then has to be remembered and reinhabited are the heterodoxies and syncretism of the past, not the Past Perfect, but the past in its dynamic untidiness, porousness, and plenitude to interrogate the neatness of Histories and their Partitions. Ghosh reminds us that religions have not always been quite so hermetically sealed from each other, that people across religious demarcations often shared 'some of the beliefs and practices that have always formed the hidden and subversive counterimage of orthodox religions'—and persist in the form of the Jewish saint, Abu Hasira, worshipped by Muslims in Egypt and the Muslim warrior who sits beneath the Vishnu idol at the Hindu temple in Mangalore.

Heterodoxy and syncretism are inconvenient in this world of Religions, Histories, and Civilizations. Detained during his trip to visit the tomb of Abu Hasira in Egypt, by officials suspicious of why a Hindu, a non-believer in any Abrahamic text, would want to visit the tomb of a Jewish saint in a Muslim land, Ghosh experiences a flashback several months later as he visits a library in America to look for information on Sidi Abu Hasira: 'I wasted a great deal of time in looking under subject headings such as religion and Judaism... Then recollecting what my interrogator had said about the difference between religion and superstition, it occurred to me to turn to the shelves marked anthropology and folklore' (ibid. 342). And sure enough, there is that material he is looking for. Syncretism, the non-Partitioned, has no place in our contemporary categorizations of knowledge and ideas.

In the aftermath of Partition, Manto tried desperately to recover moral possibilities, 'retrieving from a man-made sea of blood, pearls of a rare hue... the tears shed by murderers who could not understand why they still had some human feelings left'. Fifty-odd years later, writers like Amitav Ghosh and Mukul Kesavan would attempt another sort of archaelogy, deploying both imagination and intellect with a measure of willed optimism in the face of the pessimism engendered by the times. Theirs are projects necessarily situated at the interstices of literary and historical endeavours: lost possibilities and truths have to be reconstructed through the imagination, and the imagined, 'made precise', by what we already know of the real. This job is not one of 'rewriting history', commandeered by the mohajirs of *Shame*, but the task of painstakingly unearthing fragments of stories, slivers of the palimpsest and without imposing a false wholeness or plenitude, undoing absences and reconstructing possibilities. The search for a replenished heterogeneity, would, as we shall see in subsequent chapters, haunt the anglophone novel.

Further Reading

Alok Bhalla, *Stories about the Partition of India*; Mushirul Hasan *Indian Partitioned: The Other Face of Freedom*; Intizar Husain, *A Chronicle of the Peacocks*, and *Basti*; Abdullah Hussein, *The Weary Generations*; Manohar Malgaonkar, *A Bend in the Ganges*; Saadat Hasan Manto, *Black Margins*; Joginder Paul, *Sleepwalkers*; Qurrutulain Hyder, *River of Fire*; Prafulla Roy, *Set at Odds: Stories of the Partition and Beyond*; Rahi Masoom Raza, *The Feuding Families of Village Gangauli*; Bhisham Sahni, *Tamas*.

5

Midnight's Legacies: Two Epic Novels of Nation

> Long years ago we made a tryst with destiny, and now the time comes when we shall redeem our pledge, not wholly or in full measure, but very substantially. At the stroke of the midnight hour, when the world sleeps, India will awake to life and freedom. A moment comes, which comes but rarely in history, when we step out from the old to the new, when an age ends, and when the soul of a nation, long suppressed, finds utterance.
>
> (Nehru 1983: 76–7)

The twentieth century can be described in broad terms as the age of nationalism, particularly in those vast areas of the globe, in Asia and Africa, that came out from under the yoke of imperialism. Even as many might describe themselves in terms of identities other than their nationality, it remains the case that nation-formation has affected the lives of millions in manifold and, often, contradictory ways. If, on the one hand, nation-formation through decolonization has spelled political liberation and hope for a better life, on the other, it has often resulted in mass migration, misery, and bloodshed. There is a long tradition of writing in the Indian subcontinent that speaks to both the utopian expectations and the tragedy of Partition that marked the era of independence. In a famous lament, the celebrated poet, Faiz Ahmad Faiz, suggested that the much-awaited 'tryst with destiny' in 1947 had turned into a time of pain and mourning, blotched with the blood of people who had been incited to kill each other in the name of religion and nationalism:

> This stained, spattered light, this
> night-bitten break of day
> This surely is not the dawn we were waiting for.
>
> ('Subh-E-Azadi'/'The Dawn of Freedom', my translation)[1]

It was also a time of possibilities. In his *The Great Indian Novel*, Tharoor (1989: 246) writes: 'The India of those years...was constantly being rethought, reformed, reshaped. Everything was open to discussion.' Two famous—and instructively different—anglophone novels draw on and enrich this tradition of examining the moment and afterlife of Independence: Salman Rushdie's celebrated saga, *Midnight's Children*, which was followed just over a decade later by poet Vikram Seth's first prose novel, *A Suitable Boy*. Between them, the two novels encapsulate key preoccupations, both formal and thematic, of the postcolonial anglophone novel in India and as such, are worthy of extended consideration.

Midnight's Children was the first major publishing phenomenon for anglophone Indian fiction. Swiftly achieving canonical status, this was undoubtedly the work that put the novel from (and of) India firmly on the global literary map, paving the way for a generation of novelists to follow: 'Children being born at inconvenient times of the night who would go on to label a generation and rejuvenate a literature,' as Tharoor's narrator puts it (1989: 239). First published in 1980, *Midnight's Children* went on to win Salman Rushdie the Booker Prize and the even more distinguished James Tait Black Prize. It routinely features high in polls listing the best books of the twentieth century and, in 1993, was awarded the first 'Booker of Bookers', the best Booker Prize winner of the last quarter century, and in 2008, the best Booker of the last forty years. The novel—acknowledged to be influenced by Gabriel Garcia Marquez's *One Hundred Years of Solitude* as well as Gunter Grass's *The Tin Drum*—is also considered a classic of 'magical realist' literature, a category discussed below. It is at once a family saga, a national history, a fable, an epic, a coming-of-age story, and a political *Bildungsroman*, or a novel of political education. *Midnight's Children* also exploits a range of literary and cultural resources from allegory, satire, and surrealism to Hindi cinema, Hindu mythology, science fiction, detective novels, American 'westerns', political slogans, and advertising jingles. It is famously intertextual, alluding freely to other works, from the two novels mentioned above to Lawrence Sterne's eighteenth-century classic, *Tristram Shandy*, the *Ramayana* and the *Mahabharata*, the Koran, the short stories of Saadat Hasan Manto, the speeches of

Jawaharlal Nehru and newspaper accounts of actual incidents such as the famous Nanavati murder case, a 'crime of passion' that becomes the 'Commander Sabarmati's Baton' episode.

Intertexts: Hatterr and Trotter

Midnight's Children is often credited with putting Indian English into confident and dynamic literary use, breaking the mould not only of the nineteenth-century realism employed by most postcolonial Indian authors but also showing that English itself had been transformed in lively ways by its global disseminations. While this is undoubtedly the case, Rushdie himself has acknowledged an important precursor to his achievements in this regard. It is worth pausing briefly on G. V. Desani, from whom Rushdie learned a 'trick or two' and his 1949 novel, *All about H. Hatterr,* a work to which T. S. Eliot responded somewhat ambiguously, if honestly: 'In all my experience, I have not met with anything like it.'[2] At a time when Indian authors in English were busy attempting to reproduce standard English or, like Anand, clumsily translating vocabulary and syntax from Indian languages into English, Desani showed considerable stylistical derring-do in telling the tale of one picaresque 'Hindustaniwalla Hatterr', a bilingual and Anglo-Indian 'sahib by adoption' who decides to 'go Indian' again (thus neatly inverting Kipling's Kim, an Indian by adoption). Written in a language that 'isn't English as she is wrote and spoke', the narrative—peopled with sages, elephants, mystics, and Maharajahs—cleverly sends up Orientalism.[3] Often scatological and bawdy, Desani's Hatterr delights in puns, double entendre, riddles, jokes, and the wordplay inevitably generated by facility in English, Hindustani, Sanskrit, Tamil, and the bilingual argot known as Hobson-Jobson.[4] Desani is perhaps the first anglophone writer slyly to use 'rigmarole English, staining your goodly, godly tongue, maybe' as ironic—rather than direct—critique of colonialism and colonial discourse (Desani 1998: 37). At times, the reversal of the colonial gaze is explicit as Hatterr undertakes a reverse ethnography on the 'ways of the Occidental people':

Baw Saw: Why do the Occidental males wear neck-wear?
The Sheik: It is a mystic symbol and is called the *Necktie*...Belief in magic is universal to mankind. But the Occidental ritual is different. If their infants sneeze, instead of wiping their nose, as is done in the Orient, they utter the proscription: *Blessoo*!...
Baw Saw: Surely, Sheik, this is *witchcraft*! (ibid. 104)

Foreshadowing the guiding principle of Rushdie's aesthetic in *Midnight's Children*, Hatterr famously declares in an epigraph: 'All improbables are probable in India.' Though Hatterr's anonymous co-author hotly denies an interest in modernism or being 'involved in the struggle for newer forms of expression', a tongue-in-cheek epigraph gestures both towards the unusual form and content of this text as well as the expectations that shape marketing and reading practices:

Indian middle-man (to Author): Sir, if you do not identify your composition [as] a novel, how then do we understand it? Sir, the rank and file are entitled to know.
Author (to Indian middle-man): Sir, I identify it as a gesture. Sir, the rank and file is entitled to know.
Indian middle-man (to author): Sir, there is no immediate demand for gestures. There is immediate demand for novels....
Author (to Indian middle-man): Sir, I identify it as a novel. Sir, itemise it accordingly.

This experiment with modernism and form would open up possibilities for anglophone fiction that would culminate in Rushdie's magisterial novel of nation as well as another work that was begun around the same time but published later. I. Allan Sealy's *The Trotter-Nama* is a similarly prodigious work, bursting with bilingual puns, an excess of minor characters, and fabulous happenings. Set in 'Nakhlau' (a play on 'Lucknow'), the novel 'chronicles' the fortunes of several generations of the Eurasian 'Trotter' (once Trottoir) family. Its vaunted chronicle form, the Persianate *nama*, is homage to one among many indigenous modes of writing history (such as the *tareeq*) that preceded European historiographical influences and Hegel's and Mill's dire pronouncements. It is combined here with 'the art of kahani' or story (Sealy 1990: 148), bringing together the fictional and the historical, and a keen sense of the metafictional as evidenced in several interpolated reflections.

A thousand and one possibilities: *Midnight's Children*

A more disciplined text than Sealy's for all its 'excess' of stories, *Midnight's Children* is the saga of a family whose future sons and grandsons will *not* be biologically related to each other. The story, which commences one early spring in the Srinagar valley, takes us to the crowded streets of Agra and Amritsar where an infamous colonial massacre takes place; Old Delhi where a newly married woman learns to 'fall in love with her husband bit by bit' (1991a: 68–9); a posh estate in Bombay where the departing English owner insists that the new tenants keep everything exactly as it was in his time; Karachi in newly minted Pakistan; mangrove swamps in Bangladesh; and a 'sterilization camp' in the ancient town of Banaras. Mapping postcolonial India and its history imaginatively, *Midnight's Children* follows the fortunes of the family started by Aadam Aziz and Naseem Ghani whose middle daughter, Mumtaz/Amina marries Ahmed Sinai and gives birth to Saleem at the very second when India becomes an independent nation. It is, of course, no accident that the still-disputed terrain of Kashmir should provide the frame for a family history that is also the story of the joy and bloody birth of two nations. The novel invokes important historical moments from the infamous Amritsar Massacre to the inauguration of the sovereign, socialist, and democratic republic of India with Jawaharlal Nehru as its first prime minister, the language riots of the 1950s, the Indo-China war of 1965, the Indo-Pakistani War of 1971 and, finally, the long dark midnight of Indira Gandhi's 'Emergency' imposed in 1975. The two midnights—those of Independence and the Emergency—frame Saleem's historical account.

In 1986, the critic Fredric Jameson (1986: 69) made the controversial claim that all Third World texts were 'national allegories'. He argued that even when such texts seemed to be about individuals' private destinies, they were allegories of the public and political situations of their nations. He was criticized for this, most famously by Aijaz Ahmad, who pointed out that the literatures of countries such as India were not all exclusively defined by imperialism and nationalist resistance to it and that there were many non-anglophone texts that were concerned with other issues such as religion, sexuality, and violence. Whatever the merits of Jameson's claim with regard to *all* 'Third World' literature, it is certainly the case that *Midnight's*

Children is an explicitly allegorical text where the life of the protagonist is both inextricably linked to and represents the life of the Indian nation which is born at the same time as he is. At its outset, the narrative announces that it is not a standard issue tale, for

there is no getting away from the date. I was born in Doctor Narlikar's Nursing Home on August 15th, 1947. And the time? The time matters, too. Well then: at night. No. It's important to be more...On the stroke of midnight, as a matter of fact. Clock-hands joined palms in respectful greeting as I came. Oh, spell it out, spell it out: at the precise instant of India's arrival at independence, I tumbled forth into the world.   (Rushdie 1991a: 9)

Saleem's initial gesture as a narrator is to disavow any personal responsibility for the 'mysterious' connection between his story and that of the nation, a posture that changes over time as he starts to imagine that he has control over national events. In constant fear of falling apart completely, Saleem's mission is 'to end up meaning— yes, meaning—something. I admit it: above all things, I fear absurdity' (ibid. 9).

The links between narrator and nation that bestow his life with meaning are made possible not only by the fact of the date of his birth, but also by the enormous narrative significance that is bestowed on the hour of independence. Jawaharlal Nehru's iconic speech to the constituent assembly as the new nation comes into being punctuates the novel's account of Saleem's birth. Hailed also by Nehru's congratulatory letter to him as one whose life will be 'in a sense, the mirror of our own', Saleem comes to believe that by crafting his own narrative, he can control events in his life as well as have an effect on the life of the nation (ibid. 122). This sense of authorial power is strengthened by his later discovery of telepathic abilities:

Because the feeling had come upon me that I was somehow creating a world; that the thoughts I jumped inside were *mine*, that the bodies I occupied acted at my command; that, as current affairs, arts, sports, the whole rich variety of a first-class radio station poured into me, I was somehow *making them happen*...which is to say, I had entered into the illusion of the artist, and thought of the multitudinous realities of the land as the raw unshaped material of my gift.   (ibid. 174, original emphasis)

Saleem's role in his own narrative, however, far exceeds the symbolic brief given to him by Nehru's letter. In his understanding, he is at once a prophecy and a prophet; a historian who can 'cut up' history to suit his purposes and one who is buffeted by the winds of history; a meaning-maker and one on whom meaning is made. But his most important role is that of convenor of the Midnight's Children's Conference when, 'at a crucial point in the history of our child-nation' he discovers the gift of channelling 'a headful of gabbling tongues, like an untuned radio' (ibid. 272).

The 1,001 children 'born within the frontiers of the Infant Sovereign State of India' between midnight and 1 a.m. on 15 August 1947, of whom just over half survive, are 'endowed with features, talents and faculties which can only be described as miraculous' (ibid. 195). Their Conference gives a necessary collective dimension to the national allegory that might otherwise only be Saleem's life story. Though convened by Saleem in a Nehruvian endeavour to '"build the noble mansion of free India, where all her children may dwell"', the Midnight's Children's Conference represents the richness of the historical moment of India's transition to nationhood that brought many political and social ideas into the fray, 'a thousand and one possibilities which had never been present in one place or one time before' (ibid. 9, 200). The clash between Saleem and his alter ego, Shiva, is offered as only the most vivid example of such ideas coming into contact and conflict. Where Saleem represents a vaguely liberal democratic ideal, Shiva advocates the rule of force; if the former argues for a 'loose federation of equals, all points of view given free expression', the latter states simply: 'Everybody does what I say or I squeeze the shit outa them with my knees' (ibid. 220). Saleem, who now lives in the rich boy's home through the good offices of Mary Pereira, may be guilty of expressing a somewhat privileged point of view, where unexamined recourse to the political correctness of 'reason' is easy:

'Rich kid,' Shiva yelled, 'you don't know one damned thing! What *purpose*, man? What thing in the whole sister-sleeping world got *reason*, yara? For what reason you are rich and I'm poor?... Man, I'll tell you—you got to get what you can, do what you can with it, and then you got to die. That's reason, rich boy.' (ibid. 220–1)

Saleem's claims to historical legitimacy are shown to be bolstered by his class privilege and such articles as Nehru's congratulatory letter, while no such letter is directed to Baby Shiva at his slum address.

Nevertheless, Saleem is Rushdie's protagonist and he retains his author's acerbic sympathies. Despite its abundance of irony and satire, *Midnight's Children* is an elegy for the vision of a secular and democratic India most closely identified with Nehru. Saleem's vague advocacy of an evasive 'Third Principle' clearly echoes Nehru's own commitments to the Non-Aligned movement, which attempted to steer a course outside the polarities of socialism and capitalism: 'Do not permit the endless duality of masses-and-classes, capital-and-labour, them-and-us to come between us!' (ibid. 255). Within the liberal framework of the novel Shiva's critique of Saleem's position is caricatured as the war-cry of a dangerous rebel without a cause, one who comes to represent the forces of betrayal and annihilation. Saleem, in contrast, seems destined for heroism, even martyrdom, as he awaits the decisive encounter with the Widow (a satirical rendition of Prime Minister Indira Gandhi) who will destroy the Children and the epoch of optimism they represent: 'If there is a third principle, its name is childhood. But it dies; or rather, it is murdered' (ibid. 256).

Filiation and affiliation

The Aziz-Sinai family-nation saga of generations not linked to each other by blood has specific political resonances for Rushdie. Rather than forging a community that draws strength from its own hetero-geneity, premised on a way of being that is truly different from the divisive hierarchies of imperial rule, the story of the birth of the Indian and Pakistani nations became one of 'filiation'—where supposedly 'natural' racial, biological, and religious links are invested with a murderous sanctity. The distinction between 'filiation' and 'affiliation' is made by the critic Edward Said (1991: 17) who describes the latter as a 'way by which men and women can create social bonds between each other that would substitute for those ties that connect members of the same family across generations'. But affiliation can be turned into 'filiation', as happens in the case of those national narratives that are premised on an imagined homogeneity in the face of actual heterogeneity. Why, if the Aziz-Sinai family can function as one without an absolute need for biological links, does a nation then need to rely on narrow criteria of belonging and exclusion? When the secret of Saleem's birth is revealed, 'we all found that it *made no difference*! I was still their son: they remained my parents. In a kind of collective failure of imagination, we learned that we could not think our way out of our pasts' (Rushdie 1991*a*: 118). Saleem's later romantic love for the Brass Monkey, to whom he is not related by blood, is figured as problematic because it is, nevertheless, incestuous.

History and postmodernism

In his famous essay ' "Errata," or Unreliable Narration in *Midnight's Children*', Rushdie (1991*b*: 25). seems to imply that he is questioning the idea of 'history' itself: 'History is always ambiguous. Facts are hard to establish and capable of being given many meanings.' Rushdie's critical pronouncements on his own work are not, however, necessarily definitive. Given that the novel self-consciously deploys heteroglossia—a multiplicity of ideas and discourses in dialogue and confrontation that disrupt the apparent homogeneity of language and ideology in the novel—*Midnight's Children* does not offer us *only* a self-evidently postmodern view of history and reality (ibid. 288). As Michael Gorra has suggested, not even Saleem—with his repeated allusions to his own errors and unreliability—can claim to represent the novel's point of view, let alone its theory of history or reality. The text winds up offering as an unresolved conflict between at least two different views of history—one that we might broadly call 'postmodern' and the other, a 'critical realist' perspective that also does not see language as a simple expression of reality. Critical realism 'assumes that truth must always be open to revision as a result of experiment, but allows that in the meantime truth provides a basis for action, including collective action to transform institutions' (Wainwright 1994: 10).

'[T]here are so many stories to tell, too many, such an excess of intertwined lives events miracles places rumours, so dense a commingling of the improbable and the mundane!' (Rushdie 1991*a*: 9). Such Saleem-isms have led critics to claim that *Midnight's Children* is an unambiguously postmodern text that 'problematizes the historical novel form by demonstrating, for example, the impossibility of classifying all the data of our experience without generalization or omission' (Myers 1996). Fragments—a privileged genre in much postmodern discourse—abound in the narrative, the most famous example being that of the perforated sheet, 'which doomed my mother to learn to love a man in segments, and which condemned me to see my own life—its meanings, its structures—in fragments also' (Rushdie 1991a: 107). Saleem's lectures on memory's truth and the existence of 'many versions of India' seem to endorse the postmodernist emphasis on subjective knowledge and experience. Yet the novel appears also to interrogate its own postmodern leanings; even as it questions the ways in which the history of India has been written, it reaffirms the importance of writing history. Like Aadam Aziz, 'unable to worship a God in whose existence he could not wholly disbelieve', the novel remains caught in a limbo between commitment and scepticism (ibid. 12). In the very last paragraphs of his epic account, Saleem concedes that history is in constant need of revision and that there can be no final word, but then almost immediately proceeds to describe the novel's pickles and histories as ones that 'possess the authentic taste of truth' (ibid. 461). Indeed, at the very outset, Saleem indicates that his task as a writer is to commit history to paper for 'we are a nation of forgetters' (ibid. 37). Both silence and forgetting are dangerous, especially in the face of the impending annihilation of the Midnight's Children and the possibilities they represent. While neither memory nor writing can ever lay claim to apprehending 'truth' in its entirety, to give up on the possibility of truth and to 'secede from history' constitutes a dangerous abdication of responsibility in the context of the repression, censorship, and official distortion. *Midnight's Children* is also a novel of the Emergency, inflected by the dilemmas and concerns of the moment that spelled the 'the smashing, the pulverizing, the irreversible discombobulation of the children of midnight' (ibid. 427).

Food, more than any other image or metaphor in the novel, comes to represent the complexity of Rushdie's engagement with questions of history. The Braganza pickle factory where Saleem narrates his story is also the workroom for the 'chutnification of history, the grand hope of the pickling of time' in the form of the novel's chapters (ibid. 459). The ayah, Mary Pereira, stirs her guilt into her curries; Saleem's embittered Aunt Alia impregnates food with her emotions: 'she fed us the birianis of dissension and the nargisi koftas of discord' (ibid. 330); while the Reverend Mother 'doled out the curries and meatballs of intransigence, dishes imbued with the personality of their creator' (ibid. 139). The coming together of raw materials and cultural significance in food preparation is akin to the writing of history where facts and interpretation must also be worked together in a complicated manner so that the one ingredient is inseparable from the other (as in a chutney). Food, like writing, becomes a means of acquiring control over nature and facts:

Family history, of course, has its proper dietary laws. One is supposed to swallow and digest only permitted parts of it, the halal portions of the past, drained of their redness, their blood. Unfortunately, this makes the stories less juicy; so I am about to become the first and only member of my family to flout the laws of halal. Letting no blood escape from the body of my tale, I arrive at the unspeakable part; and undaunted, press on. (ibid. 59)

Far from privileging 'leaking' and 'fragmentation', the traditional values of postmodern aesthetics, to the exclusion of other aesthetic possibilities, this narrative seems to strive for wholeness even as it advocates a healthy scepticism about the 'longing for form'. As one critic has pointed out, the novel 'follows a more linear chronology than is usually assumed' (Singh 2000: 162). The narrator-as-cook is both creator and preserver, ' "A cook," you gasp in horror, "a khansama merely? How is it possible?" And, I grant, such mastery of the multiple gifts of cookery and language is rare indeed; yet I possess it' (ibid. 38).

Bodies—leaking, fissured, fragmented, grotesque, and constantly transforming themselves, blurring the boundaries between human and beast—are also integral to twentieth-century fiction's use of magical realism. Magical realism, 'a mode in which real and fantastic, natural and supernatural, are coherently represented in a state of rigorous equivalence', frequently deploys devices such as literalized metaphors: Ahmed Sinai's frozen 'assets'; the white skins of the postcolonial elite; and the dark fog of guilt around Amina's head (Warnes 2005: 2). The body is central to the description of the Midnight's Children and their various gifts: 'a boy who could increase or reduce his size at will'; a gender-bending child who will later be sterilized twice by the Widow; a sharp-tongued girl whose words can inflict actual physical wounds, and so on. Like food, the body is both fact and interpretation, a site where nature and culture engage with each other. Saleem's nose, which appears at first as only a freakishly outsized organ (and a misleading index of his descent from Aadam Aziz's line) is the source of both his gifts: that of telepathy before his nasal passages are drained and afterwards, of a terrific sense of smell that is an alternative source of insight.

Historiography and metafictions

'Metafiction' refers to

fictional writing which self-consciously and systematically draws attention to its status as an artifact in order to pose questions about the relationship between fiction and reality. In providing a critique of their own methods of construction, such writings not only examine the fundamental structures of narrative fiction, they also explore the possible fictionality of the world outside the literary fictional text.   (Waugh 2003: 2)

'Historiographic metafictions' according to Linda Hutcheon (1989: 285–6), highlight the intimate relationship between the writing of fiction and the writing of history. Such texts display 'a questioning stance through their common use of conventions of narrative' and 'problematize the entire question of historical knowledge'. *Midnight's Children* incorporates metafictional features such as narratorial asides that comment on the act of writing, direct addresses to the reader, and reflect on the relationship between fiction and reality. Many critics of *Midnight's Children* have, however, tended to stress the metafictional over the historiographic: while their work engages in great detail with Rushdie's interest in the structures of fiction and the fictionality of the world outside the text, much less attention has been paid to *Midnight's Children*'s sense of itself as a historical account, a committed historiography of India that offers a serious and *substantive* alternative to official histories of the subcontinent. The novel is deeply invested in the history of India as it makes its transition from colonial possession to postcolonial nation-state; as such, it is deliberately offered as the story of a generation of *children* rather than that of a lone midnight's child. If Rushdie is interested in the narrative structures of fiction, he is equally con-cerned with historiography—the ways in which history is structured and narrated—as well as what kinds of knowledge these narratives lead us to.

Indeed, without a certain passion for contradicting official narra-tives and for making visible those truths that might otherwise be obscured or repressed by 'a nation of forgetters', *Midnight's Children* would be a third of the novel that it is. It would dwindle into a series of somewhat puerile clichés better suited to bumper stickers than to powerful literary texts: 'Sometimes legends make reality, and become more useful than facts' (Rushdie 1991*a*: 47); 'Reality itself is perspective' (ibid. 165); 'illusion itself *is* reality' (ibid.); and 'There are as many versions of India as there are Indians' (ibid. 269). In a famous passage often cited as evidence of Rushdie's emphasis on the unreliability of memory and history, Saleem is fully aware of the manipulative power of philosophical and critical rhetoric:

How I persuaded them: by talking about my son, who needed to know my story; by shedding light on the workings of memory; and by other devices, some naively honest, others wily as foxes... 'What is truth?' I waxed rhetorical, 'What is sanity?' 'Did Jesus rise up from the grave? Do Hindus not accept—Padma—that the world is a kind of dream; that Brahma dreamed, is dreaming the universe; that we only see dimly through that dream web, which is Maya. Maya', I adopted a haughty lecturing tone, 'may be defined as all that is illusory; as trickery, artifice, and deceit.' (ibid. 211)

The notion that *Midnight's Children* is really only Saleem's story because it is his version of events is subtly parodied when Saleem asserts: 'Let me state this quite unequivocally: it is my firm conviction that the hidden purpose of the Indo-Pakistani war of 1965 was nothing more nor less than the elimination of my benighted family from the face of the earth' (ibid. 338).

In his incarnation as the man-dog 'Buddha', Saleem also explores the perils and pleasures of 'seceding' from history through willed amnesia, a self-preserving act in the face of trauma and subversive of the uniform historical consciousness enforced by the myth of the Land of the Pure. The 'history' that is the object of subversion here has been described by the German philosopher, Friedrich Nietzsche, as 'antiquarian', one which 'seeks to preserve traditions and pass them on to those that follow' (Price 1994: 93). The critic David Price suggests that Rushdie attempts to displace antiquarian history by writing a 'critical history' which according to Nietzsche (quoted ibid. 101) necessitated 'the strength to break up and dissolve a part of the past' by taking a knife to its roots. However, secession from history altogether is figured as unacceptable; the man-dog who 'remembers neither fathers nor mothers; *for whom midnight holds no importance*' becomes a troublingly acquiescent character: 'But how convenient this amnesia is, how much it excuses! (Rushdie 1991*a*: 356, my emphasis). Saleem's flight into the 'historyless anonymity of the forests' to escape from 'the soul-chewing maggots of pessimism futility shame', ends in a violent confrontation with the past. He recovers his full humanity only when he is 'rejoined to the past', reclaiming 'all of it, all lost histories, all the myriad complex processes that go to make a man' (ibid. 364–5).

Alternative history

The novel offers, then, the makings of an 'alternative' history of India as it makes its transition from colony to nation charting the violent excisions and exclusions that accompanied nation-formation; the resistance to these narrow conceptions of national community from both Muslims and Hindus; the inheritance of the colonial mantle by the nationalist elite who literally symbolically turn white after Independence; the gradual betrayal of the rich possibilities of independence by the postcolonial state that culminates in the 1975 Emergency; the consequent 'annihilation' of the midnight's generation by Mrs Gandhi, who also appropriates the idea of India itself through her slogan 'India is Indira'; the loss of hope after the destruction of this generation who have, literally and metaphorically, been rendered incapable of reproducing themselves; the hand-in-glove relationship of the so-called secular state with Hindu fanatics represented by Shiva and his henchmen; and the bloody birth of Bangladesh in a second partition in 1971. Anticolonial nationalism turns into postcolonial jingoism which cannibalizes its own: 'the Government even interned Indian citizens of Chinese descent—now "enemy aliens"' (ibid. 299). Not surprisingly, this moment of the 1961 Indo-China war spells the beginning of the official end of the Midnight's Children's Conference: 'In the high Himalayas, Gurkhas and Rajputs fled in disarray from the Chinese army; and in the upper reaches of my mind, another army was also destroyed by things—bickerings, prejudices, boredom, selfishness—which I had believed too small, too petty to have touched them' (ibid.).

Homage and elegy

The final episodes of Saleem's account are satirical and, yet, elegiac, as Saleem finally appears to accept the fact that his 'historic mission to rescue the nation from her fate' is doomed to failure and that he himself will be 'consigned to the peripheries of history' (ibid. 394–5). He finds himself living on the margins of society in a slum populated by folk artists and magicians who are also 'Communists, almost to a man. That's right: reds, Insurrectionists, public menaces, the scum of the earth—a community of the godless, living blasphemously in the very shadow of the house of God' (ibid. 397). While Rushdie is often treated as a pioneering Indian writer, albeit one who draws on 'traditional' literary genres such as the epic or the folktale, little attention is paid to the influence on him of modern literature in other Indian languages, a debt he appears to acknowledge here. The vibrant ghetto where artists such as Picture Singh combine artistic performances with political speeches has echoes of the IPTA or the Indian People's Theatre Association which was founded in 1942. Twentieth-century literature in India has had a long and influential tradition of radical writing that both participates in and is critical of nation-formation; many of the issues taken up by *Midnight's Children*—such as the appropriation of national history by antiquarian forces or the need to imagine the nation as a democratic and egalitarian community—had already been engaged with by writers such as Saadat Hasan Manto, Ismat Chughtai, Rashid Jahan, and Mulk Raj Anand. Manto's Partition-era stories 'Toba Tek Singh' and 'The Dog of Titwal' are amalgamated into the 'uncorroborated' description of the boatman Tai's death: '[Tai] did not die until 1947, when (the story goes) he was infuriated by India and Pakistan's struggle over his valley, and walked to Chhamb with the express purpose of standing between the opposing forces and giving them a piece of his mind. Kashmir for the Kashmiris: that was his line. Naturally, they shot him' (ibid. 37).

The 'magicians ghetto' episodes also reflect Rushdie's ambivalence towards radical cultural and political movements on the subcontinent to which he, like Saleem, feels drawn but is never quite able to 'belong'. Yet, his satirical account of the all-communist ghetto is a sympathetic one, for unlike those who would either manipulate or 'secede' from history, these artists' 'hold on reality was absolute; they gripped it so powerfully that they could bend it every which way in the service of their arts, but they never forgot what it was' (ibid. 399). Nevertheless, they are not seen as the true inheritors of the legacy of Independence for the 'midnight-given gifts of the Children' 'would not have been forgiven easily by a community which constantly denied such possibilities' (ibid. 401). For Saleem and his author, the communist artists' allegiance to literary realism (over the fabulous) deprives them of access to midnight's true potential, though they share with the children of midnight impending annihilation. The narrative that begins with a birth and the celebration of 'an infinite number of alternative realities' ends with another birth, this time of 'the child of a time which damaged reality so badly that nobody ever managed to put it back together again' (ibid. 420). Saleem's final act is to try to 'build reality' through the act of writing history 'in the face of the smashing, the pulverizing, the irreversible discombobulation of the children of midnight' (ibid. 427). The novel ends on an unmistakably elegiac note: . . . 'I shall never reach Kashmir, like Jehangir the Mughal Emperor I shall die with Kashmir on my lips, unable to see the valley of delights to which men go to enjoy life or to end it, or both' (ibid. 462). The novel's terrible conclusion is that the processes that have been set in motion by the destruction of midnight's possibilities will carry on and on 'until a thousand and one midnights have bestowed their terrible gifts and a thousand and one children have died, because it is the privilege and the curse of the midnight's children to be both the masters and the victims of their times . . .'

Middle-class self-fashioning: *A Suitable Boy*

Just over a decade after the dramatic arrival of *Midnight's Children* on the world literary scene and its establishment as one of the canonical texts of postcolonial, indeed, modern literature, Vikram Seth's *A Suitable Boy* was heralded on to a vividly international market in fiction with almost as much fanfare. By now, their way paved by Rushdie's stupendous critical success, novels by writers with connections to the Indian subcontinent had become fixtures on long and short lists for prestigious international prizes. Although, to the chagrin of some critics and readers, *A Suitable Boy* was not shortlisted for the Booker Prize, it had already attained notoriety for the hitherto largest advance offered to an Indian author. Running to nearly 1,500 pages, the novel takes the risk, by the author's own admission, of straining the reader's wrist and patience. Like *Midnight's Children*, this novel has an epochal feel to it; unlike the former, the events in Seth's saga take place over a span of less than two years—albeit two crucial years in the lives of the characters and the young nation. *A Suitable Boy* also shares with Rushdie's epic novel the form of the family saga, complete with labyrinthine family trees and detailed kinship. In both novels, the family saga is interwoven with a thematic interest in the unfolding saga of the new nation in the wake of Independence and Partition.

At the same time, *A Suitable Boy* is a determinedly, even obstinately, different kind of novel. Frequently referencing British authors such as Eliot, Austen, and Hardy, Seth determinedly recuperates nineteenth-century European realism, a genre that Rushdie's text plays with and, at times, flamboyantly subverts. Although it is possible to overemphasize the extent to which *Midnight's Children* departs from realism, it is certainly the case that Seth's text gives no quarter to the magical, the fabulous, or linguistic and formal fragmentation. Unsurprisingly, Seth's work has been compared to that of Dickens, Tolstoy, and Jane Austen and indeed, there are many possible points of comparison between the depiction of characters in *A Suitable Boy* and those in Austen's novels, not least the matchmaking mother and young, intelligent woman trying to make up her mind about love and marriage. Like *Midnight's Children*, however, *A Suitable Boy* too is steeped in an awareness of and affection for indigenous literary and cultural traditions, most notably Urdu poetry, Hindustani classical music, the performed Ramayana, the Ramlila, Shia marsiyas or lamentations, Tagore's songs ('Rabindra Sangeet'), and, of course, Hindi cinema. But the key difference between the two texts in their engagement with the moment and afterlife of India's legendary achievement of 'freedom at midnight' lies in their relationship to allegory. If allegory abounds in Rushdie's text, in Seth's it is conspicuously absent. The life of the new nation impinges on the lives of all the main characters and it forms the circumstances in which they attempt to make their own histories, but nation and character do not mirror each other in any sense. As one might expect in a realist novel, a great deal of thought in *A Suitable*

Boy goes into fleshing out the inner lives of even the more minor characters and there is little interest in making these reflect textual preoccupations, political or otherwise. Indeed, the very level of detail in the recounting of events precludes simple allegorical resonances. Two epigraphs from Voltaire duly warn the reader:

The superfluous, that very necessary thing...

The secret of being a bore is to say everything.

Seth's achievement is to have produced a novel that, for the most part, manages to hold sympathetic readerly interest in 'everything' even as there are undoubtedly digressive passages and even chapters that seem decidedly less than essential to the larger literary scheme.

On the face of it, *Boy* tells a simple story about the quest undertaken by Mrs Rupa Mehra to find a suitable match (or 'boy' in the parlance of matrimonial advertisements) for her younger daughter, Lata. The search proves interesting, funny, emotionally laden, and, at times, challenging, for all concerned. Along the way, all manner of events—some predictable, others more dramatic—take place in the lives of the four families connected by the bonds of matrimony or friendship: the Mehras, the Kapoors, the Chatterjis, and the princely house of the Nawab of Baitar. Although its telling may be linear, the structure of the novel is far from simple, alternating as it does between the lives of several key characters and between different places including the small northern town of Brahmpur, a village in the rural Rudhia district, and the city of Calcutta. There are also several moments of flashback, some offered by way of narrative explanation, others as reminiscences of characters. At all times, *Boy* is a story of human lives and loves, driven by its characters rather than overarching thematic preoccupations.

Class and the modern Indian

Nevertheless, *A Suitable Boy* is a historical novel in at least two ways. It is set, like a large part of *Midnight's Children*, in a period anterior to the time of its actual writing and publication, revisiting a formative historical moment in the life of nation and characters. Key historical events, as in *Midnight's Children*, impinge on the lives of characters,

some of whom, such as Mahesh Kapoor, are even involved in author-
ing significant events such as the only slightly fictionalized Zamindari
Act, which references land reforms actually undertaken by the Congress government in the years following Independence. At times, Seth
offers long, slightly wearying, historical disquisitions, summarizing
particular events in the manner of a textbook. But *Boy* is perhaps
most important as a thoroughly historicized imaginative exploration
of how a particular social grouping—what is today known as the
Great Indian Middle Class—constituted itself. This is a relatively new
historical grouping, one that has constituted itself in response, on the
one hand, to the formation of a formally secular nation-state and, on
the other, to the ongoing project from the nineteenth century onwards, of becoming both 'modern' and 'Indian'. In 1952, the newly
written Constitution was being interpreted in legislation and policy;
this was a project in self-fashioning that had ramifications not only in
the social and political spheres but also for familial structures, inter-
personal relations, and structures of feeling and being in the world.
The heft of a novel like *Boy* is best understood in terms of the
magnitude of the task that it sets for itself: that of understanding,
through the lives of four families, how this self-fashioning took place.

In a useful study, *The Making of a Middle Class in Colonial North
India*, the historian Sanjay Joshi (2001: 1) argues that in many parts of
the world, including India, 'the middle-classes played a crucial role in
defining what it meant to be modern'. In the wake of decolonization,
it would be this grouping, itself a diverse and fluid phenomenon, that
would replace the British ruling classes. From the late nineteenth
century into the early part of the twentieth century, Joshi contends,
middle-class standing was less an economic than a cultural endeavour: 'Being middle class . . . was primarily a project of self-fashioning'
(ibid. 2). It was a project 'predicated on the creation of new forms
of politics, the restructuring of norms of social conduct, and the
construction of new values guiding domestic as well as public life'
(ibid. 1). These processes are represented in *A Suitable Boy*, which is
very much concerned with the construction of middle-class identity
and subjectivity, both individual and collective. Joshi's study is set in
the North Indian town of Lucknow, one of the urban centres in the
'Hindi belt' that go into the making of the fictional composite Seth
calls 'Brahmpur'. Lucknow is in the Northern state of Uttar Pradesh
which is transformed into Seth's fictional 'Purva Pradesh' (Eastern

State) where Brahmpur is located. Joshi stresses the importance of what he calls 'public sphere politics' for the making of the middle classes in colonial North India, a sphere which, inasmuch as it documents and archives its own doings, is more easily accessed by the historian. Seth's novel attempts a project better undertaken by literature in dialogue with history—an imaginative reconstruction of how the project of becoming modern might have unfolded in the sphere of the personal and the emotional.

Despite appearances, the quest to find a 'suitable boy' for Lata Mehra, a young English-educated woman from an upper-caste Hindu family living in tenuously genteel financial circumstances, is anything but 'traditional' in conception and action. Becoming 'modern' puts Lata and her family in a situation where neither an older, more authoritarian mode of arranging marital alliances solely through family elders nor outright individual choice through romance are entirely acceptable. Unlike the marriages of her older brother and sister, Lata Mehra's eventual alliance must showcase the various accommodative compromises that were becoming essential to middle-class self-fashioning in North India. Here, individual choice must be given its place but cannot be allowed to replace the larger framework of familial consent and societal approval. A series of other moderating equations governs the process: Mrs Mehra rejects prospective suitors not only for being 'too dark' or 'too tall', but also for being 'far too well-to-do' although she considers a good income essential. A suitor can be too Anglicized or Westernized, but also rejected for not being able to 'speak English properly'. Within the new framework of secular nationhood, modernity entails an acknowledgement of Indian identity but a concomitant and greater insistence not only on religious, but also caste, identity: 'I think one's own community creates a sense of comfort' (Seth 2003: 594). Accordingly, to be suitable, the boy must be a Kayastha, from a North Indian trading caste ensconced in the upper echelons of the caste hierarchy.[5]

As with any project of delimiting identity, the bounds of the 'suitable' are also marked through negation, reaffirmed by that which is deemed 'unsuitable'. Lata's romance with Kabir Durrani (with his ambiguous first name, like the famous medieval poet of religious syncretism) performs this function. For Mrs Mehra, the outermost boundaries of the acceptable for the purposes of biological and social reproduction are clearly defined; it is not lower-caste, nor even Christian or Parsi: ' "A Muslim!" said Mrs Rupa Mehra more to herself now than to anyone else. . . . "Never, never, absolutely not—dirty, violent, cruel, lecherous—" ' (ibid. 196). Lata's equal and opposite response is to insist not only on the appropriateness of her love-object but also on the primacy of individual choice: ' "I *will* marry him" said Lata unilaterally' (ibid. 197, original emphasis). The larger accommodative framework of middle-class Hindu modernity allows deep-rooted prejudice to exist unproblematically alongside close, even intimate, friendships with deemed violent and cruel 'others': ' "Like Talat Khala?" demanded Lata. "Like Uncle Shafi? Like the Nawab Sahib of Baitar? Like Firoz and Imtiaz?" ' The fault-line is, of course, one that has been widened by Partition enabling the domestic drama here to converge with the most raw conflict in a new nation still reeling from the mutual bloodletting between religious communities.

Yet, as the reactions of several of the younger characters suggest, even this interdict is one that is likely to be undermined over time. Like Pran, who 'suggested mildly that they meet the boy', the new generation of middle-class Indians will at least begin to countenance the possibility of undoing prohibitions on intermarriage as they take further the project of becoming modern *Indians*, gradually allowing provincial and caste identities to be superseded by a national one. Bankers, managers, teachers, doctors, lawyers, judges, and even the odd successful author: if the firmly middle-class milieu of the novel is underscored by the chosen professions of its many characters (even so within a still wide economic spectrum), they are, nevertheless, a far from homogeneous lot and consensus is not easy to achieve, not least on the question of who is allowed to be part of this social grouping. If, for Mrs Mehra, Haresh Khanna represents a more or less ideal amalgam of tradition and innovation, for her highly Anglicized son and his wife, Lata's suitor embodies a parvenu class threat, reminding them of all they wish to transcend:

he was a short, pushy, crass young man with too good an opinion of himself. He had a smattering of the grimy Midlands over a background of the malodorous alleys of Neel Darvaza. Neither St Stephen's nor the culture of London had had much effect on him. He dressed dressily; he lacked the social graces; and his English was oddly unidiomatic for one who had studied it at college and had lived two years in the country.... Khanna was a foreman—a foreman!—in that Czech shoemaking establishment. Mrs Rupa Mehra could not seriously believe that he was fit material to marry a Mehra of their class and background, or to drag her daughter down with him. (ibid. 1018)

If Khanna offends Arun Mehra's Westernized caste sensibilities, he is, nevertheless, very much a legatee of Hindu upper-caste privilege. It is the likes of Jagat Ram, the shoemaker by trade, who will find themselves definitively beyond the boundaries of social inclusion among the Hindu middle-classes, despite the occasional nominal gesture such as the wedding invitation extended to him by Lata's successful suitor. The lower-caste man will not (yet) have meaningful access to the middle-class public or domestic sphere even if it is, troublingly, voiced as voluntary self-exclusion: 'Moved as he was, he had to refuse. The two worlds did not mix; it was a fact of life... [His presence] would cause social distress that he did not wish to be at the centre of' (ibid. 1457). It is inclusion, not exclusion, we are given to understand, that would 'injure his dignity'.

Nation and the politics of inclusion

Both the rhetorical gesture of inclusion and ultimate actual exclusion of the lower-caste man, the cobbler by labour and caste (as opposed to Haresh's vaguely comic performance of that subject-position), need to be read against the magisterial political changes that constitute both backdrop and theme in this saga of family and nation. As Sunil Khilnani (1997: 29) has observed, the years immediately following formal Independence and the adoption of a constitution for the new republic of India in 1950 were, in fact, rife with division among the ruling nationalist elites 'between differing conceptions of who the nation was and what the state should do'. The struggle took different forms and emerged across various ideological rifts, never quite disappearing even after the so-called Nehruvian victory in the battle between Nehru and his political opponent within the Congress, Sardar Patel:

Diametrically opposed in character, the two waged an emblematic struggle between rival conceptions of modern India. One wanted the state simply to express and tend the existing pattern of India's society, with all its hierarchy, particularity and religious tastes; the other hoped to use the state actively to bring it in line with what it took to be the movement of universal history. (ibid. 33)

It is this struggle and the extremely tenuous nature of the victory of the latter, Nehru's reformist agenda, that *A Suitable Boy* both draws on and dramatizes, most visibly in its accounts of Mahesh Kapoor's political fortunes and the fiery debates on the floor of the Brahmpur Assembly.

In what may well be the only nod to national allegory in this novel, this legislative assembly is a microcosm of the larger national political canvas. Like his leader, Nehru, Mahesh Kapoor is besieged by 'good people, bad people, happy people, unhappy people...people who wanted to pull him to the right, people who wanted to push him further towards the left, Congressmen, socialists, communists, Hindu revivalists, old members of the Muslim league who wanted admission into Congress' (Seth 2003: 51). In the Brahmpur Assembly, the chief players in the struggle are Begum Abida Khan, who represents the landed Muslim gentry and their interests, L. N. Agarwal, the Hindu nationalist, and, of course, Kapoor himself, embodying the developmental and reformist thrust of Nehruvianism. He is the author of the Zamindari Bill for his state, which, like the historical Zamindari Abolition Acts, entailed 'abolition by state legislation between 1950 and 1954 of intermediary rights and tenures...Proprietary rights over vast agricultural estates...were transferred from a handful of absentee landlords to state governments' (Frankel 1978: 190). For Mahesh Kapoor, this entails putting even close personal friendships at risk: 'If the lifestyle of a few good men like the Nawab Sahib had to be sacrificed for the greater good of millions of tenant farmers, it was a cost that had to be borne' (Seth 2003: 283). As with the historical legislation that, while allowing for some redistribution, 'fell far short of an agrarian transformation', Kapoor's Bill is derided by both right and left as either too radical or too conservative. Like the moves that govern Lata Mehra's marital future, these legislative changes too 'bore the obvious marks of political compromise' (ibid. 191).

Like *Midnight's Children*, *A Suitable Boy* is cognizant, at one and the same time, of the utopian tenor of the moment of Independence and the whiff of betrayal that begins to emanate from the nationalist vanguard, represented by the Congress party, as the decade unfolds into the realities of postcolonial existence. For Rushdie, the betrayal is embodied by the figure of the Widow; for Seth, it has begun much earlier and its tragedy is the marginalizing of incorruptible idealists such as Masterji:

When he was in jail, his wife, with no one to support her, had died of tuberculosis, and his children, reduced to eating other people's scraps, had suffered near fatal starvation. With the coming of Independence he had hoped that his sacrifice would result in an order of things closer to the ideals he had fought for, but he had been bitterly disappointed. He saw the corruption that had begun to eat into the rationing system and the system of government contracts with a rapacity that surpassed anything he had known under the British.   (ibid. 348)

To turn insult into injury, this corruption is theorized as pragmatism: 'Politics is like the coal trade. How can you blame people if their hands and face become a little black?' (ibid. 349). It is a familiar situation in the wake of decolonization, one described by the radical anti-colonial intellectual, Frantz Fanon, as the 'transfer into native hands of those unfair advantages which are a legacy of the colonial period' by a bourgeoisie 'which is stupidly, contemptibly, cynically bourgeois' (Fanon 1963: 152, 150).

Seth's novel captures a moment in the saga of India when the oppositional becomes the mainstream through a 'slow slide into complacency', justifying Gandhi's warning against English rule without Englishmen. The Indian National Congress, a vibrant anti-colonial organization, turns into a 'great, shapeless, centrist [lump]' that demands rather than commands political allegiance (Seth 2003: 884). The political scene itself is dynamic, 'alive with aspirations' in Khilnani's term, and shaped by the antinomies of 'post-Independence romanticism and post-Independence disillusionment' (ibid. 885). The necessary separation of the Congress party from its role as vanguard of independence from its role as one more party on the democratic scene is strenuously resisted by many within its ranks, as suggested by the face-off between the local politician and the honest administrative officer over fundraising. As in some of the novels discussed in Ch. 3, Nehru, the 'imperious democrat' himself makes a cameo appearance in the novel to give a speech that is a composite of actual speeches. There is an unmistakably elegiac—and perhaps, even defiant tone—in the face of the fashionable contemporary repudiation of the idea of secularism—in the narrator's final comments on the man: 'a man whose greatness of heart won the hearts of others, and whose meandering pleas for mutual tolerance kept a volatile country, not merely in those early and most dangerous years, but throughout his own lifetime, safe at least from the systemic clutch of religious fundamentalism' (ibid. 1355). This much is indisputable.

Though emphatically not a subaltern history, the novel does, in passing, take note of those marginalized by the sweeping movement of the nation towards realizing its own modernity and vaunted place in world history: the low-caste man, the peasant (Kachheru, who will be further disenfranchised by the compromises of agrarian reform) and those like the nameless farmer who will be left out by something as simple as language:

'Do you speak English?' he said after a while in the local dialect of Hindi. He had noticed Maan's luggage tag.

'Yes,' said Maan.

'Without English you can't do anything,' said the farmer sagely.

Maan wondered what possible use English could be to the farmer.

'What use is English?' said Maan.

'People love English!' said the farmer with a strange sort of deep-voiced giggle. 'If you talk in English, you are a king. The more people you can mystify, the more people will respect you.'

He turned back to his tobacco.   (ibid. 543)

The quiet death of idealism represented by the tragedy of Rasheed, young Muslim socialist, a man committed to sacrificing part of his own inheritance to enfranchise such subaltern figures, finally occupies only a footnote at the end of the novel, a passing sad mention in the shortest of chapters and few lines of poetry: 'O my creature, you gave your life too soon. I have made your entry into Paradise unlawful' (ibid. 1438). Faithful, like his character, the writer Amit Chatterji, to Jane Austen, Seth ends his blockbuster with a wedding, not a funeral. It is a Hindu wedding but in keeping with the accommodations of the times, one also undertaken under the protectively egalitarian auspices of the state and its civil laws, 'much fairer to women' (ibid. 1458). This same state and its often unfulfilled promises with regard to the rights of women and other disenfranchised groups, including cultural minorities, is the subject of many of the novels discussed in the next two chapters.

Further Reading

Vikram Chandra, *Red Earth and Pouring Rain*; Amitav Ghosh, *The Circle of Reason* and *The Glass Palace*; Ruchir Joshi, *The Last Jet Engine Laugh*; Jawaharlal Nehru, *The Discovery of India*; Shashi Tharoor, *Riot.*

6

Bombay and the Novel

Midnight's Children's evocation of the infinite possibilities of post-colonial India had a paradigmatic location: they were embodied by what its protagonist, Saleem, describes, in opposition to the 'flat-boiled odours of acquiescence' of Karachi, as 'the highly-spiced non-conformity' of Bombay. In Rushdie's fifth novel, *The Moor's Last Sigh*, he would expand on this idea: 'Bombay was central, had been so from the moment of its creation: the bastard child of a Portuguese English wedding, and yet the most Indian of Indian cities . . . all rivers flowed into its human sea. It was an ocean of stories; we were all its narrators and everybody talked at once' (Rushdie 1997: 350). There is no doubt that this port metropolis—with its self-conscious commingling of cultures and commodities, fabulous wealth and unimaginable poverty, and teeming tensions and transformations—has provided writers with compelling literary material, particularly in what has come to be known as 'the Bombay novel' in English.[1] In its polarities and contradictions, this vibrant city embodies both the promise and the betrayals of Independence, a theme that would emerge repeatedly in the spate of anglophone fiction inspired by *Children*. The modern city enabled encounters across classes, castes, communities, and genders in hitherto unprecedented ways that gestured towards, without necessarily realizing, egalitarian possibilities. As the political scientist, Sudipta Kaviraj (1998: 149), has remarked: 'Democracy in the decades after independence . . . had a clearly marked space of residence. . . . The city, Bombay and Calcutta, par excellence, had that mysterious quality, liberating and contaminating at the same time.' Bombay, however, has specific qualities that has made it particularly compelling for anglophone novelists exploring questions of nation and Indianness: at once cosmopolitan and parochial, it appeared to seek, like their own work, to assimilate the 'outside' while laying claim to a home 'inside' the nation. Like

Bombay, the anglophone novel is itself a site and product of cultural encounter. The 'Bombay novel' is inspired by the city and draws imaginatively on its resources, notably, that most famous of Bombay's industries, the popular Hindi film—another genre that evinces a preoccupation with the question of what it means to be Indian.[2]

Though all Indian cities can claim a certain constitutive diversity, Bombay is distinguished by the presence, in significant numbers, of a variety of minority or marginalized communities from Parsis, Muslims, and Jews (of different denominations), to Protestants, Roman Catholics, and Dalits. Their complex relationship to the larger project of 'India'—at once integral but often sidelined—generates unique stories which can evince critical and questioning attitudes to both nation and community. *The Moor's Last Sigh*, peopled by 'Christians, Portuguese and Jews' insists that it too is an 'Indian yarn'. In danger of being relegated to the periphery, it must stake its own claim to the postcolonial nation: 'Are not my personages Indian, every one?' (Rushdie 1997: 87). Situated centrally on the western Malabar coast of India, Bombay was once an island fishing village included in the dowry of the Portuguese princess, Catherine of Braganza, when she married Charles II. Leased by the English ruler to the East India Company, its economic potential was recognized and exploited by British merchants who then shaped this small port into a great city tailored to the needs of British commerce. By the early twentieth century, Bombay also became a manufacturing base, particularly for textiles, creating an indigenous class of capitalists and industrialists. After Independence, Bombay retained and developed this role as India's premier commercial city. In its capacity as an industrial, financial, and commercial centre, it has attracted waves of largely rural migrants from elsewhere in the subcontinent, escaping rural poverty and looking for work, at first in the great dockyards and textile mills set up in the early twentieth century and later, in the many service industries and informal economy that sprang up to look after the needs of the city's better-off: 'cobblers, painters, masons, sign painters, construction workers, watchmen, public transport workers, vendors, sellers of flowers and vegetables . . . domestic servants, hotel, restaurant and catering workers' (Seabrook 1987: 88). With the arrival of successive waves of migrants, ethnic, caste, religious, and linguistic diversity has become a constitutive aspect of the city. As early as 1832, visitors to the city remarked on its heterogeneity: 'In twenty minutes' walk through the bazaar of Bombay, my ear has been struck by the sounds of every language that I have heard in any part of the world...in a tone which implied that the speakers were quite at home' (B. Hall cited in Kosambi 1986: 38).

Though diverse in this way and perhaps because of it, the city is also prone to communal tensions. Although Bombay (renamed Mumbai under chauvinist pressure) is the capital of the state of Maharashtra, only a minority of the city's residents are native Marathi speakers. Groups such as the anti-Muslim Shiv Sena also seek to assert ethnolinguistic Marathi dominance over 'foreigners' from the south and other parts of India, a phenomenon that once again suggests that shared Indianness is more often a question than a given. As English continues to reign as the language of commerce and professional advancement, Bombay has become a self-conscious cocktail of cultural heterogeneity, cosmopolitanism, and chauvinism:

On the one hand, the colonial authorities stamped the official public space with their representations and encouraged the use and spread of the English language, Gothic, and later other styles, of architecture, Western music and theatre. On the other, the native migrant communities developed their own community cultures, their languages through their community associations...By the late nineteenth and early twentieth centuries, a distinct form of upper class cosmopolitan culture had developed in Bombay as much as its opposite.   (Patel 2003: 7)

Unsurprisingly then, the Bombay novel is preoccupied with both this cosmopolitanism and the stories generated by migrants and minority communities. Writers from minority communities within India, such as Rushdie himself, Rohinton Mistry (of Parsi background), the poet, Nissim Ezekiel (Jewish), and Shama Futehally (from a Muslim family), have found Bombay a familiar and productive, if not always congenial, space to write about. A degree of marginality can afford an analytical vision that is at a tangent to dominant discourse on India and Indianness. Some of Bombay's communities, like the Parsis, once refugees from medieval Persia, have a relatively longer history of engagement with the West and English education and as a likely consequence have produced a proportionately larger number of writers in the language.

Real and imagined citizens: *Such a Long Journey*

'What kind of life was Sohrab going to look forward to? No future for minorities, with all these fascist Shiv Sena politics and Marathi language nonsense. It was going to be like the black people in America—twice as good as the white man to get half as much' (Mistry 1991: 55). Arguably the most talented such writer in a list that includes Ardashir Vakil and Bapsi Sidhwa, Mistry grew up in a *baag* or Parsi residential association, in which he sets some of his most engaging fiction. His first novel, *Such a Long Journey*, is also set in one such run-down residential complex, somewhat euphemistically named Khodadad Mansions. *Journey* is about fraught family ties and male friendships, as the promises of independence begin to show clear signs of corrosion under Indira Gandhi's increasingly authoritarian rule. Gustad Noble, the novel's main protagonist, lives a lower-middle-class life as a bank clerk, teetering along with his family on the edge of genteel poverty. In this perilous economic situation, anchorage is provided by religious and cultural rituals, dreams of a better future for his progeny, and his friendship with Major Jimmy Billimoria who, as the novel opens, has disappeared mysteriously. Gustad's own disappointments are sublimated by the hope that his son will be able to partake of The Great Indian Dream, with its firmly developmental thrust, in ways that have eluded him: 'Daddy never made pronouncements or dreamed dreams of an artist-son. It was never: my son will paint, my son will act, my son will write poetry. No, it was always: my son will be a doctor, he will be an engineer, he will be a research scientist' (ibid. 66).

Gustad's sense of peril is not simply economic: if the state is failing to live up to its promise of social justice and equal opportunity, then the sense of alienation is doubled for those who do not fit comfortably into normative categories of citizenship where, despite official secularism, 'Indianness' seems dominated by one community. Published in 1990, six years after the assassination of the woman satirized by Rushdie as the 'Widow' in *Children*, Mistry's *Such a Long Journey* is also a novel of the Emergency as the culmination of an ongoing erosion of the democratic and socialist principles to which Nehru had, rhetorically at least, committed himself. As Sunil Khilnani (1998: 41) points out, by the time of his death, Nehru's state and its promises had 'etched itself into the imagination of Indians in a way that no previous political agency had ever done', largely by infiltrating every-day life on an unprecedented scale through 'jobs, ration cards, educational places, security and cultural recognition'. The Nehruvian vision of secular pluralism had also put in place a compelling, though contested, framework for a multifaith society: juridical equality within a secular framework but with the state as the guarantor of political and cultural rights of minorities. The betrayals of the time provide a whetstone that sharpens the pain of what Gustad feels most keenly as a personal and an affective betrayal, the disappearance of Jimmy Billimoria from his life. In this novel that is part political thriller, the two betrayals are, as it turns out, connected in chilling ways. For all its unflinching scrutiny of the rot that has set into state and extended into civil society, *Journey* is also a poignant evocation of the strong, if fractious, bonds between Gustad and his male friends, Jimmy and Dinshaw, both of whom he will lose in different ways.

'What hope for the country? With such crooked leaders?' (Mistry 1991: 279) What the powerful do is, we are told, 'beyond the common man's imagination'. So can imagination itself provide then for the triumph of the common man? In the mural painter's joyous hetero-doxy that transforms 'a stinking filthy disgrace' of a piss-soaked wall into 'a beautiful fragrant place' with a multifaith mural, we sense an affirmative answer to this question. But imagination and faith can also be manipulated by those in power, as in the canny conflation, for instance, of 'Mother India/Mother Indira'. In the end, it is a real and local, rather than imagined national, community that bands together to fight, not because 'our beloved country is a patient with gangrene at an advanced stage' but because everyday life must be sorted out: 'Overflowing sewers, broken water-pipes, pot-holed pavements, rodent invasions, bribe-extracting public servants, uncollected hills of garbage, open manholes, shattered streetlights'. The ensuing protest march provides a feisty catalogue of Bombay's unique citizenry:

All manner of vendors and tradespeople, who had nothing in common except a common enemy were waiting to march. There mechanics and shopkeepers, indefatigable restaurant waiters, swaggering tyre retreaders, hunch-shouldered radio repairers, bow-legged tailors, shifty transistors-for-vasectomies salesman, cross-eyed chemists, sallow cinema ushers, hoarse-voiced lottery ticket sellers, squat clothiers, accommodating women from the House of Cages.   (ibid. 312)

Though Mistry feels the need to translate them into rather bloodless English versions of themselves, the narrative does capture the utopian thrust of the Hindustani slogans demanding a reclamation of polis and nation. An old film poster hoarding for the patriotically named film *Jis Desh Mein Ganga Behti Hai* is modified to 'The Land where the Ganga Flows—and the Gutter Overflows'. The events of the day culminate, however, not in triumph but tragedy as the painted wall is brought down by a municipal demolition squad while the clash between police and protesters claims a lone victim: the symbolic innocent and bystander, the man-child Tehmul. 'We the people' dissolves into his jabbering: 'Bigbigbigmachine. Bhumbhumbhum. BigbigloudloudmachinebigshoutingbigGustad' (ibid. 328–9). In a presaging of the greater horrors to come, Tehmul—marginalized, mocked, and powerless—inadvertently becomes the ritual sacrifice for the angry crowd.

The story-factory: *A Fine Balance*

Sacrificial scapegoats, usually the marginalized and disenfranchised, find epic representation in Mistry's justly acclaimed second novel, *A Fine Balance* (1997), a powerful literary rendition of ordinary lives in the metropolis. Over half the city's population of millions live in the gigantic slums of Bombay; the richest urban centre in India is also home to Dharavi, Asia's largest slum. In the trope suggested by the novel itself, what is sewn together is a patchwork quilt of lives and stories connected by chance encounters and shared experiences and yet each distinctive in its own right. This too is a novel of Bombay, the near-mythic 'city by the sea', and the encounters it fosters, but its stories are in turn set against the even larger canvas of the postcolonial nation-state, its caste tensions and class divisions further distorted by the strangulating reach of the Emergency. *Balance* tells of the making of a small and unlikely refugee community in a cramped tenement flat rented by Dina Shroff, a Parsi widow struggling to hold on to her 'fragile independence' from her domineering and financially successful brother. She is joined by Maneck, a paying guest escaping dingy student accommodation, and Ishvar and Om, two tailors fleeing rural caste violence. After a difficult period of adjustment, the foursome manage—for a brief and fragile moment in time—to create a space of sustenance and hope for themselves, a bulwark against the vicious combination of economic, social, and political forces arrayed against them in the world outside.

Though its historical canvas spans the period from just before Independence and Partition to the 1984 assassination of Indira Gandhi, which was followed by pogroms against Sikhs, the novel opens in 1975, just as the Emergency is declared. The forces of the state are authorized to act with brutal force against anyone deemed to undermine 'democracy'. The novel explores the issue of how these cataclysmic historical events unfold in insistently personal terms. The grand sweep of communal violence, caste oppression, patriarchy, agrarian politics, economic exploitation, and urban migration all make their presence felt through small, but powerful, individual stories of loss, despair, pain, small victories, quiet resistance, and the occasional triumph. The making and breaking of families, friendships, and small communities are unique affairs deriving from specific encounters and dynamics, yet they are inexorably shaped by forces and histories that extend well beyond them. *Balance* also draws on a familiar narrative of Bombay which it makes very much its own, a Bombay written about in other Indian literatures as well as the Hindi cinema which is itself one of the emblematic industries of this metropolis. In these cinematic stories—iconic films such as *CID*, *Awara*, and *Shri 420*—Bombay is figured as a place bristling with paradoxes. A city of dreams where nightmares lurk everywhere, Bombay is luxurious and gritty; full of promise, it is sure to betray. Cold-hearted and impersonal, its stories are full of human warmth.

Though Mistry's own literary vision is compellingly realist, Bombay's fantastical contradictions as well as the nightmarish quality of the Emergency itself push at the boundaries of the plausible nudging the novel's realism to the edges of pastiche, the surreal, and the burlesque; tragedy played out on a national stage is often acted out by characters of comic dimensions. It is only at the end of this epic tale, peopled by extraordinary characters, that the significance of the cautionary epigraph from Balzac's *Le Père Goriot* becomes clear: 'And after you have read this story of great misfortunes, you will no doubt dine well, blaming the author for your own insensitivity, accusing him of wild exaggeration and flights of fancy. But rest assured: this tragedy is not a fiction. All is true.' The Emergency provided a ghastly fount of chilling aphorisms ('to make a democratic omelette you have to break a few democratic eggs') and twisted logic often spouted by loyal middle-class followers of the regime: 'at least two hundred million people are surplus to requirements, they should be eliminated' (Mistry 1997: 367). The brunt of massive state-inflicted violence was, as always, borne by the most vulnerable.

Balance is also a literary legatee of the attempts in the 1930s to render what the subaltern historian Ranajit Guha (1987: 138) describes as 'the small drama and fine detail of social existence, especially at its lower depths'. Unlike Anand's forays into the lives of coolies and sweepers or Kamala Markandaya's mannered agrarian novel, *Nectar in a Sieve*, however, this is an anglophone novel that generally manages to imagine and delineate subaltern existence without recourse to condescension or artifice (even if some quite unlikely English formulations issue from the mouths of the two tailors). If the Emergency was an exercise in sinister burlesque with deadly material consequences, through the eyes of the dispossessed we also see how it drew on and intensified existing social fissures into human tragedy on a colossal scale. Integral to the novel's tragic power are the tender and beautifully nuanced portraits of the indigent tailors, Om and Ishvar, uncle and nephew. When they arrive in the big city, they discover that in the eyes of the state and its stratified welfare laws, they have no visible existence and in a reductio ad absurdum, they cannot inscribe themselves into existence without its cooperation:

'A jhopadpatti is not an address. The law says ration cards can only be issued to people with real addresses.'

'Our house is real,' pleaded Ishvar. 'You can come and see it.'

'My seeing it is irrelevant. The law is what matters. And in the eyes of the law, your jhopdi doesn't count.' (Mistry 1997: 177)

Ordinarily, 'jhopadpattis' or shacks that 'are not recognized have no legal existence, which means that the Bombay corporation has no obligation to provide any amenities at all' (Seabrook 1987: 57). Under the bizarre machinations of the Emergency's population control measures, however, if the already disenfranchised will make themselves incapable of reproducing by agreeing to state-sponsored vasectomies, their 'application can be approved instantly' (ibid. 177).

Invisibility and poverty are twinned with inexorable force and it is the novel's achievement, in some sense, to inscribe these otherwise invisible lives into narrative and history. As Sandeep Pendse (1995: 9) has shown in his discussion of labouring communities in Bombay, it is the 'toilers of the city' who are 'relegated to the periphery of existence in the city, both literally and figuratively; actually and ideologically'. But ironically, the city itself depends on their labour for its existence—'proper addresses' are constructed by them, machines and trains operated by them and all manner of tasks—including the factories and shops that underpin its urban economy life—depend on their toil. This novel of Bombay is necessarily also a novel of India, as Bombay's elastic borders are forced to respond to 'developments in the villages and countryside [that create] new reservoirs of landlessness and poverty' (Mistry 1997: 86). While it is not clear whether Mistry is familiar with these works, it is worth noting also that there is a substantial body of Dalit literature in Marathi that speaks powerfully of caste and economic exploitation in the city and beyond, 'of men's bodies in which shame and sensitivity have been wiped out...where leper women are paid and fucked on the road while children cry nearby' (Vijay Tendulkar cited in Bhagwat 1995). In works by writers such as Namdeo Dhasal and Anna Bhau Sathe, Bombay is again depicted as structured by vicious contrasts, a space of both temptation and betrayal. Dina Shroff's life and circumstances enable the telling of a different kind of existence, one that is distinctly more privileged than that of the two tailors and is yet marked by its own (in this case, profoundly gendered) forms of penury and struggle on the fringes of middle-class life, itself a fragile category subject to economic and social vicissitudes. What the city does make possible, it seems, are encounters, solidarities, and even relationships across class boundaries in the crucible of the struggle to survive and assert human needs. These are not easily achieved: Dina and her employees' relationship is marked by mutual distrust and even hostility in the early days; it is through the force of shared experience—particularly a shared vulnerability to the powerful combine of legal, commercial, and criminal forces who run the city—that a bond is forged, albeit one that is never simply trustful or egalitarian. There is a self-conscious if not entirely happy sense of being part of an epic story:

'It's not us, it's this city,' said Om. 'A story factory, that's what it is, a spinning mill.'

'Call it what you like, if all our customers were like you, we would be able to produce a modern Mahabharat—the Vishram edition.'

'Please, bhai, no more adventures for us,' said Ishvar. 'Stories of suffering are no fun when we are the main characters.' (Mistry 1997: 77)

Ironically, it is those who suffer the most who will find a means to survive if not to triumph over adversity. In the end, the novel suggests, it is to bear witness to such suffering that might prove to be the most unbearable pain of all.

Millenarian dreams: *The Death of Vishnu*

'Not wanting to arouse Vishnu in case he had not died yet, Mrs Asrani tiptoed down to the third step above the landing on which he lived, tea kettle in hand' (Suri 2001: 1). As the opening lines of Manil Suri's *The Death of Vishnu* suggest, witnessing and compassion do not always go together. Bombay is also a city where proximity does not mean either intimacy or community. The last hours of a callously neglected man dying on a staircase provide the frame narrative within which are interwoven the stories of all the denizens of the claustrophobic confines of one of the housing complexes that provide shelter for Bombay's large middle classes. Like the pavement dwellers who pay 'rent' to sleep on a square of pavement, Vishnu has 'inhabitation rights' to a staircase landing in return for his sporadic labour—'perfectly entitled to store his meager belongings there, to eat, drink, and sleep there, even to spit paan juice on its crumbling walls if he wanted. (He did)' (ibid. 6). The novel blends social satire, domestic fiction, soap operatic slices of family drama, individual tragedy, and a documentary of city life from a subaltern perspective with doses of Hindu mythology leavening the whole, at times successfully and at others with heavy-handed exoticism. The satire is inflected by Suri's sense of the moral void that shapes relations between haves and have-nots in the city, a void that leads to ritual atonement and stingy pieties in place of genuine empathy and shared human concerns: '"Vishnu?" he called. "Are you alive?".' Then he realized how absurd his question sounded' (ibid. 27). A quotidian indifference to the lives of others allows Vishnu to die alone and soiled on the landing he calls home.

Yet, the novel's attempt to inhabit the mind and soul of a dying subaltern is also only occasionally successful. Vishnu remains a construct: a disenfranchised member of Bombay's lowlife imagined by an author whose own milieu is very different. In this regard, there are similarities between Suri's Vishnu and Anand's powerful, yet flawed, imaginings of an untouchable's life and feelings. This is perhaps most evident in Suri's use of non-realist or magical-realist narrative modes and stylistic devices when relaying Vishnu's pespective: dream sequences, Hindu mythology and legend, hallucinatory cinematic visions rather than the more straightforward realism of other sections. Although the novel is not magical-realist as such, it flirts with the narrative possibilities of myth and magic, particularly towards the end as the dying Vishnu and the religious seeker Jalal appear to commune in a shared religious vision of apocalypse where Vishnu the man and Vishnu the god merge into a single awful avatar. The avatar of Kalki in Hindu mythology 'has been a recurrent and powerful vision of the world turned upside down and a variety of millenarian dreams' although ultimately, a divine order is restored (S. Sarkar 1989: 35).

Whose home? *Baumgartner's Bombay*

A Bombay of loneliness, scarred by communal tensions, violence, class hostilities, and a struggle over scarce resources, is also the adopted home of the Jewish refugee who is the protagonist of Anita Desai's unusual and disturbing novel, *Baumgartner's Bombay*. The eponymous protagonist's city of refuge is a place where posh hotels, glittering racecourses, and wealthy gallery owners exist alongside dilapidated apartment blocks, grimy Irani restaurants, pavement-dwellers, and drug-addled hippies. Babies are born on a piece of sacking on the pavement with relentless traffic in perpetual motion like 'an all-devouring monster on the move'. As in *Balance*, Bombay is a place where even the disenfranchised feel relatively privileged for there is always someone living in a greater degree of degradation. Interwoven with descriptions of the ageing Jew's shabby life in a dark and dank flat overrun by his beloved cats is the reconstruction of his extraordinary personal history: a childhood and adolescence in

Germany during the inexorable rise of Nazism, exile to colonial India as World War II breaks out; internment by the colonial government along with other 'German' citizens; and, finally, the decision to stay on in independent India in the absence of anywhere to return to. Baumgartner becomes an Indian by default: 'He had lived in this land for fifty years—or if not fifty then so nearly as to make no difference' (A. Desai 1998: 19). For Desai, the figure of Baumgartner—an iconic Wandering Jew—serves to interrogate Indianness itself: on the one hand, Baumgartner and the land he lives in, 'more utterly familiar than any other landscape on earth' belong to each other by virtue of long habitation (ibid.). On the other, he perceives himself as doomed to be the eternal foreigner wherever he lives—the dark-eyed Jew in Germany and now the too pale 'firanghi' in Bombay: 'Accepting—but not accepted; that was the story of his life, the one thread that ran through it all' (ibid. 20).

Despite this somewhat romanticized figuring of the eternal exile, Baumgartner emerges as a powerfully etched character. Resigned to a lonely existence relieved by the company of refugee felines, Baumgartner tussles with a sadness and exhaustion that is at once existential and situational. The story of his internment along with other Germans brings to light a forgotten episode in the history of colonial India when, ironically, Jewishness is ignored in favour of a decreed 'German' identity. As Baumgartner's memories of his youth are evoked through snatches of German song and speech woven generously into the linguistic fabric of the novel, *Baumgartner's Bombay* turns away from the anglophone novel's traditional preoccupation with England to examine other encounters between India and Europe. Even in Hugo's childhood, the quasi-mystical figure of the poet, Tagore, enthralls the German literati, including his mother, who, however, is not immune to her own form of racism: 'Silly Hugo, that was written by Goethe, it was about the Mediterranean, not about some dangerous land in the East, *mit den Schwarzen*' (ibid. 57). Like E. M. Forster, Desai herself appears to both be aware of Orientalism and its attendant dangers and yet not entirely invulnerable to it herself. When Baumgartner first arrives in Bombay, his initial impressions are distinctly reminiscent of Mrs Moore's experience of India as a mystical yet recalcitrant trickster in *A Passage to India*:

Was it not India's way of revealing the world that lay on the other side of the mirror? India flashed the mirror in your face, with a brightness and laughter as raucous as a street band. You could be blinded by it. But if you refused to look into it, if you insisted on walking around to the back, then India stood aside, admitting you where you had not thought you could go. India was two worlds, or ten. She stood before him, hands on her hips, laughing that blood stained laugh: Choose! Choose!   (ibid. 86).

In a clear echo of Adela Quested's mysterious experience in the Marabar caves, Baumgartner also undergoes a moment of mystical passage in a cave in barren, hot countryside.

The spilling of blood that marks the birth of Independent India and Pakistan brings Baumgartner, not normally given to historical or political reflection, to a painful recognition of shared suffering with others who lose their homes and loved ones. He sees his situation and that of the fleeing Muslims as 'not very different—and equally hopeless'. Ironically, it is the violent consequences of perceived difference that provides shared human experience: 'Everyone engaged in a separate war, and each war opposed to another war. If they could be kept separate, chaos would be averted. Or so they seemed to think, ignoring the fact that chaos was already upon them' (ibid. 173). He flees the pre-Partition bloodshed in Calcutta to arrive in Bombay which offers 'the possibilities, the opportunities, the sanguine nature of a port', though as riots rend the new nation, Bombay too '[bulges] with refugees who streamed in from over the border' (ibid. 191). The 'sanguine' nature of Bombay takes on a macabre irony towards the end of the novel as the refugee who fears both bloodshed and history is forced to confront the apparently consanguine ties of nationhood in the form of a drug-addled young German. Though consciously Baumgartner refuses any such ties, he finds himself questioning his own motives for providing an unaccustomed and reluctant hospitality: 'Not because he was German, no, but simply because he was in need. Well, the man on the pavement downstairs, the family that lived there, was in need too; did he think of asking them up here and cooking for them? . . . Why? Baumgartner, Baumgartner, he sighed. Ask your blood why it is so, only the blood knows' (ibid. 151–2).

The urban and the pastoral: *Tara Lane*

Bombay can also deceive, requiring us to read it against the grain. The opening chapters of Shama Futehally's *Tara Lane* is one that appears to be an almost pastoral idyll. Here, the coming-of-age for the protagonist, Tara, entails moving, both literally and conceptually, out of the dusty incandescence of Tara Lane and its cobwebby hedges into something more troubled, restless, and urban. The story of a Muslim industrialist family's shift in fortunes in the years immediately following Independence, *Tara Lane*'s imaginative power derives precisely from the juxtaposition of the pastoral-timeless and the urban-historical. The city is on the edges of the child's sheltered and privileged consciousness. It is there in the space between the factory and the home, audible in the distance as women fight over water from the pump, 'pinky pools' of streetlight illuminate children playing with scraps of bunting or wrapping paper, and the rare journey to school in the train in 'a press of bodies': 'I could never, after that, see a train without wondering at the difference between the train as it looked from a distance and as I knew it to be in truth' (2006: 20–1).

The urban has a hint of menace but also a moral claim as the abode of the Other—the labouring and the disenfranchised. Early on, the child Tara becomes vaguely aware that her life of pastoral privilege is underpinned by something not altogether comfortable 'pricking its way across my mind. I despaired of this worm—whatever you did it was there—crawling or turning or still, but it was there' (ibid. 28–9). Even as a teenager taking the train to college, Tara manages to block out the city and all it implies by taking refuge in 'an alternative world' provided by her beloved dog-eared Penguins: 'In a daze I raised my eyes and gazed at the dark flash of buildings as they thundered past. What did it matter that they were grimy and mildewed, with clothes hanging anyhow... I walked on the street feeling that nothing could touch me' (ibid. 53). It is only with romance and marriage that Tara finds herself with no choice but to confront the tensions that had merely lapped at the edges of her childhood and adolescence. Ironically, this is precipitated by extreme happiness: ' "I feel, deep down, that things can't be totally... they can't be... *real*, I mean," I said desperately to my bewildered husband, "for instance our lovely house and garden. When they are surrounded by such slums and such

squalor...they can't be *real*"' (ibid. 81). The existential crisis, the
'*can't* exist', is profoundly tied up with a moral one, the '*shouldn't*
exist', that can no longer be kept at bay. The heightened normalcy of
perfect wifehood and domestic bliss ironically highlights the fissures
between her home and the world of the city outside.

Tara Lane is a novel that does not so much interrogate as articulate
a sense of unease with the rickety resolutions of the Nehruvian model
of the 'mixed' national economy, socialism combined with capitalism. Within this framework, the workers are ostensibly looked after
by the industrialist as benevolent patriarch: 'It was surprising, really,
considering how entirely he could be trusted, that I was so very
nervous of our being collectively and unwittingly in the wrong.
Perhaps I felt an unconscious fear because the source of all
good seemed to be so entirely my father...' (ibid. 30). The menace
that Tara perceives to be lurking at the borders of her childhood
pastoral emerges precisely from those who are not willing signatories
to this form of paternalism, the obstreperous militant unionism
of those described by the loyal family retainers as 'ungrateful good-
for-nothings'. Although Tara ultimately manages the inevitable
crisis by making a distinction between her father's brand of 'honest'
Nehruvian industrialism and the more sleazy managerial attitude
embodied by her husband, the questions she confronts are more
wide-ranging: 'Deep down I had known that our world was an erratic
one' (ibid. 120). Despite this coming to knowledge, the novel provides no easy moral victory: as an upper-class woman, it is possible
for Tara to find shelter and avoidance in motherhood and the 'warm,
muffling quilt' of her marriage. Indeed, upper-class feminine angst
is used to justify the morally questionable end to the crisis, with
the patriarch 'doing things that we would not otherwise have done'
(ibid. 171). The pastoral will return but with a difference 'so the
picture was black instead of white' (ibid. 174). The city can no longer
be made to stay out of the picture.

In praise of the bastard: *The Moor's Last Sigh*

If *Midnight's Children* was, among other things, a rejection of the idea
of purity through filiation, it is in *The Moor's Last Sigh*, Rushdie's fifth
novel, that the themes of 'impurity' and 'heterogeneity' are amplified

into what the author elsewhere calls a 'love song to our mongrel selves' (1991: 394). Bombay is integral to this engagement, itself, on the one hand, a port city where cultures meet and interact and, on the other, a terrain of struggle between the forces of 'purity' and those of plurality. The novel begins in another port city, however, with an even longer history of the commingling of cultures: Cochin, which Rushdie sees as 'the site of the first contact between India and the West' ('Interview', n.d.). It is here that the young Catholic heiress and painterly genius, Aurora da Gama (descended from the famous Portuguese explorer), meets her 'beloved Jew', the older man Abraham Zogoiby, to form a liaison that scandalizes both communities. They move to Bombay to set up house and create a family of three girls and a boy, the last being the eponymous 'Moor'. Like Salim Sinai, the Moor is born with distinct physical differences: a club-shaped hand that will serve him as a deadly weapon and the misfortune of ageing at twice the rate of ordinary mortals. The narrative spans, in one sense, the centuries between the eviction by Christian zealots of Sultan Boabdil from medieval Granada to the destruction by Hindu fanatics of the Babri mosque in 1992. At the same time, like *Children* this too is a twentieth-century family saga with a particular emphasis on the complex and tormented relationship between Aurora and her son, the Moor.

The Moor's Last Sigh is self-consciously written as the story of a family with ties to the religious and ethnic minorities that, albeit less visibly, are also a part of postcolonial India. The narrative pauses early on to reflect on itself, offering a manifesto that is also a challenge to readerly expectations:

Christians, Portuguese and Jews; Chinese tiles promoting godless views; pushy ladies, skirts-not-saris, Spanish shenanigans, Moorish crowns...Can this really be India? Bharat-mata, Hindustan-hamara, is this the place?...is this not the most eccentric of slices to extract from all of that life—a freak blond hair plucked from a jet black and horribly unraveling plait? (Rushdie 1997: 87)

Answering his own rhetorical question, the narrator refuses to allow those not part of the standard Hindu–Muslim binary to be marginalized: 'Majority, that mighty elephant, and her sidekick, Major-Minority, will not crush my tale beneath her feet. Are not my personages Indian, every one? Well: this too is an Indian yarn.'

Despite his disclaimer—'To hell with high affairs of state, I have a love story to tell'—this too is a novel that braids together the stories of individuals and their nation. In a narrative that celebrates 'mongrel selves', both protagonist and city are figured as defiantly 'bastard' twins. Born to unmarried parents, the Moor 'was raised neither as Catholic nor as Jew. I was both and nothing: a jewholic anonymous, a cathjew nut, a stewpot, a mongrel cur' (ibid. 104).

Just as *Midnight's Children* is elegiac about the promise of freedom for the newly born India, *Sigh* is at once praise song and lament for the city that has long mythologized itself as cosmopolitan, plural, and tolerant unlike other more parochial townships. For Rushdie, still committed to the pluralism envisioned by Nehru and others who were part of the process of making the political entity of the post-colonial nation, Bombay *is* India, both reality and ideal. Writing in the wake of bomb blasts attributed to Islamist groups and ensuing riots, Rushdie seems to wonder if Bombay's very strengths are what lead to its downfall: 'Those who hated India, those who sought to ruin it, would need to ruin Bombay' (ibid. 351). The enemies of Bombay's heterogeneity are, of course, chauvinists of various hues, particularly those who would reclaim India in the name of majority religious community with the slogan, 'Hindu-stan, the country of Hindus!' (ibid. 295). The novel explicitly refers to actual events—the destruction of the Babri mosque, which unleashes a sectarian poison 'even the great city's power of dilution could not weaken . . . enough'. This novel also brought controversy in its wake, this time for its depiction of Raman Fielding or 'Mainduck', the underworld boss and sectarian Hindu leader, loosely based on Bal Thackeray, the leader of Bombay's militant Hindu 'army', the Shiv Sena.

He was against unions, in favour of breaking strikes, against working women, in favour of sati, against poverty and in favour of wealth. He was against 'immigrants' to the city by which he meant all non-Marathi speakers, including those who had been born there. . . . He spoke of a golden age 'before the invasions' when good Hindu men and women could roam free. (ibid. 299)

The degradation of the gloriously impure Moor yoking himself to the service of anti-pluralism evokes the crisis in the Moor's relation-ship with his mother, the defiantly pluralist Aurora, but is also a shrewd comment on the apparently cosmopolitan supporters of such chauvinism, the city's 'blue bloods' and 'eager young things from Malabar Hill' who come to pay homage to the likes of Mainduck. Mainduck's observations about 'the need to tame the country's minorities, to subject one and all to the tough-loving rule of Ram' fall on receptive elite ears (ibid. 309).

Curiously, the author who is often read as the embodiment of postmodern writing from the postcolonial world offers here a meditation on the relationship between certain kinds of postmodern performativity, ethical relativism, and religious/racial chauvinism. This relationship is vividly evoked in the figure of the Moor's lover, Uma Sarasvati, 'young, beautiful and driven by her strong religious faith' in Hinduism, who refuses to see the difference between a 'metaphor' and a 'lie':

For in the matter of Uma Sarasvati, it had been the pluralist Uma, with her multiple selves, her highly inventive commitment to the infinite malleability of the real, her modernistically provisional sense of truth, who had turned out to be the bad egg and Aurora had fried her—Aurora, that lifelong advocate of the many against the one, had discovered some fundamental verities and had therefore been in the right.   (ibid. 272)

Although the Moor opines that this constituted a 'defeat for the pluralist philosophy' on which he and other secular Indians had been raised, the point here is that there is a difference between secular pluralism and the relativism espoused by proponents of Uma's 'postsecularism'. Though minorities are entitled to their own identity, not to be subsumed or 'crushed' by 'the flap-eared trumpeting herds' of majoritarianism, trouble begins when each group sees its 'fiction' as more true than that of the other group—rather than as knitted together into a greater yarn: 'The followers of one fiction knock down another popular piece of make-believe, and bingo! It's war' (ibid. 151).

Sigh shares with earlier Rushdie novels features such as a protagonist marked by physical deformities that can also be turned into an advantage (in the Moor's case, a deformed hand that can be used as a club; he also ages twice as quickly as other human beings) and extensive use of filmic imagery and allusions. There is also intertextual engagement with a wide range of other genres: Shakespeare, seashanties, fairytales, Dante's *Inferno*, and the Bible. The use of Indian English extends not only to 'bastard' sentences with mixed vocabulary and different syntax, but also the altered morphological structure of individual words, most prominently in Aurora's verbs— 'killofy,' 'scrubofy,' 'chokeofy,' 'run-o it'. Single words, accordingly, can be punned on in two languages: '*Bastard*, I like the sound of the word. *Baas*, a smell, a stinky-poo. *Turd*, no translation required. Ergo, Bastard, a smelly shit. Like, for example, me' (ibid. 104, my emphasis). As in *Shame*, female characters, particularly mothers— Epifania, Flora Zogoiby, and Aurora herself—come to take on monstrous qualities; so too

> Mother India, with her garishness and inexhaustible motion, Mother India who loved and betrayed and ate and destroyed and again loved her children, and with whom the children's passionate conjoining and eternal quarrel stretched long beyond the grave...a protean mother India who could turn monstrous, who could be a worm rising from the sea with Epifania's face at the top of a long and scaly neck; who could turn murderous, dancing cross-eyed and Kali-tongued while thousands died... (ibid. 60–1)

This description of one of Aurora's own paintings draws our attention to the novel's use of art and painting as a resource in contrast to the metaphors of writing (and rewriting) that are a feature of Rushdie's earlier novels. Paintings—and descriptions of paintings—allow not only for epic scale, but for the simultaneous narration of stories that are otherwise separated by time and space. India's own story, for instance, can be witnessed in one sighting rather than through sequential narration: the same epic mural juxtaposes St Thomas the Apostle and King Asoka, the building of the Taj Mahal, the battle of Srirangapatnam, 'the coming long ago of Jews', the arrival of Vasco da Gama, and modern nationalists such as Gandhi and Nehru.

Indeed, writing and narration seemed doomed to failure when attempted on such an epic scale as the concluding and somewhat messy chapters of the novel itself (inadvertently) suggest. The Moor arrives in Benengali in Spain in search of his now dead mother's last four paintings (thus completing the circle that starts with the Moorish Sultan's expulsion). After a series of surreal experiences in a village where everything is out of joint, not unlike a Dali painting, the Moor is held prisoner in a folly. What happens to him remains unclear though it would seem that his time has come as he lays himself down to die in the very graveyard in which his Moorish ancestors are buried. In this paean to plural cities and human beings, what ultimately also dies is a dream of recreating 'the fabulous multiple culture of ancient al-Andalus' (ibid. 398). Bombay approximates that ideal, but it cannot be made to conform to specifications. Nor is it clear that this city will survive the threats posed by entities such as Abraham's mafia, Mainduck's Army, and the so-called Islamic Bomb. India no longer seems hospitable to the dream of being just human: 'there was no room for a man who did not want to belong to a tribe, who dreamed of moving beyond; of peeling off his skin and revealing his secret identity—the secret, that is, of the identity of all men' (ibid. 414). With grim humour, the Moor also writes an epitaph for secular Nehruvian India in the fate of Jaw-Jaw, the dog: 'His had been a long journey too, and it deserved a better end than a broom-cupboard in a foreign land. But a broom-cupboard it had to be . . . and Jawaharlal had, after all, become just another abandoned Andalusian dog' (ibid. 407).

Meditations on neighbours: *Ravan and Eddie*

Although many anglophone writers, including Rushdie, possess a bilingual sensibility that enriches their literary use of English, few have actually produced novels in more than one language. It is perhaps unsurprising that the one successful exception is a writer from and of Bombay. One of the most innovative twentieth-century novelists in Marathi, Kiran Nagarkar is also the author of English language fiction, translating his own work into English as well as writing original works in it. His most distinctive anglophone work— and the story of how it came to be written—are symptomatic of Bombay's transformative heterogeneity. Nagarkar writes that it began life as a screenplay for a serious Hindi film and, over the course of thirteen years, changed into a script for a 4-hour English film, a half-written Marathi novel, and, finally, into *Ravan and Eddie*, a carnivalesque Bombay novel. Although begun before the publication of *Children* in 1981, *Ravan and Eddie* shares identifiable modernist features with some of Rushdie's early works and modernism more generally: twinned protagonists who are 'not twins' but whose 'lives ran parallel'; multiple narrative perspectives; internal monologue; satirical riffs on mythologies and religious epics; and surreal dream sequences. This is the English novel as 'Hindi film story... not bound by the petty logic and quibbling of the colonizer's tongue' (Nagarkar 1995: 195). Nagarkar's and Rushdie's texts also share a wryly passionate engagement with history and the stories it generates, the nuances of which are profoundly literary: 'If history is the teeter-totter dialectic between heroes or villains and social forces, then chance, the stray remark and the accidental encounter are often the under-rated instruments which shape and reshape the contours of individual lives' (ibid. 16).

Ravan and Eddie is set in that quintessential Bombay institution, the 'chawl', which houses those of the city's vast labouring underclass fortunate enough to have more than makeshift accommodation. The 'floor-plan' of a chawl, Nagarkar writes, is essential to understanding the psyche of its denizens and the novel duly provides a thickly descriptive mapping of these warren-like tenements:

Each room was twelve feet wide and twenty-four feet deep with a wooden partition separating the drawing-room-cum-bedroom-cum-study, library, playpen or whatever from the kitchen which doubled as dining-room, bed-room, dressing room... It is uncommon to have only two people staying in the one long but partitioned room. The average is between six to eight. Patriarch and wife, sons and daughters-in-law, and grandchildren.

(ibid. 67)

The novel unfolds as 'a meditation on neighbours' with the narrator reflecting on both the conjoinings and the separations engendered by these dense proximities where 'it's almost impossible to pick the lice out of your own hair without picking a few out of somebody else's' (ibid. 54). Bombay's own contradictions, which are perhaps also those of a nation aspiring to secular pluralism, are embodied here: majority and minorities live in close proximity without necessarily always understanding or engaging with one another. Like Ravan and Eddie, their communities, Hindu and Goan Catholic respectively, live parallel lives: 'And there is no greater distance on earth than that which separates parallel lines, even if they almost touch one another. One city, two floors, two cultures, two languages, two religions and the enmity of two women separated them' (ibid. 195). Nagarkar's take on communal differences and conflict is often Swiftian in its satirical thrust: 'Hindus bathe in the morning, Goan Catholics in the evening.... Hindus didn't think that spitting was peeing through the mouth. Catholics did...Hindu women wore saris, Catholic women dresses except on special occasions when they switched to saris' (ibid. 174–5).

For all its self-conscious bawdry, the narrative, like the other Bombay novels considered here, is also a serious examination of community identities, histories, and relations in a city and nation both defined by and uneasy with their own heterogeneity. Even as majoritarianism—in the form of the Hindu Sabha which flourishes in the chawl—is seen for the dangerous chauvinism that it is, relations between majority and minority do not map on to a simple binary of oppressor and oppressed. The denizens of this Mazagaon chawl all share the condition of economic marginalization and while the Catholics are clearly a minority, their ability to speak the language of power complicates this condition. Like Seth, Nagarkar reflects on the power bestowed by the very language in which he writes this novel: 'English was the thorn in the side of the Hindus....It gave caste-Hindus a taste of their own medicine. It made them feel like untouchables. It also turned the tables. The former outcastes could now look down upon their Hindu neighbours' (ibid. 179). There are continuities between Brahminical tyranny and colonial domination; if the former identified the command of Sanskrit with culture ('sanskriti') and power, the latter simply did the same with English. The Goan Catholics' English may be unrecognizable in England but in a postcolonial era, as the Marathi novelist writing in English undoubtedly knew, it nevertheless 'opens up new worlds and allows you to cross from one universe to another' (ibid. 180).

Ultimately, it this city's capacity to juxtapose worlds and allow for such crossovers that makes Bombay a compelling subject and setting for Nagarkar and many of his fellow writers in postcolonial India. Bombay both enables and complicates the pluralism through which the postcolonial nation-state articulated itself. In Nagarkar's account of Goan history, for instance, 'liberation' itself is a complicated affair: colonized once by the Portuguese, the people of Goa develop a distinctive identity. Some years after India's achievement of freedom at midnight, Nehru's state takes on the task of liberating Goa from the Portuguese. Though many Goans had been involved in the Indian freedom struggle, the 'liberation' in 1961 is not without its ambivalences, 'a sense of loss, nostalgia, upheaval' as three small islands 'lose themselves in a land mass a hundred times the size of Portugal and among 350 million Hindus and Muslims'. What does it mean to 'become' Indian and 'of India', to find national communion with millions of others even as differences are fostered and proliferate? This is the question that Bombay poses and that its writers attempt to answer in a myriad stories.

Further Reading

Vikram Chandra, *Love and Longing in Bombay* (short stories) and *Sacred Games*; Amit Chaudhuri, *Afternoon Raag*; Arjun Dangle (ed.), *Poisoned Bread: Modern Marathi Dalit Literature*; Shashi Deshpande, *The Dark Holds No Terrors*; Farrukh Dhondy, *Bombay Duck*; Rohinton Mistry, *Tales from Firozshah Baag*; Kiran Nagarkar, *Seven Sixes are Forty Three*; I. Allan Sealy, *Hero*; Shashi Tharoor, *Show Business*; Ardashir Vakil, *Beach Boy*.

7

Family Matters: Domesticity and Gender in the Novel

This book has argued that since its inception, the anglophone novel in India was markedly preoccupied with questions of nation and history, events necessarily played out in the public sphere even as they inflected domestic spaces and personal relations. Critical observations to the effect that 'all Third World texts' are 'national allegories' are, to some extent, underpinned by readings of such texts, more widely available and read, certainly in the Anglo-American literary establishment, than works in Hindi or Bengali. Aijaz Ahmad (1991: 118) claims that modern literature in indigenous languages such as Urdu is far less concerned with the 'nation' as a category or 'primary ideological problematic' and much more with 'our class structures, our familial ideologies, our management of our bodies and sexualities, our idealisms, our silences'. While it is certainly true that epic narratives of nation and history are particularly salient in anglophone Indian fiction, transformations of the public sphere made their presence felt in private lives and fiction inevitably engaged with these. As Tagore suggested almost a century ago, the world and the home can impact each other in strong, often unexpected ways, and out of this emerge unique stories. It is also true that as the anglophone novel diversifies across readerships and writers its concerns have also proliferated.

This chapter examines novels in English that can be described, in a necessarily provisional and partial categorization, as 'familial' or 'domestic' fiction in so far as they are set in the home and concerned mainly with personal relations, emotional lives, and 'affect' more generally. A genre in which women writers are salient, the family story is is also one where the anglophone is eclipsed in volume and, often, in quality, by writing in other Indian languages. As we noted in

Ch. 2, domestic fiction in India emerged towards the end of the nineteenth century preceded by women's life writing which generated 'an extraordinary number' of memoirs and autobiographies (Tharu and Lalita 1991: 160). (Male writers such as Bankim Chatterjee and Sarat Chandra Chatterjee and Tagore himself, of course, were also writing what might be described as familial fictions, tracing the changes wrought in family life and gender relations by colonial modernity.) Women's domestic fiction, as it began to emerge in several Indian languages, also bears imprints of the autobiographical mode, emphasizing personal relations, love, sexuality, family tensions, and the drama of everyday life. Early anglophone fiction by women shared many of these features but also had roots in ethnographic fictions where the author often functioned as a kind of 'native informant' for an assumed European or American reader; traces of this function would persist in the fiction to come. As it evolved over the twentieth century, domestic fiction in English often also became the vehicle for tales of life in particular communities including minorities such as Muslims and Parsis. This development may well be connected to the ways in which the codification of 'personal law'—which governed family and civic affairs—itself came to define community and community identities during the colonial period and into the postcolonial era. As historians and political scientists have shown, this process was inevitably gendered with 'women and the family becoming emblematic of "authentic" cultural traditions constituting these identities' (Mukhopadhyay 1994: 108).

Narrating change: *Sunlight on a Broken Column*

One such novel of family life that is also the story of an upper-class Muslim milieu in transition is Attia Hosain's *Sunlight on a Broken Column*, published by Chatto & Windus in 1961 and then reprinted by Virago in 1988 with an introduction by Anita Desai. A long, often rambling, text, *Sunlight* falls somewhere between memoir and novel in its fictionalized account of young women growing up in a feudal Muslim family in North India. Hosain herself was born into one such family in Lucknow in 1913 and received an English education at La Martinière girls' school and the famous Isabella Thoburn College for women. Like many other women writers from that milieu, she spoke Urdu at home and was educated in English, Arabic, and Persian but is one of the few, however, who chose English as her literary language. Contemporaries such as Rashid Jahan, Ismat Chughtai, and Razia Sajjad Zaheer wrote in Urdu, a language in which there is a vast and engaging body of fiction by women, much of which—including Chughtai's remarkable 1942 novel, *The Crooked Line*—is more accomplished and inventive than *Sunlight*. In part, Hosain's novel is vulnerable to its own attempt to render, in Raja Rao's formulation, a spirit that is the author's own in a language that is not (quite) her own or that of her milieu, the 'begumati zuban' or upper-class Muslim women's sociolect which Chughtai, for example, took to new literary heights. Nevertheless, *Sunlight* is an important document of its time, one marked by profound changes in family, community, and political life. The transitional period to provincial autonomy in 1935 and then complete Independence in 1947 was, for landed Muslim families, also a period of great turmoil. With Partition in 1947, these families also fractured as many branches migrated to the newly formed nation of Pakistan, only to remain irrevocably divided by the hostile border between the two countries.

Narrated by Laila, a young orphan raised by her uncle and aunt, the text seems bifurcated: the first two-thirds of the narrative are relayed in ethnographic mode, as a series of almost—but not quite—timeless vignettes of household practices, family tensions, wedding dramas, eccentric relatives, and sombre funerals; the last third is taken almost unawares by the momentous events that take place from 1935 onwards, a breathless succession of happenings on a national scale which impinge on every household discussion and decision. If, at first, politics and historical events seem only to hover on the edges of the novel's leisurely descriptions of meals, rituals, and festivities, in the last several chapters nothing takes place that is not profoundly shaped by events outside and beyond the family's control. In her introduction to the Virago edition, novelist Anita Desai (1992: p. vi) proposes somewhat problematically that Hosain's text captures a society that was 'not then in flux, it was static and it was a feudal society'. Societies, however stable, are generally in a process of transformation, at times gradual and at others at a more dramatic pace. As the novelist Shashi Deshpande (1989: 47) observes of her own family stories, 'it is stasis that is the aberration'. The very *raison d'être* of *Sunlight* is narrating change which, often in the minutest ways, provides an unending supply of grist to the mill of family drama.

The very opening chapters of the novel depict a clash of views between the family elders about marriages and marital alliances. 'Tradition' is constitutively contested terrain even if traditionalists try to depict it as unchanging and beyond questioning; 'traditions' are, in practice, rarely agreed upon or deployed smoothly. By suggesting that in the novel's India 'it has always been so, it must continue to be so', Desai employs a 'magisterial approach', 'inferences dominated by rigid preconceptions', that confuses discourse about tradition with the practice of tradition (Desai 1988: p. v; Sen 2005: 143). The novel, by contrast, suggests that in 1935 there was no simple correlation between breaks in tradition and what Desai (1988: p. v) terms the 'downfall of the family, of society, of religion, of the motherland, India herself'. The links between these various entities were themselves being worked out and a variety of perspectives, in particular, on the relationship between religion and nation, jostled with each other for legitimacy. For a young woman in a Muslim landowning family that is privileged in many ways and marginalized in others, figuring out the relationship between individual and family, and between community and nation, is not an easy one: 'What was "wrong" in itself, and what was "right"? Who was to tell me?' (Hosain 1988: 31). Where Laila herself comes to a recognition of the artifice often involved in the construction of 'tradition' and 'Indianness', Desai's approach illustrates how *not* to read such a text, by taking anthropological explanations at face value, un-selfconsciously invoking so-called 'ruling concepts of Indian behaviour—Izzat/honour, and Sharam/dishonour'. Indeed, for Desai, Hosain's texts are very much authoritative ethnographic monuments rather than narrative constructs with their own selections and omissions: 'To read them is as if one had parted a curtain, or opened a door, and strayed into the past' (Desai p. vi).[1]

Although *Sunlight* is, unusually for its context, written in English, its author's debts to an Urdu literary milieu are evident. Like Rashid Jahan, Ismat Chughtai, Razia Sajjad Zaheer, and other women writers, Hosain acknowledged the radicalizing influence of the Progressive Writers Association: 'I was at the first Progressive Writers Conference [in 1936] and could be called a "fellow traveller" at the time' (cited ibid. p. viii). Family commitments, she recalls, made active engagement with politics difficult but did not mean a refusal of it. What Desai describes as 'the tenderness' that Hosain 'shows for those who served her family, an empathy for a class not her own' is better understood in terms of the critical questioning of class relations and subjugation encouraged by the radicalizing atmosphere created by the PWA. The character of Nandi in Hosain's novel—a feisty and attractive servant who becomes the target of lascivious male attention—may well have been inspired by 'Dulari', written by PWA founder-member, Mahmuduzzafar.[2] Laila's description of her cousin Zahra in her bridal finery as a 'glittering scented bundle, no longer Zahra but the symbol of others' desires', is distinctly reminiscent of Ismat Chughtai's description of a cousin's wedding in *The Crooked Line*. At the same time, the influence of the afsana, or romance, staple reading for young women of her generation, is evident in Hosain's somewhat saccharine treatment of Laila's romance with Ameer, mildy subversive though it is of class boundaries: 'The moment when Ameer kissed me had no beginning; it was as pure and eternal as the snows we had been watching in communicative silence' (Hossain 1988: 222).

Writing in the 1960s, Hosain is able to reflect back on Partition with the benefit of some temporal distance while conveying the remembered immediacy of the personal and political turmoil that marked the division of the subcontinent. Partition is relayed as an event that has already taken place with Laila revisiting the site of familial division as she bids one last farewell to her old home now taken over by Hindu refugees from Pakistan. The concomitant dissolution of Muslim landholdings and feudal lifestyles is relayed with an awareness of its political inevitability yet with a sensitivity to the human drama of these transformations, the pain of which echoes most persistently in the domestic sphere. Underneath their 'prejudices and absurdities' even traditionalists carry within them 'a real core of suffering' which has to be acknowledged through all the revolutionary sloganeering (ibid. 279). For Laila, the 'futility of arguments which involved beliefs' is underscored by the enormous irony of defining of one's ideological 'homeland' away from the land of one's birth and actual existence, the tragic separation of the familial and the national. Ultimately, the domestic, 'the ordinary elements of everyday life', finally provides a transcendent refuge; Laila is 'happy to have a home of my very own, to live in it as I pleased without dictation, though it was small and simple' (ibid. 314). Nevertheless, the dialectic of domestic seclusion and public engagement will culminate in Laila's union with Asad, the human face of an idealism she comes to admire.

Outside history: *Twilight in Delhi*

Another well-known novel of transition, also set in a feudal Muslim family, provides a telling counterpoint to *Sunlight*. Ahmad Ali's *Twilight in Delhi*, a somewhat mannered and ponderous novel, is, in its author's view, about 'the decay of a whole culture, a particular mode of thought and living' (1966: p. vii). The domestic world of Delhi, now the 'old' city, superseded by the New Delhi built to its south, is the theme of this novel, which laments the passing of the glory of the Mughals and, consequently, the decline of a way of life for elite Muslim families; 'the old inhabitants though still alive, have lost their pride and grandeur under a foreign yoke' (ibid. 2). In Ali's evocative delineation of its spaces, Delhi has been 'reduced' to a domestic sphere in itself, the public and the political having moved to new spaces and new custodians.

Only narrow by-lanes and alleys, insidious as a game of chess, intersect the streets and the city like the deep gutters which line them on either side, and grow narrower as you plunge into them, giving a feeling of suffocation and death, until they terminate at some house front or meet another net of by-lanes as insidious as before.   (ibid. 4)

Peppered with explanatory footnotes and elaborate translations, *Twilight* is written in the ethnographic mode and assumes a primarily English-speaking audience. Significantly, what might have once been a novel of politics is now figured as a domestic novel precisely because Delhi is feminized in defeat, a place history has left behind. The women's quarters or zenana too are figured as a place that history passes by: 'The world lived and died, things happened, events took place, but all this did not disturb the equanimity of the zenana ... secluded from all outside harm, the storms that blow in the world of men' (ibid. 39–40). Unlike the zenana, however, Delhi is figured not as the sphere of female experience but that of male desire, as embodied by the work of its great poets, Mirza Ghalib and the last emperor, Bahadur Shah Zafar, translations of whose ghazals pepper the narrative. As suggested by the doomed romance that provides the novel with one of its thin plotlines, this is a world where poetry generates romance rather than the other way around.

Like Hosain, Ahmad Ali was briefly involved with the PWA, co-authoring one of its early manifestos, and was one of the original contributors to *Angarey*, a controversial collection of short stories by young Muslim writers that inspired literary radicalism in Urdu. Never entirely comfortable with the left-wing politics of the PWA, Ali soon broke away from the group, accusing his fellow writers of sectarianism and in turn, drew criticism for his perceived reactionary elitism. On the evidence of *Twilight*, it is certainly the case that Ali was more drawn to an aesthetics preoccupied with sadness and longing than revolution and change. While mourning copiously the loss of Mughal grandeur and the 'purity' of Delhi's language, the novel nevertheless places this defeat within a World-Historical schema where empires routinely rise and fall, vulnerable to 'the ravages of Time which has destroyed Nineveh and Babylon, Carthage and Rome' (ibid. 206). And if fatalistically, defeat has been conceded in the political sphere, the intrusion of the foreign-colonial into domestic spaces occasions patri-archal anger. Small items and gestures such as soap-boxes, dressing-gowns, leather shoes, and handshakes are met with 'suspicion and ridicule': 'I will have no aping of the Farangis in my house!' (ibid. 203, 11). Amid the elaborate descriptions of clothes, rituals, meals, and pastimes, the novel briefly engages with the most powerfully unavoid-able spectacle staged by the British Raj to declare and consolidate its triumph—the famous Delhi Durbar of 1911, which also marked the shift to Delhi from Calcutta as the capital city. As a holiday and occasion for a family outing, it allows for a more explicit interface of the domestic and the political; for the patriarch, Mir Nihal, it also marks his relegation to the margins of history: 'The past, which was his, had gone, and the future was not for him' (ibid. 152).

Pushing the perimeter: *The Walled City*

Cityscapes are texts that yield knowledge and stories; they provide places where people and communities come together but are also marked by spatial divisions, both metaphorical and literal. These are typically the spaces of domestic and family life where communities affirm and renew themselves. It is unsurprising then that the novel of family life, as in the two novels above, is often the chosen literary vehicle for narratives of minority cultures and communities, the stories that Rushdie insists must not be crushed beneath the feet of that mighty elephant, 'Majority', and even 'Major-Minority', the large Muslim population of India. If it is Parsis who have notably given their community high-profile literary representation in anglophone fiction, one unusual novel makes visible the lives of a family who belong to the fast-dwindling numbers of Indian Jews, a diverse community (including the Bene Israel and the Baghdadi) who have been part of the fabric of the subcontinent for several centuries. Esther David's *The Walled City* combines an evocative account of the everyday life of a Jewish family living in the older quarter of Ahmedabad city with a haunting story of tragic secrets, troubled filial relationships and a rebellious girlhood in a patriarchal community. David, also an artist and academic, herself comes from an Ahmedabadi Bene-Israel Jewish family.[3]

Although the title gestures towards a snapshot of life in the ethnographic mode, the novel itself suggests that neither the city nor the lives of its communities and denizens can be captured in simple vignettes. Even within the extended family, spaces and identities are always under negotiation and subject to transformation. Jewishness, for instance, is the object of reflection for the narrator rather than an identity that can be taken for granted; it is often honoured in the breach of 'a series of don'ts' as in the case of dietary laws:

Uncle Menachem cannot imagine lunch or dinner without gulab jamuns or pedas. He winks and says it is not permissible to mix milk and meat, but he cannot help it. We do not know what he is talking about. His son Samuel explains to us the rules of traditional cooking, shamelessly eating a milk peda with a meat samosa. He says, 'In our house, we do not marinate meat in curd. We do not cook the lamb in its mother's milk. In a way we obey the law, or at least try to. (David 1997: 13)

In a heterogeneous India where a multitude of cultures and faiths jostle next to each other, the curious gaze each casts on the other also returns as self-scrutiny: 'I wonder whether the great flood and Noah had anything to do with the third eye' (ibid. 24). Hinduism, of course, dominates the imagination of all around it and, for the narrator, takes the form of an obsession with the forbidden bindi: 'In my dreams, I draw the bindi in a thousand and one ways' (ibid.). The public and private meanings of symbols cannot be kept neatly separate any more than cultures themselves can be sutured from each other. Jewishness in India flourishes as a quietly syncretic practice, symbolized by the Shabbat meal: 'the flaked rice, washed well and mixed with rose petals, raisins and sugar. There are dates to remind of the desert, bananas and applies, unsalted omelettes and sweet puris made of wheat flower and jaggery, deep fried in pure ghee' (ibid. 30).

For the family, Hinduism is both deeply familiar and determinedly alien. If, for the narrator, it is easier to pray in a temple than a synagogue, for her adulterous grandfather Hinduism had once held the 'lure of the unfamiliar' (ibid. 61). For the desperate grandmother who visits a Hindu charlatan to help win her husband back, it embodies the zone beyond the familial/familiar:

She was crossing the thin line that had always separated her from things that were not Jewish. She knew she was pushing back the perimeter of her world to include another dimension about which she knew nothing, to go beyond the limits of a life which had extended from the kitchen and the garden to the synagogue, the gymkhana club and the few houses she had been invited to. (1997: 65)

Yet out in the street, Leah recalls an age 'where the enlightened gave potions that brought back stray husbands, drove ghosts away from heads and houses, cured illnesses and offered hope to barren women' (ibid. 66). As Ghosh (1992: 263) points out, such 'beliefs and practices have always formed the hidden and subversive counter-image of the orthodox religions of the Middle East'. Although little is said in this novel about the public world of politics, its impact is registered in quiet but meaningful changes to domestic life as Parsi and Jewish families leave the old walled city behind to set up more secure homes 'behind high walls' (David 1997: 173). Like the Parsis of Sidhwa's novels, Jews are not directly targeted by communal violence, but 'difficult times' underscore their sense of numerical smallness and vulnerability to being proclaimed 'alien'. As everywhere, it is women's bodies upon which the battle against encroaching change and difference is fought, but the women here are also agents, participating in transformation. In the ultimate act of resistance, the narrator and her cousin, 'the last of what is referred to as "the family"', choose to allow the community to dwindle further: 'We have decided to lock our wombs' (ibid. 202). Choosing not to have children, particularly when the community reproduces itself through the maternal line, is both an act of resistance and an attempt to put an end to the endless recyling of gendered suffering: 'According to our laws she would be Jewish and it would be torture for her and for me' (ibid. 204).

The woman I am now: *Difficult Daughters*

Complicated and fraught relationships between daughters and parents, particularly mothers, are also powerfully evoked in Manju Kapur's story of growing up in the pre-Independence era in an Arya Samaj family.[4] Of all the novels by women writers considered here, *Difficult Daughters* is the closest to the tradition of women's life writing initiated in the nineteenth century in languages such as Bangla and Marathi. Kapur's novel, like many of those works, is an account of the shifting complexities of social reform and modernity as experienced by wives, daughters, and widows in Hindu families that were attempting to define and stabilize a new Hindu identity in relation to nation-building and modernity.[5] Concerned with the ways in which history, both familial and national, shapes subjectivities in the present, Kapur's narrative revisits the not so distant past of the freedom struggle years as a daughter's reconstruction of her mother's childhood and youth. As though exploring a version of the poet Audre Lorde's question—'To whom do I owe the woman I have become?'—Kapur's narrator writes: 'This book weaves a connection between my mother and me, each word a brick in a mansion' (Kapur 1998: 259).

The novel is as much about the historical experience of female education and emancipation in an upper-caste Hindu family in colonial India as it is about the affective texture of filial relationships, particularly those between different generations of women in an 'undivided Hindu family' that will also experience divisions and changes. If liberating moves such as higher education for the daughters of the family generate anxieties about carefully constructed domestic and sexual boundaries, they also evoke conflicts *within* the subject of emancipation. At a time when the nation and its freedom seem to dominate all ways of being, personal freedom may well come into conflict with the insistently collective project of political liberation: 'Am I free, thought Virmati. I came here to be free, but I am not like these women. They are using their minds, participating in conferences, politically active, while my time is spent being in love. Wasting it. Well, not wasting time, no, of course not, but then how come I never have a moment for anything else?' (1998: 131). Freedom has multiple meanings, and even if the personal is not always at one with the national, each inflects the other, at times, in indeterminate and evasive ways. Like national freedom, choices made in matters of love and desire, even transgressive ones, are never simple nor do they take place in a vacuum.

Tragic transformations: *Family Matters*

Minority communities are particularly susceptible to the shifting vicissitudes of history. It is with a characteristically humane eye for detail that Rohinton Mistry's 2002 novel, *Family Matters*, explores in greater depth than his previous two novels, the shifts and tensions of Parsi identity in contemporary India. An account of a painful family feud, the novel is the story of the ageing Nariman Vakil, who lives with his two stepchildren, Jal and Coomy, and suffers from Parkinson's disease. After breaking his ankle, he requires extensive nursing and, unwilling to continue caring for him, Coomy arranges for him to be sent to the small flat where his biological daughter, Roxana, lives with her husband and two children. As his children wrangle about arrangements for his care, the saddened Nariman lies confined to bed, dependent on them for help with his most intimate bodily functions. His mind revisits his youthful love affair with a Catholic girl, Lucy, that eventually tore his family apart, leaving scars that still flare up and hurt. In the several months between Nariman's move to Pleasant Villa and eventual return to the equally ironically named Chateau Felicity, much happens in the lives of the characters, leaving all of them changed in one way or another, not always for the better. Although most of the novel is narrated by an omniscient voice, the epilogue takes the form of a memoir written by Nariman's younger grandson, Jehangir, who witnesses these events as a child who had even then decided to write 'a big fat book when he grew up, called The Complete History of the Vakeel and Chenoy Families' (Mistry 2002: 47).

Although very much concerned with the characters and emotions that characterize the life of these two families, linked by marriage, *Family Matters* is also more engaged than either of Mistry's earlier novels with the politics of being Parsi in India. Through the stories of Nariman's doomed love affair with Lucy, and his son-in-law, Yezad's, transformation into a religious fanatic, Mistry engages frontally with ideologies of purity and the ensuing bigotry that afflicts the community, itself a vulnerable minority where majoritarian thugs hold political sway in the form of the Shiv Sena. If Hindu chauvinism represents an aggressive attempt to claim India solely for the majority religious community, orthodox Parsis mirror this aggression in their deprecation of racial 'deterioration' and impurity. Though Parsis are usually more preoccupied with whether their egg should be on the keema or on the side, Mistry suggests, bigotry rears its head in an insistence on 'the purity of this unique and ancient Persian community' and the assertion of 'unshakeable arguments for prohibiting relationships between Parsi and non-Parsi' (ibid. 132). As in the *Moor's Last Sigh*, it is Bombay that exemplifies the opposite of purity, providing the antidote to hatred masquerading as community identity. One of the most memorable characters in the novel, Yezad's boss, Mr Kapur, is a Partition refugee who describes, in Shakespearean tones, Bombay as a religion and himself as a devotee:

This beautiful city of seven islands, this jewel by the Arabian Sea, this reclaimed land, this ocean gift transformed into ground beneath our feet, this enigma of cosmopolitanism where races and religions live side by side and cheek by jowl in peace and harmony, this diamond of diversity, this generous goddess who embraces the poor and the hungry and the huddled masses, the Urbs Prima in Indis, this dear, dear city now languishes—I don't exaggerate—like a patient in intensive care. (ibid. 160)

Although his flights of idealism are gently ironized by a sceptical Yezad ('fourteen million people, half of them living in slums, eating and shitting in places not fit for animals', ibid. 159), Kapur remains something of a secular hero, albeit a tragic one, in this novel about the survival of love and decency in the most extreme circumstances.

This is why Yezad's unexpected transformation from Bombay man to Parsi bigot is also figured as a tragic one. Defeated by circumstances and the uphill task of keeping his family fed and clothed, the witty and fiercely secular ironist becomes a dour man of religion. Though not entirely explained by the narrative, Yezad's is clearly the transformation of a man defeated by history and the public sphere, one who believes that only family and community will provide him with a platform from which to assert himself. It is the next generation, in the form of Murad and Jehangir, who are left to remind their father and others of the more expansive meaning of being Parsi with links to more universal and humane ways of living. It is this expansive sense that animates this most overtly 'Parsi' of Mistry's novels, steeped as it is in unexplained cultural references and untranslated linguistic detail without seeming to exoticize it for the ethnographic gaze. In what may well be a manifesto for the familial novel, Mistry suggests that the cultural particular and human universal are not so much opposed as interdependent categories: 'In fact, not matter where you go in the world, there is only one important story: of youth, and loss, and yearning for redemption. So we tell the same story, over and over. Just the details are different' (ibid. 228).

'Irrelevant, middle class'? Shashi Deshpande and Anita Desai

A different kind of manifesto underpins the work of Shashi Deshpande, one of the most prolific women writers and writers of women's lives in English, whose novels deal with the breakdowns in communication, the silences, and the lies that marriages and families contend with. In many ways, the imperative to write is a troubled one for the middle-class woman writer, aware as she is of relative privilege, and yet driven by the need to break silences. The writer and character seem to share a crisis: 'Middle class. Bourgeoise. Upper-Caste. Distanced from real life. Scared of writing. Scared of failing' (Deshpande 1989: 148). Deshpande's best novels are resonant with the tensions and fears that mould the inner lives of her female protagonists and their relationships, the hidden stories of women abused and hurt in these families, and an insistence, through her own doubts, of their relevance to 'real life, real problems . . . As if women's experiences are of interest only to women' (ibid. 147). In *That Long Silence*, the 'huge words screaming out TOTAL REVOLUTION contrast powerfully with the silences in a marriage: In fact, we had stopped speaking, except for the essentials of daily living' (ibid. 148). Even as it is profoundly, compellingly aware of the wretchedness of greater economic and social disenfranchisement, the text cautions against too great a sense of being 'distanced from suffering', like the glossy ads for Vicks and Farex: 'That the way we lived and what we were was no talisman against all the terrible, ugly things we imagined happened only to other people' (ibid. 4, 6).

Few such reflections trouble the work of Anita Desai, who, when she began her writing career in the 1960s, was set apart by her undoubted command of English as a literary language even as most of her contemporaries were still working with an awkward combination of Indian English and ponderous English archaisms. Desai was soon established as a major anglophone writer. Often described as 'Chekhovian', Desai's fiction is largely restricted to an upper-class English-educated milieu with cosmopolitan aspirations. Within this narrow slice of Indian life, however, Desai often creates engaging characters and compelling stories of sibling rivalry, marital alienation, troubled romances, and filial conflicts. Her insider's sense of the tensions, achievements, and preoccupations of this milieu shields her work from the caricaturing that afflicts the work of her close friend, Ruth Prawer Jhabvala. *Fire on the Mountain* is a short but unnerving novel that tells of an upper-class dowager, Nanda Kaul (always referred to by her full name), whose attempts to hold herself apart from the world are trumped by her great-granddaughter, an unexpected and dour claimant to her hospitality. If subaltern characters—servants, ayahs, villagers, shopkeepers—are generally reduced to vaguely humorous or sinister cameos in the novel, there can be no doubt about Desai's ability to draw powerful portraits of women from relatively privileged backgrounds.

The chatelaine of a large house improbably named 'Carignano' in the once British 'hill-station' of Kasauli, Nanda Kaul bestows upon herself the status of a refugee, a curmudgeon in glorious exile from domestic duties and familiar commitments: 'All she wanted was to be alone, to have Carignano to herself, in this period of her life when stillness and calm were all she wished to entertain' (Desai 1999: 17).

Thus, the announcement that her young great-granddaughter is to be sent to live with her for a while precipitates something of an existential crisis, with attendant anxieties, of having to 'bow again, to let that noose slip once more round her neck that she thought was freed fully, finally' (ibid. 19). Nanda's reflections on her practice of the art of stillness, against the grain of her former existence as a wife and mother, provide a compelling portrait of the demands of motherhood and domesticity even for a relatively privileged woman: 'All right, she would say, sitting up on the edge of her bed and letting down her feet to search for her slippers, then straightening her hair—all right, she'd sigh, come, come all of you, get me, I'm yours, yours again.... Had they never been silent? Never absent?' (ibid. 24–5). Desai's description of Nanda's life as a mother is strikingly reminiscent of a passage in the first known autobiography by an Indian woman who had to teach herself how to read and write. In Rassundari Debi's *Amar Jiban* (*My Life*), the author describes a similar sense of having to give of herself physically and mentally in the care of others, once going without food for two whole days: 'After everybody ate, I thought I'd finally have the time to have something for myself. But that was not to be' (ibid. 198).

Like Rassundari, Nanda Kaul too professes to have had too many children and grandchildren to remember the surfeit of details specific to each one: 'She had suffered from the nimiety, the disorder, the fluctuating and unpredictable excess. She had been so glad when it was over' (ibid. 30). Raka, the unwelcome guest, turns out to be no Goldilocks, no child to charm and mellow her grandmother. In an unpredictable turn, it is Nanda instead who will resort to spinning 'charmed fantasies' of an idyllic existence in order to draw her reluctant descendant into her emotional ambit. But as the shock ending of the novel suggests, there is little, in the end, that is idyllic either in the family or in the belated attempts of its members to connect with each other.

In *Fire*, the one woman who has fallen on hard times, Ila Das, is rendered as a caricature of the spinster teacher, meeting a melodramatically brutal ending at the hands of a 'savage' villager. In a later novel, Desai creates a more nuanced character in the shape of Aunt Mira, the poor widowed relation who comes to live with the family in their Old Delhi home. In *Clear Light of Day*, possibly her most accomplished novel, Desai picks up the skein of troubled memories and emotional wounds hinted at in *Fire* to knit together a delicately textured tale of four siblings and the ways in which they grow apart even as the bonds of a shared childhood stake their claims. The narrative of *Clear Light* is gently inflected by the historical moment of its telling and the demands of the world beyond the crumbling mansion on the banks of the Yamuna river that is its *mise-en-scène*. At the same time, it is a sense of stasis—in opposition to the apparent dynamism of the world beyond them—that provides the sisters, Bim and Tara, the opportunity for forensic reflections on their past and present. In tones that recall Ali's dirge for the old city, Bim observes:

Old Delhi does not change. It only decays ... And here, nothing happens at all. Whatever happened, happened a long time ago—in the time of the Tughlaqs, the Khiljis, the Sultanate, the Moghuls—that lot. She snapped her fingers in time to her words, smartly. 'And then the British built New Delhi and moved everything out. Here we are left rocking on the backwaters, getting duller and greyer, I suppose. Anyone who isn't dull and grey goes away—to New Delhi, to England, to Canada, the Middle East. They don't come back.

Old Delhi is a place outside history because history has moved out and happens elsewhere.

There is some irony, then, in the fact that it is Bim, the history teacher, who stays back and that it is she, not Tara, now the outsider, who deconstructs the governing myths of family to which the latter clings. To live in the actual grittiness of the old is also to reject antiquarian aspirations and self-Orientalizing:

'The Taj Mahal—the Bhagavad Gita—Indian philosophy—music—art—the great, immortal values of ancient India. But why talk of local politics, party disputes, election malpractices, Nehru, his daughter, his grandson—such matters as will soon pass into oblivion? *These* aren't important when compared with India, eternal India—'

'Yes, it does help to live abroad if you feel that way,' mused Bim.... Over here I'm afraid you would be too busy queuing up for rations and juggling your budget, making ends meet—' (Desai 2001: 35–6, original emphasis)

Aestheticism and insulation from the exigencies of the present also turn out to be something of a male privilege. The claims of history are at their most insistent in relation to the Partition, 'the great event of our lives—of our youth' (ibid. 43). Relatively sheltered from its worst excesses, Bim and her siblings nevertheless find its divisive legacy reverberating in their lives in unexpected ways. While it makes their brother, Raja, both a hero and a narcissist, it is Bim who is left to cope with the minutiae of everyday life, the 'small things' that patriarchal heroics sets itself above:

'Oh Bim, Bim,' he said, dramatically gesturing towards the door that opened out into the thick, dusty twilight. 'Look there—look,' he said, 'the city's burning down. Delhi is being destroyed. The whole country is split up and everyone's become a refugee. Our friends have been driven away, perhaps killed. And you ask me to worry about a few cheques and files in father's office.' 'No, that's only for me to worry about,' said Bim . . . 'That, and the rent to be paid on the house, and five, six, seven people to be fed every day, and Tara to be married off, and Baba to be taken care of for the rest of his life, and you to be got well again—and I don't know what else.' (ibid. 66–7)

Clear Light is also a wittily unsentimental tribute to small histories— the challenges of everyday domestic and family life—the burden of which is largely carried by women. Ultimately, it is the small things, her tasks and responsibilities rather than the 'vast, warm ocean' of emotions, that will provide Bim with a refuge, as will the teaching of history rather than the making of its grand narratives. She will 'return to what she did best, most efficiently, with least expense of spirit—the keeping to a schedule, the following of a timetable, the application of the mid to facts, figures, rules and analyses' (ibid. 169).

Of 'Small Things'

The image of brother and sister spooning into each other to form a healing whole is not the only point of similarity between Desai's novel and Arundhati Roy's *The God of Small Things* published in 1997 to wide, occasionally hyperbolic, acclaim. Almost two decades after *Midnight's Children* changed the face of the anglophone Indian novel, this was a different kind of work to burst upon the international literary scene, an arrival also marked by bestowal of the Booker Prize. If the former ranged across the epic scale of 'India' as subject and setting, the latter self-consciously refuses grandeur of scale in favour of the story of two small people and the shattering of their lives as initially minor actions come to take on gargantuan tragic significance. The difference in scale between public-national and private-familial tragedies itself underwrites the telling of the story, which suggests that:

> in some places, like the country that Rahel came from, various kinds of despair competed for primacy. And that *personal* despair could never be enough. That something happened when personal turmoil dropped by at the wayside shrine of the vast, violent, circling, driving, ridiculous, insane, unfeasible, public turmoil of a nation. That Big God howled like a hot wind, and demanded obeisance. Then Small God (cosy and contained, private and limited) came away cauterized, laughing numbly at his own temerity.
>
> (Roy 1997: 19)

Marking its own setting and story as one that is inherently distinct from that of the Rushdie-esque epic nation described above, *Small Things* represents a coming-of-age for the anglophone family novel. With its emphasis on sensory and emotional experience as well as its deft knitting together of the familiar and the exotic, this novel was received by both critics and a wider readership, long accustomed to wrestling with epic novels and magical-realist semiotics, with relieved enthusiasm. This was, at long last, a novel with a clear storyline, empathetic characters, identifiable villains, and an original literary style that was both musical and completely accessible. The family dynamics seemed both identifiably universal and pleasingly culturally particular. After the stylistic pyrotechnics of magical realism, Roy's novel proffered a masterly command of realism and the pleasures of seemingly unmediated experience: 'After you turn the last pages ... you can still feel against your skin the lush vines and grasses, smell the pickled mangoes and sweet banana jam, hear the children singing as their uncle's car carries them home to disaster' (cited in Swami 1997: 101).

If the great historical narratives of nation provide the resource that structure the telling of *Midnight's Children*'s tale, *Small Things*, by contrast, makes brilliant use of personal memories to reconstruct the events of a childhood at once idyllic and tragic and in particular, the fateful evening when three children set out on an unsupervised boating expedition. The novel's power derives from the vividness with which the child's impressions and voice are relayed, mediated though they undoubtedly are by the adult narrator. Literary childhood is always a construct but here it is brilliantly crafted. The juxtaposition of the relatively innocent juvenile consciousness of the twins and the adult Rahel's disabused mind is also compelling: 'Anyway, now she thinks of Estha and Rahel as Them, because separately, the two of them are no longer what They were or ever thought They'd be. Ever.' Childhood is a time without divisions whereas now: 'Edges, Borders, Boundaries, Brinks and Limits have appeared like a team of trolls on their separate horizons' (Roy 1997: 3). The grand narratives of Nation and History are part of this team, legislating and dividing human experience; history, in the poet Agha Shahid Ali's words, gets in the way of memory. To the extent that it repudiates History (capitalized in this way) and concomitantly, grand narratives, aspects of God overlap with Guha's theorizing of the 'small voice of history' (Dingwaney Needham 2005). Indian history, Guha (1996: 3) argues, is fixated on the nation-state, which determines how the past is to be read; this can be undone by listening to the myriad 'small voices' in civil society.

Indeed Roy's narrative is emphatic in its evocation of the small, in doing what literature can often do more powerfully than historiography—bending its ear low to hear whispers and even thoughts, invoking the texture not only of thoughts, but feelings and desires, as well as what Rushdie's Saleem terms 'memory's truth'. It is, Roy (1997: 19) suggests, the very smallness of personal despair in the face of great national turmoil that makes it the source of powerful stories. Where Big God controls the writing of official histories, Small God 'climbed into people's eyes and became an exasperating expression'. If the nation is the dominant story, then individuals are constitutively subaltern. Roy's command of metaphor and imagery flourish in her invocation of the aesthetics of the small: 'a bird in flight reflected in old dog's balls'; silences sitting between two people like a 'third person'; childhood fleeing while 'flailing its thin arms'; fear lying 'rolled up on the car floor like a damp cheroot'. If Big God and his discursive epics obscure the despair and pain that sit in people's eyes, it is through reading silences that these stories can be recovered, at least partially. At the heart of this narrative, relayed through the consciousness of one twin, is the living silence that envelopes the other:

Once the quietness arrived, it stayed and spread in Estha. It reached out of his head and enfolded him in its swampy arms. It rocked him to the rhythm of an ancient, foetal heartbeat. It sent its stealth, suckered tentacles inching along the insides of his skull, hoovering the knolls and dells of his memory, dislodging old sentences, whisking them off the tip of his tongue.   (ibid. 11–12)

The 'reason for his silence' prompts the telling of the story, the novel's excess of language perhaps compensating for the words he has lost to the 'inky tranquillizer' that coats his mind. The child who unwittingly betrays a beloved adult comes to so terrifying a realization of what he had done that it can neither be contained within nor resolved through language, the very stuff of writing History. The telling of the story falls then to Rahel and the resultant narrative revels in speech and the glories of language, at times with thrilling inventiveness and at others with clumsy excess. A bilingual sensibility where English is not taken for granted as a first language opens up literary possibilities in this novel, which is constantly aware of the joys and pitfalls of language acquisition:

> 'Thang God,' Estha said.
> 'Than*k* God, Estha,' Baby Kochamma corrected him.
> … Their Prer NUN sea ayshun was perfect.   (ibid. 154)

It is not language, however, that brings about an apparent resolution at the end of the novel but a mystical sexual union between the twins of which nothing can be said but 'Only that what they shared that night was not happiness but hideous grief' (ibid. 328).

Although *Small Things* is overtly a paean to all that eludes large narratives, official histories, and even articulation through language, it is curiously reliant on these very categories in making sense of the tragic events that shape the lives and deaths of its protagonists. Thus, the brutal killing of Ammu's 'Untouchable' lover, Velutha, by 'Touchable' policemen begets a series of schematic explanatory maxims: 'a blind date with history'; 'History walking the dog' (ibid. 288); 'History's twisted chickens come home to roost' (ibid. 283); 'History in live performance'; and 'history's henchmen. Sent to square the books and collect the dues from those who broke its laws' (ibid. 308). The persistent underscoring of 'History' not only as a determining force but as a self-evidently explanatory category has the paradoxical effect of emphasizing the workings of Big God. The reader is shepherded insistently towards a large and somewhat reductive framework—complete with biological rules and historical laws—for reading the events of that tragic day in Ayemenem. Caste oppression—the contours of which have changed historically even if its workings have been undiminished in brutality—is figured as something of an eternal verity. Other generalizations proliferate: 'civilization's fear of nature, men's fear of women, power's fear of powerlessness. Man's subliminal urge to destroy what he could neither subdue nor deify' (ibid. 308). At the heart of the tragedy, Roy suggests, are 'Love-Laws' that were made 'thousands of years ago' when, in fact, desire, proscription, and family structures are entities that change historically.[6] At its best, the novel connects the personal to historical and social realities; at its crudest, it dwindles into a schematic history lesson in which the reader is bludgeoned into accepting rather than reflecting on the relationship between the two. History, in Roy's hands, becomes curiously ahistorical and the novel, a 'clinical demonstration under controlled conditions' (ibid. 309). This was, as we shall see in the next chapter, a pitfall negotiated by other writers, particularly those of the diaspora, who sought to find both history and identity in an imagined homeland.

Further Reading

Amit Chaudhuri, *Afternoon Raag and A New World*; Venu Chitale, *In Transit*; Zeenuth Futehally, *Zohra*; Kamala Markandaya, *Nectar in a Sieve*; Manju Kapur, *A Married Woman and Home*; Kaveri Nambisan, *The Scent of Pepper*; Shashi Deshpande, *The Dark Holds No Terrors and Small Remedies*; Ismat Chughtai *The Crooked Line*; Qurrutalain Hyder, *Fireflies in the Mist*.

8

Imagining 'Origins': The Literature of Migration

The idea of India in the literary imagination was, as we have seen, usually tied to a specific geographical locale, inhering powerfully in cities such as Bombay that appeared to encapsulate its most fundamental cultural and political realities. It was often explored in its contradictions and tensions, particularly as these emerged through the juxtaposition of small stories with the larger epic of nation, or private narratives of everyday life with the great sweep of public History. The question of 'Indianness' is never far away in these anglophone novels but often elucidated through its messy elusiveness. But over the years, the question of what it means to be Indian has been posed not only by novelists whose work was set in the geographical terrain that has come to be known as India, but increasingly and with different resonances, by those who belong to the growing Indian 'diaspora' or communities generated by the experience of migration, many of whom fall under the governmental category, 'Persons of Indian Origin'. The question of 'origin', however, is never a simple one, particularly when posed by writers of second, third, and later generations of migrant communities whose passports, location, sense of belonging, and cultural affiliations are not always congruent. It is unsurprising then, that 'Indianness' has become a compelling topic for imaginative explorations of the existential, cultural, and historical aspects of identity in (once) migrant communities. On the links between India and its diaspora, Amitav Ghosh (2002: 248) writes: 'It is precisely because this relationship is so much a relationship of the imagination that the specialists of the imagination—writers—play such an important role in it.' The Indian diaspora has produced a great many writers in recent years and although a full study of this diverse body of work is outside the scope of this book, this chapter will examine how 'India' is refracted in the work of some key writers of 'Indian origin' from four different global locations. All the texts considered here address versions of a question posed by Rushdie (1991: 17–18): 'What does it mean to be "Indian" outside India?'

The making of a diaspora

Although inhabitants of the Indian subcontinent have been travelling for centuries, for trade, seamanship, work, or study, sometimes as slaves, occasionally resettling in other parts of the world, it was not until the nineteenth century that mass migration to distant parts of the globe made its impact on this region. In the mid-nineteenth century, hundreds of thousands of rural poor were shipped to and resettled in the British and French sugar plantations of the Caribbean and Indian Ocean to replace the labour lost by the abolition of slavery: hence their presence in Trinidad, Guyana, Fiji, and Surinam, as well as Mauritius and the Seychelles. It was only after 1890 that large numbers of indentured labourers from the subcontinent were brought by the British administration of these regions to the East Africa Protectorate (present-day Kenya and Uganda) to work on building the great Uganda Railway and other projects. Thousands of free immigrants also began to come to the region, attracted by the economic possibilities which included clerical work, teaching, and small businesses. From the seventeenth century onwards, many had begun to travel to England in larger numbers, often as servants or lascars, Indian seamen, who, over time, were exploited in increasingly larger numbers. But it was during World War I that Indians arrived in Britain in the largest numbers, brought to fight for Britain on the Western front. In subsequent years South Asians continued to come to Britain as imperial citizens, as soldiers in World War II and, in another large wave, during the post-war years when there was a demand for labour. As a result of this long and variegated history, there are now large communities of peoples of South Asian descent living in regions from Fiji, Mauritius, the West Indies, and South Africa to Britain, Tanzania, and Kenya. (Post-independence expulsions of Asians from Kenya and Uganda, however, resulted in another wave of migration to Britain). Since the 1960s, the economic prosperity of the United States and Canada have made them sought-after destinations for those who are able to get through stringent immigration restrictions.

The Caribbean: *A House for Mr Biswas*

Though he remains a controversial figure in Indian literary circles, no discussion of the writing of the Indian diaspora, or indeed, the novel of India more generally, can ignore the work of V. S. Naipaul. With an œuvre divided between fiction and non-fiction, Naipaul is also the only figure connected with the Indian subcontinent, after Rabindranath Tagore, to have received the Nobel Prize for Literature (and, like Rushdie, a British knighthood). The young Naipaul was beset by an anxiety that the Caribbean, much like Hegel's India, was a place without history and, therefore, a place that would afford the writer nothing to imagine or write about: 'The history of the islands can never be satisfactorily told.... History is built around achievement and creation; and nothing was created in the West Indies' (Naipaul 1962: 29). For the young writer, disenchanted with his own biographical and cultural context, the 'India' of which his elders spoke longingly had come to have the promise of presence, plenitude, and historical form. Born in Trinidad into what has come to be known as the 'girmit' diaspora, the Indo-Caribbean communities descended from those who were transported to the sugar plantations of the West Indies as ill-paid indentured labour, never to be able to buy their passage back.[1] As such, a 'deep, dislocating rupture' marks the community's sense of itself and, indeed, a profound awareness of historical—and physical—dislocation marks Naipaul's Caribbean works (Nandan 2001: 52). Where other writers have celebrated the hybrid and mixed cultures of the region, Naipaul goes so far as to suggest that the islands suffer from 'an *unnatural* bringing together' of peoples (my emphasis). Even as it remains unique in its often unrelenting cynicism, Naipaul's work did foreground themes that would recur in the writings of others who engaged with India as a distant homeland: a sense of cultural and historical loss, the experience of being 'in-between' cultures, and emotional and intellectual alienation from both 'imaginary homeland' and actual residence. His greatest novel, the autobiographical *A House for Mr Biswas* (2000 [1961]), is a complex and compelling exploration of precisely these themes as they play themselves out in the life of one Mohun Biswas, journalist and father of three by the age of 30.

That *Biswas* is widely read as a 'quest' novel is not surprising and indeed, that quest seems to take various forms for both character and author. For Naipaul, the Caribbean was 'without shape and embarrassing', unpromising material for the novel which, to his mind, needed a stable, 'knowable' social context and a defined sense of the kind of History available to Europeans: 'Unlike the metropolitan writer, I had no knowledge of a past. The past of our community ended, for most of us, with our grandfathers; beyond that we could not see' (2004: 20). This was a 'historical darkness' against which Naipaul would struggle, bringing his quest to India to have it dispelled. Deeply disappointed by this country he would give it the vicious appellation, 'an area of darkness'. But for the early Naipaul, immigrant time was 'undated' and 'mythical' time; only the 'India where Gandhi and Nehru and others operated was historical and real' (ibid. 89). This keen sense of lacking a history, of living in a void would shape—and distort—Naipaul's vision of the Caribbean, but it also gave him important insights into the poignant self-perception of 'people who have been cut off': 'To be an Indian from Trinidad is ... to be a little fraudulent. But so all immigrants become' (ibid. 41). Though *Biswas* was written before Naipaul's notorious voyage to India where he claimed to find 'layers of wretchedness', there is an incipient awareness here that for the migrant, 'India' was already a mythical place, honoured more in the longing than in actual return. 'India' serves to underscore the migrant's sense of himself as cut off from a homeland and, thus, distinct in his marooning. But ironically for the old men of *Biswas*, the void, ultimately, is not 'here' where they live but 'there' in India: 'They continually talked of going back to India, but when the opportunity came, many refused, afraid of the unknown, afraid to leave the *familiar temporariness*' (2000: 195, my emphasis). This is the paradox inhabited by the migrant, a recognition of his own history and reality that Biswas comes to in the wake of breakdown: 'If there was a place for him, it was one that had already been hollowed out by time, by everything he had lived through, however, imperfect, makeshift and cheating' (ibid. 316).

Despite Naipaul's claims that his early fiction was 'concerned only with story and people and getting to the end and mounting the jokes well', *Biswas*, arguably his best work, ends up doing something more (ibid. 22). It transcends Naipaul's own perception that it is the migrant's destiny to be cut off from history—which always happens elsewhere—and 'hung in a void, without a context' (ibid. 20). As it charts the struggle of its protagonist to make his mark, *Biswas* unwrites this void and elaborates 'the larger self-knowledge' that Naipaul assumed was ineluctably tied to the metropolitan novel. Despite its author's gloominess about the migrant's and the Caribbean's exilic fates, the novel broadens the definition of what it is to have a history, crafting the space of diaspora as a third space, neither homeland nor metropole, but a place where a history of its own is unfolding. In a rare moment, the text acknowledges that the Caribbean and its original inhabitants are not so much lacking history as brutally *deprived* of historical existence: 'And Mr Biswas found it easy to imagine the other race of Indians moving about this road before the world grew dark for them' (ibid. 397). He himself is a figure who reckons with the loss of land, father, family, and language, the quintessential migrant:

he was to be a wanderer with no place he could call his own, with no family except that which he was to attempt to create out of the engulfing world of the Tulsis. For with his mother's parents dead, his father dead, his brothers on the estate at Felicity... it seemed to him that he was really quite alone.

(ibid. 40)

History threatens to reject him too by refusing to inscribe him into the archives of officialdom, so that there is 'no witness to Mr Biswas' birth and early years' though he does eventually acquires the 'buth suttificate' which constitutes a historical record of his existence (ibid. 45). Biswas's struggle to have a history is, significantly, bound up with his campaign to 'paddle [his] own canoe' and thus retain his independence from his in-laws. Resisting a sort of indenture, Mr Biswas insists on controlling his own labour power by refusing to work on the family estate. Yet Mr Biswas, like his creator, is beset with the anxiety that his is not the context where such independent subjectivity is possible. In this, he reaches the limits of his identification with Samuel Smiles's literary heroes who 'had rigid ambitions and lived in countries where ambitions could be pursued and had meaning' (ibid. 78–9).

The novel's passionately rebarbative account of life in the Tulsi household and Mr Biswas's resistance to it can be read as a deflected, if notional, critique of indenture and servitude within the plantation economies of the islands. It is also a rejection of the rituals and hierarchies that define Hindu Indian identity in this immigrant milieu and, as such, the oppressive Hinduism and matriarchy of the Tulsi household are the targets of satire. 'The husbands, under Seth's supervision, worked on the Tulsi land, looked after the Tulsi animals, and served in the store. In return, they were given food, shelter and a little money; their children were looked after' (ibid. 97). To live in Hanuman House, therefore, is to endure the lot of slaves and the indentured: the extraction of free or cheap labour; use as a 'stud' to father children on the Tulsi women; and political subjection whereby any deviance from the official norm is to elicit charges of sedition and disloyalty: 'This house is like a republic' (ibid. 123). The rebellious Biswas is repeatedly forced into his place as 'troublesome and disloyal...weak and therefore, contemptible' (ibid. 102). But at times, he too is not beyond the seduction of belonging to a defined culture and political entity: 'The House was a world...everything beyond its gates was foreign and unimportant and could be ignored' (ibid. 188). Belonging, however, generates an ambivalence whereby neither surrender nor secession feel right, but which yields insight: 'The past could not be ignored; it had never been counterfeit; he carried it within himself' (ibid. 305, 316).

England: *The Satanic Verses*

Duality, a sense of division within the self, and ambivalence about both belonging and exile are also central to another novel that explores questions of both Indianness and Englishness as they shape each other: 'from Indianness to Englishness, an immeasurable distance. Or, not very far at all, because they rose from one great city, fell to another' (Rushdie 1988: 41). One of the legacies of colonialism is that Indian and English identity seem to have become oddly twinned. If Bombay is the paradigmatic site of India's heterogeneity,

London becomes the exemplary site of exploration of what happens to cultural identity and historical consciousness when it is taken outside its comfort zone and natural habitat. With this novel, Rushdie placed himself in a long line of immigrant writers from colonial or ex-colonial countries who reflected on the experience of coming to England and negotiating the challenges thrown at them by their new home. Though all his novels evince an interest in the ontological and philosophical condition of being a migrant, or what Rushdie somewhat abstractly calls 'a migrant's eye view of the world', *Verses* is given historical heft by Rushdie's own experiences as an Indian immigrant in London and his activist engagement with the politics of immigration and race in Britain during the 1970s and 1980s (Rushdie 1991*b*: 394). Like the novels that preceded it, *Verses* has two protagonists who can be figured as representing divisions within the postcolonial anglophone Indian self: the self-hating Anglophile Saladin Chamcha (literally, Saladin the 'spoon' or 'sycophant'), complete with bowler hat and pin stripes, and the celebrated film icon, Gibreel Farishta (literally, Angel Gabriel), who sings of his heart that will always remain Indian. Gibreel's tortured dreams of faith and doubt comprise the two secondary narratives set in twentieth-century India and tenth-century Jahilia. More people have heard of *The Satanic Verses* than have read Rushdie's notorious and significant fourth novel. Thanks to the infamous 'fatwa' issued by Iran's late Ayatollah Khomeini, the novel became a flashpoint for controversy that more often than not rehearsed a tired opposition between a presumed liberal, freethinking West and a despotic, repressive East.

For Rushdie, typically, being a migrant is, at one and the same time, a highly specific condition and one that is universal. Accordingly, the novel's tongue-in-cheek yet poetic meditation on the mid-air explosion as a 'universal beginning, a miniature echo of the birth of time' shifts in one fluid movement into a quietly charged and historically specific invocation of the institutionalized racism and humiliation faced by Asian migrants to Britain in the 1970s, including the infamous 'virginity tests' conducted on women coming to the country to join their husbands: 'Also—for there had been more than a few migrants aboard, yes, quite a quantity of wives who had been grilled by reasonable-doing-their-job officials about the length of and distinguishing moles upon their husbands' genitalia, a sufficiency of children upon whose legitimacy the British Government had cast its ever reasonable doubts' (Rushdie 1988: 4). The cheerfully savage satire on eminently 'reasonable' anti-immigrant practices then morphs into a softly poetic enumeration of the emotional and spiritual costs of migration, at once tangible and evanescent: 'mingling with the remnants of the plane, equally fragmented, equally absurd, there floated the debris of the soul, broken memories, sloughed-off selves, severed mother-tongues, violated privacies, untranslatable jokes, extinguished futures, lost loves, the forgotten meaning of hollow, booming words, *land, belonging, home*' (ibid. 4).

For Rushdie (1991*b*: 11), the 'migrant's eye view' is inescapably fragmented, obliging the immigrant writer 'to deal in broken mirrors, some of whose fragments have been irretrievably lost'. Evoking the Hinduism that, like Islam, is also part of his Indian heritage, Rushdie suggests that migration can also be seen as a kind of reincarnation, sometimes desirable and desired, at other times bewildering and painful. It is not a process that the migrant is always in control of and transformations are far from seamless. Chamcha, who aspires to a 'dream-Vilayet [meaning "Britain" or "abroad"] of poise and moderation', leaving behind 'that Bombay of dust, vulgarity, policemen in shorts, transvestites, movie fanzines, pavement sleepers', is terrified when he finds his 'Angrezi' accent overcome by his old Indian self 'bubb[ling] up, in transmogrified vowels and vocab' (Rushdie 1988: 34, 37). He will eventually face a more terrifying transformation, one that forces him to confront the disjuncture between his dream-Vilayet and the reality of life in Britain for most black and Asian immigrants. Like Rushdie's own, Saladin's journey begins with a humiliating and hostile rite of passage in an English boarding school, learning to eat the unfamiliar kipper as his 'fellow pupils watched him suffer in silence; not one of them said, here, let me show you, you eat it in this way' (ibid. 44).

As he begins his imagined conquest of England, Chamcha duly learns 'contempt for his own kind', sealing his imagined triumph by pursuing and marrying an Englishwoman in a symbolic act of reverse conquest: 'England yields her treasures with reluctance . . . if she did not relent then his entire attempt at metamorphosis would fail' (ibid. 49–50). Like some of Naipaul's characters, Chamcha creates and inhabits new selves; like them, in order to become English he must undertake a willed repudiation of Indianness, even when he is back in Bombay with Zeeny:

'Give up on me,' he begged her. 'I don't like people dropping in to see me without warning. I have forgotten the rules of seven-tiles and kabaddi, I can't recite my prayers. I don't know what should happen at a nikah ceremony, and in this city where I grew up I get lost if I'm on my own. This isn't home. It makes me giddy because it feels like home and is not.' (ibid. 58)

His disaffiliation from India and his fellow Asian migrants is so extreme that when he is taken for an illegal immigrant and subjected to police brutality, his first reaction is not to decry the violence but to dissociate himself from its usual targets: '—there's been a mistake, he cried, I'm not one of your fishing-boat-sneakers-in, not one of your ugando-kenyattas, me' (ibid. 140). Given shelter, complete with newly sprung horns and sulphurous breath, by a kindly Bangladeshi and his family, Chamcha's response is distinctly ungracious: '"I'm not your kind," he said distinctly into the night. "You're not my people. I've spent half my life trying to get away from you"' (ibid. 253). But the lesson that Chamcha, like many other migrants, will have to learn is that between the aspiration to belong and the reality of immigrant life falls the shadow of a hostile state and society. *Verses* can be read, at one of its many levels, as the story of Chamcha's brutal coming to political consciousness of the England in which he lives, a place he has imagined as all 'cricket, the Houses of Parliament, the Queen' (ibid. 175). Chamcha's disbelief at what is happening to him is a powerful discursive tool in demystifying this picture-postcard version of life in England. Forced to confront 'Improper' England, Chamcha's disbelieving protest, 'This isn't England' is undermined by reality: 'Why did Purgatory, or Hell, or whatever this place might be, look so much like that Sussex of rewards and fairies which every schoolboy knew?' (ibid. 158). Chamcha becomes the protagonist of a type of anti-racist *Bildungsroman* as his 'old certainties [slip away] by the moment, along with his old life' (ibid. 259).

The Ellowen Deeowen of *Verses* is a city comparable to, even implicitly twinned, with Bombay: teeming with migrants from across Asia, the Caribbean, Africa, and Eastern Europe, it is vibrant with cultural mixings and seething with racial and communal hostilities. As the critic Sukhdev Sandhu has suggested, Rushdie's literary rendition of London can be placed in a longer tradition of black and Asian writing about the city. This 'tradition of black metrography' involves an imaginative mapping of the city: 'something all immigrants from time immemorial have sought to do—to give shape and meaning to a metropolis that at first terrifies them in its noisy chaos and formlessness' (Sandhu 2003: p. xxi); this is also a form of self-exploration. The metrography attempted by *Verses* comes up against two Londons: the 'Proper London', picture-postcard capital of Vilayet ('Blighty' or Britain) and the 'demon city' that is its 'Improper' and often violent, racist, and chauvinist underbelly. In the tellingly titled section, 'A City Visible but Unseen', London, like Delhi once upon a time, is figured as the scene of another epic, another Mahabharata or 'mythological battleground', where Chamcha learns the 'fables of the new Kurus and Pandavas, the white racists and black "self-help" or vigilante posses' (Rushdie 1988: 283). This 'Mahavilayet', as Rushdie terms it, is an epic struggle for the soul of Britain. Despite himself, Chamcha becomes an unlikely anti-racist icon, a rallying point for the very anti-racist agitators he professes to despise. Whatever he comes to mean for different people, he takes on a reality that exceeds them all: 'Illegal migrant, outlaw kind, foul criminal or race-hero, Saladin Chamcha was getting to be true' (ibid. 288).

For Rushdie, the greatness of such cities as Bombay and London are the opportunities they provide for people and cultures to mix and mingle; to uncompromisingly reject the 'foreign' and refuse to be part of the city, as the Imam does, is what Fanon (1965: 130) might call a 'disturbed' relationship to tradition and culture. To refuse to engage with the present is a refusal to engage with history which, for Rushdie, is always a dangerous move: 'History is the blood-wine that must no longer be drunk. History... is a deviation from the Path, knowledge is a delusion, because the sum of knowledge was complete on the day Al-lah finished his revelation to Mahound' (Rushdie 1988: 210). The opposition between law, revelation, purity, and timelessness on the one hand, and ambiguity, multiplicity, hybridity, and history on the other, is central to the narrative. London and Bombay embody Rushdie's sense of the messiness of history and ways in which it reflects constant change: 'How does newness come into the world? How is it born? | Of what fusions, translations, conjoinings is it made?' (ibid. 8). The use of fabulation in the novel, Rushdie argues, is a device for undertaking such questioning about the nature of revelation and the sacred—as opposed to history, which allows for the new. In the end, it is Chamcha, not Gibreel, who finds renewed existence and meaning—not, ironically, in his migrant life—but in his return to the heterogeneous India of his birth: 'the entire national culture based on the principle of borrowing whatever clothes seemed to fit, Aryan, British, Mughal, take-the-best-and-leave-the-rest' (ibid. 52). Ironically, in a novel which radically challenges ideas of origins and essences, resolution is enacted through a return, albeit to the heterogeneous and constantly transforming country, rather than a mythical homeland.

Britain: *The Buddha of Suburbia*

If *Verses* depicts a complex and elusive journey from Indianness to Englishness for first-generation immigrants such as Saladin Chamcha, there is now a substantial body of literature that speaks of the experience of second- or third-generation Asian Britons who see themselves as British but, with their ties to the subcontinent, 'a new breed as it were, having emerged from two histories' (Kureishi 1990: 3). While this burgeoning body of work by such writers as Hanif Kureishi, Suniti Namjoshi, Romesh Gunesekera, Monica Ali, Tahmima Anam, and Nadeem Aslam necessitates separate study, it is useful to pause on another text where it is not only India that is subjected to reflective scrutiny, but also ideas of Englishness and England. Hanif Kureishi's well-known novel, *The Buddha of Suburbia*, examines an England that is fraught with alienation and tension and where, like Central London itself, 'the rotten was being replaced by the new, and the new was ugly. The gift of creating beauty had been lost somewhere' (ibid. 258). In the suburbs where Karim's narrative begins it is not the migrants alone who are experimenting with the selves they might eventually inhabit. The denizens of suburbia are also dislocated, seeking out the possibilities and new identities posed by 'mysticism, alcohol, sexual promise, clever people and drugs' (ibid. 15). The 'Buddha' persona adopted by Karim's father, Haroon, is not so much fraudulent as the performative culmination of his lifelong 'loneliness and desire for internal advancement' undertaken against the grain of the normative Asian immigrant trajectory to ownership of a corner-shop: 'toilet-rolls, sardine tins, sanitary pads and turnips' (ibid. 27). Haroon's invocation of 'an entirely new way of life', seen through Karim's sardonic but affectionate gaze, resonates with the lost souls of suburbia and for all of them, India is the imagined locus of spiritual realization. The imagined India, however, has far more power than the real one for both Haroon and his friend Anwar, who is obsessed with preserving 'tradition': 'It was puzzling: neither of them expressed any desire actually to see their origins again. "India's a rotten place," Anwar grumbled. "Why would I go there again?"' (ibid. 64).

Though Haroon's forays into Oriental philosophy and yoga elicit comic rather than satirical treatment from Kureishi, returns to imaginary homelands can also have real and dangerous consequences, as Jamila, Anwar's daughter, finds out. Clinging to his own notions of Indian and Muslim traditions, which is not necessarily reflective of subcontinental realities, Anwar goes on a fast unto death in order to coerce Jamila to marry a bridegroom of his choice from Bombay. Surrounded by a racist culture that is all too willing to cast Asian immigrants into stereotypes, the feisty Jamila finds herself in a difficult position where even describing her situation seems to 'expose our culture as being ridiculous and our people as being old-fashioned, extreme and narrow-minded' (ibid. 71). Her generation finds itself not so much 'in-between' cultures as in the difficult position of working against two sets of mythologies, 'Indian' and 'English', sometimes competing and sometimes collaborating in the production of fixed (and false) cultural identities. 'Truth' becomes an elusive goal, as Karim discovers when he plays a character based on Anwar and is criticized by Tracey, the lone black woman in his drama group:

> She spoke to me as if all I required was a little sense. 'I'm afraid it shows black people—'
> 'Indian people—'
> 'Black and Asian people—'
> 'One old Indian man—'
> 'As being irrational, ridiculous, as being hysterical. And as being fanatical.' (ibid. 180)

It is difficult in this context to find an individual identity outside the generalized 'us' or 'them'. For Tracey, as for Jamila, Karim's 'picture is what white people already think of us' and is not so much a truth as a 'white truth'. In a sense, *what* Buddha articulates is the paradox of 'minority' writing itself: it must counter the falsities of 'majority' discourse while refusing the straitjacket of defensive cultural identity and yet retain space for the specificities of individual artistic and literary sensibilities.

Kenya: *The In-Between World of Vikram Lall*

'What makes a man leave the land of his birth, the home of those childhood memories that will haunt him till his deathbed?' (Vassanji 2005: 18) While M. G. Vassanji's *The In-Between World of Vikram Lall* shares the general preoccupations of much diasporic writing, its concerns are also quite specific to Kenya as that nation made its transition to independence and postcolonial statehood. The 'in-between' here is not a generic 'migrant's-eye' view of the world but derives from the specific historical and political place of Asians in Kenya as well as Vikram's own ambiguities and predilections. Despite his uncompromising assertion, 'We have been Africans for three generations', Vikram is dogged by a profound sense of not quite belonging to the land of his birth, hoping secretly that his ancestors had cohabited and had children with Masai women: 'my fantasy has partly to do with desperate need to belong to the land I was born in' (ibid. 67). But at the same time India has no real claim upon him and remains an abstraction, even as he is bequeathed a Hindu sensibility by his Indian mother. Indeed, his father, like Naipaul during his infamous visits to the land, repudiates this aspect of his heritage, finding 'everything in India dirty and poor' (ibid. 21). Ironically, the novel suggests, it is this very repudiation that might account for the 'in-between' status of Kenyan Asians, for it also results in a refusal of the solidarity of the colonized. It is no accident that Vikram's radical Uncle Mahesh, who is one of the few Asians to openly espouse the Mau-Mau cause, also identifies profoundly with India and the Indian freedom struggle: '*We* fought for the independence of India, dammit, he would say. The Africans are just doing the same!' (ibid. 55).

An East African writer of Asian descent, now living in Canada, Vassanji belongs to a community descended from Indians who migrated to Africa from the nineteenth century onwards, many of whom were, like Naipaul's ancestors, indentured skilled labour. Labour, for Vassanji, provides its own claims to belonging:

The railway running from Mombasa to Kampala, proud 'Permanent Way' of the British and 'Gateway to the African Jewel' was our claim upon the land. Mile upon mile, rail next to thirty-foot rail, fishplate to follow fishplate, it had been laid down by my grandfather and his fellow Punjabi labourers... recruited from an assortment of towns in northwest India and brought to an alien, beautiful and wild country at the dawn of the twentieth century.

(ibid. 17)

The narrative alternates between the 1950s and 1960s youth of the eponymous narrator and his sister, and the late 1990s, when Vikram finds himself living in exile in Canada. Vikram's accounting of his life and misdemeanours begins in the 1950s when the Lall merchant family is living in the small town of Nakuru alongside European administrators and a black African underclass. While the black, brown, and white children play together, tensions simmer among the adults: the European administrators and officials, the African servants suspected by the whites of loyalty to the militant independence movement known as 'Mau-Mau', and the Asians trying to retain the favour of their colonial rulers, though there are those among them who sympathize with the freedom fighters. In the aftermath of a tragic incident where their European playmates are brutally murdered, the Lall children relocate with their parents to Nairobi. 'In-between-ness' here is experienced as a problematic subject position, unique to the Asian in Africa: 'I couldn't help feeling that both Bill and Njoroge were genuine, in their very different ways; only I, who stood in the middle, Vikram Lall, cherished son of an Indian grocer sounded false to myself, rang hollow like a bad penny' (ibid. 54). Ambiguity here is also the enemy of intermingling and mixing: 'they were too inconsistent and confused about where they stood and who they were even as they called themselves Kenyan' (ibid. 172–3). If, for Rushdie, the city (Bombay or London) allows for the ultimate triumph of migrant sensibilities and the mixing it calls for, Vassanji's insights into Kenyan urban life are more sober: 'every evening from the melting pot of city life each person went his long way home to his family, his church, his folk' (ibid. 311). Where being in-between might have allowed the 'Asian Shylock' the buffer position in colonial times, as anti-colonial nationalism turns into ethnic chauvinism in postcolonial Kenya, it is a liability that forces an exodus of thousands of Asians, 'few and frightened and caricatured', to a Britain that will also soon shut its doors on them (ibid. 330).

As for Saladin Chamcha, so for Vassanji's characters, London, experienced in the imagination before the actuality, takes on the curious role of affective touchstone, providing the setting for an unexpectedly intimate communion between father and son. They spend their days together 'walking the streets of London, seeing places which had once carried powerful meaning in our lives' (ibid. 348). But when it is time for Vikram to 'return' to make peace with his past, like Saladin, it is to Kenya, *not* India, that he must come 'home'. It is no accident that he takes this decision in Canada and at the point at which he asks himself the questions that all immigrants seem to ask of themselves: '*Belong*, I echoed her word and asked myself, Can I too learn to belong here?' (ibid. 404, original emphasis). It also marks a fundamental shift in Vikram's psyche, a decision to abandon the space of the dispassionate in-between, both emotionally and physically, in favour of the difficult but unambiguous task of reclaiming a homeland and ethical commitment:

This cold moderation should after all be conducive to my dispassion? No. I feel strongly the stir of the forest inside me; I hear the call of the red earth, and the silent plains of the Rift Valley through which runs the railway that my people built, and the bustle of River Road; I long for the harsh familiar caress of the sun.   (ibid. 405)

Whether the end of Vikram's narrative represents a homecoming or another kind of leaving is, however, left for the reader to decide.

United States: *Jasmine*

Of the many sites from which writers with connections to the Indian diaspora have emerged, the experiences of Indian immigrants and their descendants in the United States have generated little longer fiction that is worthy of note. It is dwarfed in quantity and quality by novels from Asian American writers of Chinese, Japanese, and Korean descent, and where it does exist such fiction seems to follow fairly predictable trajectories that, drawing on the founding myths of American nationhood, figure Americanness as the emancipatory apotheosis of a life seeking freedom. In work that is reminiscent of nineteenth-century ethnographic 'purdah' fiction, Indian American writers have, by and large, addressed themselves to a liberal American readership eager to consume multiculturalism through details of life in immigrant ghettos and the exotic countries from which these immigrants come. In the work of the most well-known Indian-American writer, Bharati Mukherjee, India is figured simultaneously as the sphere of spirituality and wisdom and as a deeply and homo-geneously oppressive culture which the female protagonist must leave behind in order to find personal freedom. In Mukherjee's most well-known works, a young Hindu woman moves from India to the United States, which, though fraught with problems, is typically figured as a fundamentally liberatory move. Stifled by marriage to an Indian man or Indian domesticity more generally, she begins a process of becoming American, which usually involves finding com-fort and transformation in the arms of an American man. Coming to America, Mukherjee's work suggests, invariably enables the produc-tion or liberation of new, freer selves than is made possible by India. Though there are some conflicts and difficulties the characters may face, including occasional racism, Mukherjee's America is that idealized zone of individual freedom mythologized by official histories of America where the Statue of Liberty gives shelter to the 'huddled masses' fleeing other nations. What *might* have been nu-anced and interesting accounts of the gendered experience of migra-tion and of self-transformation across national and cultural borders generally dwindle into melodramatic psychodramas or implausible romances. As such, it is an archetypal narrative of immigration to North America, 'founded on a belief in the redemptive power of the land ahead' (Ghosh 2002: 311).

Mukherjee's highly regarded novel, *Jasmine* (1991 [1989]), for in-stance, is the story of Jyoti/Jasmine who arrives in America and transforms herself first into 'Jase,' a New York nanny, and then into Jane, a mid-Western housewife. Though its opening chapters are set against the backdrop of the militant struggle for a separate Sikh state in India during the 1980s, the novel's understanding of the social and political context of postcolonial India is both trite and instrumental, allowing mainly for the plot device whereby Jasmine is widowed by a bomb blast. (There is a suggestion that the bomb is aimed at her by Sikh militants who hate her for being a modern woman and a 'whore', a suggestion with little historical basis). The same 'exoticism' praised by some reviewers of the novel provides a substitute for a careful engagement with time, place, and context. Thus 'ravishing' Jasmine's India is replete with stereotypes, a place of astrologers under banyan trees, mud huts, prophecies, patriarchs, women attempting 'sati' on funeral pyres, shaven-headed widows, random terrorists, child-brides, and 'cut-rate husbands' who are 'jealous, drunken men'. Appropriately, the novel is peppered with aphorisms intended to evoke 'Eastern' wisdom: 'Enlightenment meant seeing through the third eye and sensing designs in history's muddles' (ibid. 52). However, history and its actual complexities are themselves given short shrift in *Jasmine* even as the migrant's complicated biography seems to demand a nuanced engagement with it: 'We've been many selves. We've survived hideous times. I envy Bud the straight lines and smooth planes of his history' (ibid. 190).

Apart from the occasional insensitive remark, America poses few institutional or social challenges to this illegal migrant who, the reader knows, is also the runaway murderer of the man who rapes her. Under the loving gaze of an American man, declares Jasmine: 'I bloomed from a diffident alien with forged documents into adventurous Jase' (ibid. 165). If India is figured as oppressed woman, America is her male rescuer: 'I mean, I fell in love with what he represented to me, a professor who served biscuits to a servant, smiled at her, and admitted her to the broad democracy of his joking, even when she didn't understand it. It seemed entirely American' (ibid. 148). India for Mukherjee, is not so much imagined homeland as imaginary foil for mythologies of America; both nations are evacuated of complexities of their respective histories and realities. But for other writers of India and the diaspora, including Vassanji and Ghosh, India would continue to provide a rich historical and imaginative resource for thinking through the challenges of identity, self and society as the twenty-first century came into being.

Further Reading

Arun Joshi, *The Foreigner* and *The Strange Case of Billy Biswas*; Jhumpa Lahiri, *The Namesake*; V. S. Naipaul, *The Mystic Masseur* and *The Enigma of Arrival*; Santha Rama Rau, *Home to India*; Salman Rushdie, *East, West*; Meera Syal, *Anita and Me*; M. G. Vassanji, *The Gunny Sack*.

Conclusion:
The Contemporary Scene

The anglophone novel of India and its diaspora continues to flourish, as each year scores of titles emerge out of presses in India and abroad. As is to be expected with such productivity, many of these titles are interesting, others are unexceptional or mediocre, while a small number constitute real achievements. Many of the most significant works that have emerged in recent years pick up and rework the themes discussed in this study, albeit in fresh ways and in different contexts. History and historical consciousness, far from receding as concerns, are, if anything, even more central. Stories of family and community continue to compel the writer's imagination. The 'idea of India' is also integral to the novel, but often with a different, increasingly sombre emphasis on communal and sectarian religious tensions. Hindu majoritarianism, Islamism, and movements of secession, all of which put pressure on the idea of a unitary postcolonial nation-state, also emerge as prominent concerns. With a strong sense of itself in a global frame, the anglophone novel now asks: what shape does 'India' take fifty or more years after the independent nation-state officially came into existence on the world stage? How are older narratives of nation being rewritten or replaced by new ones that seek to break, remould or interrogate the former in the face of migration and globalization? Who owns 'the past' and what is the writer's responsibility in relation to it?

The rewriting of the idea of a plural and secular India in the ferocious image of communal and majoritarian forces constitutes a recurring theme in a great deal of recent anglophone fiction. Dedicated to 'all those who speak up in times of siege', Githa Hariharan's third novel, *In Times of Siege* (2003) is distinctly reminiscent of J. M. Coetzee's *Disgrace*, a narrative in the present tense shaped by the consciousness and reflections of its middle-aged academic male protagonist. Both Coetzee's Lurie and Hariharan's Shiv are relatively privileged men trying to negotiate personal passions and unexpected political exigencies, albeit of quite different kinds. Shiv too negotiates an erotic attraction to a younger woman and, partly under her influence, finds himself compelled to take a political stance against the forces of 'Hindutva' or Hindu chauvinism. Hariharan's is a political novel with a very real sense of urgency, written as it is in the early years of the new century as Hindu chauvinism gains an unprecedented foothold in academia. With the electoral success of the BJP or the Bharatiya Janata Party, the political arm of Hindu nationalism, its academic allies are 'crawling out of the woodwork now it's their season' (Hariharan 2003: 30). These are times that make demands on even those, like the mild-mannered Shiv, who have hitherto considered themselves apolitical. Significantly, Shiv is a historian and it is, once again, history—'become a live, fiery thing'—(ibid. 134) that is the terrain of struggle, as thinly fictionalized Hindu fundamentalist groups such as the Itihas Surakhsha Manch or the Forum for the Protection of History challenge his depiction of Basava, a medieval poet and social reformer:

But why this sudden anxiety about a historical figure we have safely consigned to textbooks till now? And from such unlikely quarters? I can only think of one answer—a fear of history. A fear that our history will force people to see that our past, like our present, always had critics of social divisions that masquerade as religion and tradition. So what do these frightened people do? They whitewash historical figures, they seize history.

(ibid. 97)

The battle is also, of course, for the nation and how it narrates itself, whether as a plural and critical polity that Shiv describes or as a 'Hindu Rashtra' that will 'entertain no ideas but those of the glorification of the Hindu race and culture' (ibid. 100).

For Shiv, the crisis has painful personal resonances, sharpening his unresolved sense of loss around the father who disappeared mysteriously when he was a child. Personal memories contend with the apparently more dispassionate act of writing history: 'his father's life—incomplete, cut off without a legible end' (ibid. 82). Passion and courage, the qualities Shiv attributes to his father rather than to himself, may well have dispatched him to an unknown destination:

'for him the freedom movement didn't end in 1947. In fact, the burdens of the new world—the travails of a free India—sat heavy on his shoulders' (ibid. 34). Although little is said about what these travails might have been, Shiv's journey towards finding a voice and renewing his commitment to critical history in times of siege is, in some sense, an acknowledgement of the claims made by the father's struggle for a progressive and plural nation: 'But how do you seize hold of the past and make it yours? Who owns the past?' (ibid. 82). Shiv's scholarly engagement with the work of the medieval 'poet-saint', Basava, a questioning voice, is shown to be richly laden with imaginative possibilities countering those who would claim that the nation needs to be either homogeneous or owned by a single community: 'a new community, a new ethos, that provoked people to experiment' (ibid. 104). Basava, poet (*vachanakara*), and reformer, brings together imaginative and political work in a combination that has much relevance for the present day. One of his *vachanas* or short poems provides an epigraph to Hariharan's novel: 'Look at them, | busy, making an iron frame | for a bubble on the water | to make it safe!'

Egalitarian movements for cultural and social reform on the subcontinent—richly embodied by the poetry and songs of the Bhakti and Sufi poets of the twelfth and thirteenth centuries—have provided an important resource in recent years for scholars and writers who see their task as one of reclaiming deeply embedded indigenous traditions of social justice and tolerance. In Hariharan's novel, the life of Basava, an actual historical figure, itself becomes a site of contestation between history and mythology. In M. G. Vassanji's fourth novel and the first to be set mainly in India, the lives of a fictionalized Sufi sage and his twentieth-century descendants provide material for reflections on history, nation, and community. *The Assassin's Song* moves between a precolonial Indian past figured as laden with the subversive possibilities of ambiguity, and a present in which identities have become sharpened and violently polarized. Occasioning Vassanji's turn to writing about the Indian state of Gujarat in past and present are the infamous pogroms of February 2002, when thousands of Muslims were slaughtered en masse as reprisal for the burning of a train compartment carrying Hindu activists. Those who would rewrite history textbooks in Hariharan's novel had now also shown themselves willing to undertake genocidal violence, 'violence to curdle the blood' (Vassanji 2007: 359).

The aggressive majoritarian self-assertion of Hindu religious nationalism is answered by an equally ferocious, if outnumbered, minority fundamentalism. If the former seeks to conflate 'our nation's glorious history' with a mythical Hindu 'Golden Age', the latter repudiates common ground in favour of 'pure' Muslim identities. As in Rushdie's *Midnight's Children* and *The Moor's Last Sigh*, Vassanji's critique of religious purity and communal chauvinism is faintly elegiac, invoking the moment of Nehru and Gandhi: 'They were our gods, they had gone to jail for the independence of our country. But I knew that not everybody cared for them' (2007: 126). The life of Nur Fazal, the sage of Pirbaag, like that of Basava, provides an imaginative means of exploring alternatives to the sectarian boundaries that generate such grief in the present. It allows Vassanji to pose and attempt to answer the anguished question that arises after the Gujarat bloodshed of 2002, 'What is an ordinary, secular Indian, after all? Is such an entity possible?' (ibid. 260). As an immigrant writer in Canada, Vassanji can juxtapose this question next to those raised by multiculturalism in Canada, 'a young country excited by its new identity' producing 'confessional poetry of wintry exile' (ibid. 285). Multiculturalism in these contexts is often little more than what some scholars call 'plural monoculturalism', leaving little space for overlap and fuzziness of the sort that Pirbaag seeks to foster:

—But we should choose, nai, Bapuji—between Hindu and Muslim? Everybody chooses.
—There's nothing to choose, Karsan, we have been shown our path, in which there is neither Hindu nor Muslim, nor Christian nor Sikh, just the One. Brahman, the Absolute, Ishvar. Allah. God.

But, in Gujarat in the year 2002, the choice to 'bow neither to Kashi not to Kaaba' is no longer theirs to not make; Pirbaag, 'a centuries-old neutral sanctuary' is deemed a 'Muslim abode' on which vengeance can be wrought (ibid. 93).

As in *Siege*, fraught father–son relationships are central to the narrative and its engagement with questions of memory, history, and the act of breaking silences (whether of the 'detached' or the 'fearful'). In both novels (as in the *Satanic Verses*), the younger man is alienated from the patriarch only to return circuitously to a place of resolution, albeit a fragile one. In *Song*, the son repudiates the spiritual calling of the father but comes, nevertheless, to an acceptance of his responsibility to work against the grain of religious sectarianism and communal violence. He will make 'a bookish shrine of songs and stories. This is my prayer, if you will, this is my fist in the air my anger, so unlike his; it is my responsibility, my duty to my father and all...whose stories are intertwined with ours' (ibid. 116). A similar filial relationship preoccupies the narrator of Siddharth Deb's *Point of Return* (2003), set in the contested terrain that is the Indian North East region, the region near its border with China. If Hindu and Islamic chauvinism threaten to undo the fabric of the entity that calls itself India, the 'tribal' peoples of the North East—the Mizos, Nagas, Khasis—have arguably never been fully knitted into the nation as idea and reality even as the Indian state lays claim to the land in which they live. The 'spectre of secession' thus underwrites the historical context of Deb's novel, one where 'new tribal states' are carved out of the large state of Assam accompanied by 'growing uncertainty about the relationship between the hills and the plains', 'armed insurrections and kidnappings', and 'negotiations between ministers and bureaucrats from Delhi and tribal leaders' (Deb 2003: 29). The moment and afterlife of Independence and Partition generates three nations but very many more nationalisms.

Like Naipaul's Biswas, Deb's Dr Dam cuts a lonely figure as he struggles to make not only a house but a home for himself in this hostile landscape. Here, he is an 'Indian', a 'Bengali', an 'outsider' and a 'foreigner' even within the sovereign boundaries of the nation-state to which the family have fled in the wake of Partition. 'You cannot be an exile in your own country', insists the narrator, even as he attempts to reconstruct the life of a man who may have been precisely such a paradoxical subject. What then is 'home', asks the novel, as boundaries shift, new lines are drawn between ethnic groups and states, and landscapes become unexpectedly hostile. Like Thamma in Ghosh's *The Shadow Lines*, the narrator's grandfather too copes with displacement by conceptualizing home differently with 'the landscape of his past...permanent and unchanging, not something that was historical and therefore open to perpetual revision but a place beyond the vagaries of time' (ibid. 26). As he himself turns to it to fill the lacunae in his father's story, the narrator is confronted by a disjuncture between history (with its national moorings) and something more evasive. It is particularly so in the margins of the nation-state where this novel is set: 'History, dragged so far from the metropolitan centres, from the rustic mainlands, will tell you nothing. In the North-East...history lies defeated, muttering solipsistically from desultory plaques put up to commemorate visiting politicians' (ibid. 157).

Unlike Hariharan's and Vassanji's novels, Deb's narrative ends on a note that speaks of failure and alienation, of a return to nothing. It is a condition at once historical and existential and one that raises questions for narrative itself:

It was not a question of roots or origin, you understand. That was not possible, not now, not fifty years after the notional ancestral village had ceded its place to the nation-state. If we were all to do that, we whose lives are flung around in Pakistan, India, Bangladesh, if we were to let loose our songlines, our routes of memory, our pilgrimage paths, we would find them faltering against the documents and borders and guns. (ibid. 187)

Deb is all too aware that clinging to notions of origin might render his nostalgia akin to that of Hindutva's followers who insist that 'the crack of 1947 will be layered over again some day, but on their terms'. Yet there is an unmistakable note of bitterness around what the narrator sees as the failure to foster 'non-tribal rights in a protected tribal state' (ibid. 208). While the questions raised by the novel are important in their seeming intractability, it is ultimately—and iron-ically—undermined by an embittered refusal to engage with history with greater complexity. Despite the many invocations of history and historicity, the account of alienation and exile is rendered with very little sense of what the other side of the story might be. Indeed, the indigenous inhabitants of the contested landscapes that the novel charts so beautifully are rendered in somewhat colonial terms as faceless, nameless, and often somewhat sinister, 'tribals'. Deb's narra-tor concedes his own biases in a passing justification: 'I could have taken the side of the people here, agreed with them that they had for too long been treated as exotic props in their own land, had I not been denied that possibility by being who I was' (ibid. 178). In his critique of nativism as bordering on the fascist, drawing on 'the symbolism of the Third Reich as a way towards self-assertion', the novel fails to consider the ways in which the region interrogates the constitution of the nation-state of India as a powerful, self-constituting entity that does not always have the consent of those it annexes.

'What was a country but the idea of it,' asks a character in Kiran Desai's Booker Prize-winning novel, *The Inheritance of Loss*, which is set in an India declared to be 'coming apart at the seams' (Desai 2006: 236, 108). As in Deb's novel, the uneasy relationship between the postcolonial nation-state and its north-eastern territories provides the context for an often moving study of loneliness and pain as a historical and emotional legacy as it structures both private and social relations. Large and small histories, the larger-than-life and the commonplace, intersect; 'extraordinary hatred' is also commonplace (ibid. 295). In Kalimpong, a small town in the Himalayas where 'India blurred into Bhutan and Sikkim', the shabby lives of its Anglicized middle-class denizens intersect with those of the less privileged as they are drawn into the ambit of a fictitious 'gathering insurgency' with Nepali Indians agitating for their own 'country or state' (in the author's rather vague formulation). If individual characters like the judge struggle with the profound self-hatred that is their inheritance from colonialism, the Nepali disenfranchised now confront an India that appears to be a colonizing power in its own right, occupying land and capable of inflicting its own humiliations and hurt. At the same time, India's own history of struggle bequeaths a nationalist 'hunger' that renders it, in turn, vulnerable to challenge: 'If a nation had such a climax in its history, its heart, would it not hunger for it again?' (ibid. 158).

'India' as 'a concept, a hope, or a desire' is also defined in acts of rejection and loss (ibid. 236). India is the cultural and emotional sensibilities—'Indian love, stinking unaesthetic love', that the judge works so hard to keep at bay, even separating 'himself away from himself' in the process. It is also the economic and political disenfranchisement that causes the cook to insist that his only son emigrate to America somehow: 'Stay there. Make money. And don't come back here' (ibid. 191). Unlike many narratives of 'coming to America', *Inheritance* tracks the sheer desolation, hard graft, humiliation, and loss—of lives, families, respect—that this journey entails for many thousands of poor and illegal migrants each year. America is not the opposite of India as it is in Mukherjee's novels; it is a place, not of self-realization, but of self-decimation and invisibility. India too, however, is capable of its own cruelties, in sudden excisions of those who have lived and loved here for many years as in the case of Father Booty who 'knew he was a foreigner but had lost the notion that he was anything but an *Indian* foreigner' (ibid. 220, original emphasis). In a nation where all exist in a state of simultaneous belonging and alienation, Booty, the wonderful oxymoron, might well even be the quintessential Indian, the novel suggests, one who will tragically be expelled from his homeland, one more debtor among the many who must now 'pay the debt that should be shared with the others over many generations' (ibid. 242). In the end, Biju's return is also a paradoxical one: a loss that is also, finally, the only gain—of home, homeland, and the merest glimmer of hope.

A provisional 'return' to India also ends Amitav Ghosh's *The Hungry Tide*, which brings together the preoccupations of his earlier work: language and communication, fluid faith practices, indigenous and subaltern knowledge, translation, and the persistence of the past—the links between events that take place at different historical moments and the ways in which individual lives are inflected by those pasts. This accomplished novel also picks up on the theme of migration and return, figured not only through the migratory *Orcaella Brevisrostris* or Gangetic dolphins that compel much of the narrative's interest, but also the woman who studies them for her calling, Piya, the American-born daughter of Indian parents. The narrative, like many of Ghosh's other works, is complexly layered, weaving together archival materials, scientific insights, different narrative perspectives, poetry, and folk legends. It is also set in the powerful and treacherous terrain of the mangrove swamps and river islands of the Ganges delta, a terrain that resists colonization and generates conflict between different ideologies of land, conservation, ownership, and settlement. It is a landscape that provides an extended metaphor for the fluid interaction between languages, knowledges, and faiths:

How could it be otherwise? For this I have seen confirmed many times, that the mudbanks of the tide country are shaped not only by rivers of silt, but also by rivers of language: Bengali, English, Arabic, Hindi, Arakanese and who knows what else? Flowing into each other they create a proliferation of small worlds that hang suspended in the flow. And so it dawned on me: the tide country's faith is like one of its great mohonas: a meeting not just of many rivers, but a circular roundabout people can use to pass in many directions—from country to country and even between faiths and religions. (Ghosh 2004: 247)

These are not, however, simple movements when they involve human beings for whom translation and communication are at once complex and fraught, laden as much with the possibility of misunderstanding as of communion. If Piya and the fisherman, Fokir, find themselves caught up in a non-verbal attraction, the city slicker, Kanai, for whom translation is a career, finds himself a non-comprehending outsider when faced with the challenges of the tide country. In the clash between the human struggle to survive and the ideologies of conservation, complex—even intractable—moral dilemmas appear to arise, rendering human life and nature seemingly incommensurable if, at other times, interdependent.

Although 'nation' and 'Indianness' are not explicitly foregrounded as themes, the novel is, nevertheless, inflected by questions of home, belonging, and community. The utopian community once attempted in the tide country 'could be a model for all of India; it could be a new kind of country' (ibid. 52). The settlement at Morichjhapi, which will come to a tragic destruction at the hands of the state, is figured in passing as a nation of the oppressed, a subaltern community, 'if not a Dalit nation, then at least a safe haven, a place of true freedom for the country's most oppressed' (ibid. 191). In a 'return' that echoes those of Saladin Chamcha and Vikram Lall, Piya, 'the American', comes back to the tide country, not out of racial or cultural affiliations, but more simply because: 'for me, home is where the Orcaella are; so there's no reason why this couldn't be it' (ibid. 400). Transient habitation also provides space for reflection and regrouping in Shama Futehally's poignantly rendered last novel, *Reaching Bombay Central* (2006 [2003]), where communal tensions are evoked with the lightest of touches that does not, however, make them any less sombre. Set in a railway carriage—that quintessential temporary home and place of intimacy with strangers—the domestic novel intersects here with the larger sweep of the nation's narrative as, towards the end of the twentieth century, the Hindu majoritarian BJP gains electoral power and legitimacy. Even as she makes small talk and tiny exchanges with strangers—'what is there in giving tea to somebody', the Muslim woman narrator, a Mrs Dalloway-like figure, reflects on the psychic costs of communal tension: 'it made you spiral downwards and end up in a small dark place where you were all alone' (Futehally 2006: 122).

Though devoid of the linguistic pyrotechnics of a Rushdie novel, Futehally's narrative makes evocative use of the colloquial English that middle-class Indians use with each other: 'How much Aunty was worrying! Too much she was worrying' (ibid. 15). As its narrator's mind freely associates small phrases and more dramatic events, the novel reminds us that the texture of communalism is often benign until it becomes larger than life. Her husband's fall from grace around which the narrator's anxieties centre remains an ambiguously sinister event and the question remains unanswered: 'Would this have happened if he didn't have a Muslim name?' The uneven but determinate relationship between private and public is reflected in the way in which the conversation connects suddenly with a discussion of direction of nation: 'We are a hopeless people'... 'betrayed the vision of Gandhiji'... 'We must have faith that we will finally go the right way... in the end we are reaching Bombay Central' (ibid. 117–18). The narrator reflects wryly on how even a liberal-minded 'fearing for the nation' becomes something of a majority privilege: 'And how very pleasant it must be to fear for the nation when you did not have to fear for yourself' (ibid. 119). As Mukul Kesavan (2001: 12) writes, secularism in contemporary India often becomes a form of 'benign Hindu' patronage and gallantry, a form of 'behalfism, where skeptical Hindus act as proxies for believing Muslims'.

The persistent reach of the idea of India in contemporary fiction is perhaps best underscored by a novel that claims for itself a certain ironic distance from it: 'Some people thought that the whole conception their country had been based on was flawed; so they must start again. Speeches were expended on the "idea" of the country and what the meaning of that idea was' (Chaudhuri 1998: 85). Amit Chaudhuri, described by one critic as the author of 'fiction very different from the kind being written by other writers', begins his novel, *Freedom Song*, with an invocation of the religious tensions that inflect even quiet middle-class lives in Calcutta.[1] As the *azaan* issues from a local mosque, two elderly Hindu ladies grumble: 'it really isn't Indian, it sounds like Bedouins' (ibid. 3). Comprising lyrical vignettes of a lazy Calcutta under 'one of the last Socialist governments in the world' and peopled with characters who 'eked out the days with inconsequential chatter', the novel is, nevertheless, aware of the tensions that simmer across the nation, news of 'atrocities in other cities' that swirls around them in the days following the demolition of the

Babri mosque in 1996 (ibid. 99). Also quietly shaping the transformation in the lives of its characters is the economic 'liberalization' that changes the contours of the nation's economic life in the 1990s, embraced even by the official Left that rules in Calcutta. Even in a novel that embraces, like the young married couple, 'the unknown and the inconsequential' (ibid. 182), 'India' figures as an idea becoming variously a honeymoon itinerary—'a series of small hotels, connecting routes, different climates existing at once, peculiarities of cuisine' and the 'INDIA IS GREAT' graffiti that mark the landscape on which they travel. It lurks at the edges of the imagination, one way or another (ibid. 187).

With some notable exceptions then, the anglophone novel from and of India has liberated itself from a sense of address to the West and from 'anxieties of Indian-ness', taking its place in the Indian literary landscape with confidence but without complacency. It is undoubtedly a genre that has come into its own, exuding now a sense of belonging to a cultural and political context that is at once marked by very specific histories and constantly evolving. Its most important writers (themselves bi- or multilingual) are attentive to and remain troubled by the politics of linguistic faultlines and the skewed dynamics of working in a language accorded disproportionate cultural and economic privilege. In a national context where literacy itself remains an elite skill and literacy in English still more so, this is not a problem that will find resolution in the near future. Celebratory claims for the democratization of the anglophone novel in India are not yet in order. What can, however, be said is that this is a genre that began with an interest in how to read the past and continues to remain concerned with the question of the 'burden of history' (Ghosh 2002: 312). In its attempts to understand through reading the past, 'the sufferings of the present', the anglophone novel is, finally, an engaged and dynamic participant in a conversation that is taking place across the literary spectrum of India.

NOTES

INTRODUCTION

1. A recent article in India's *Outlook* magazine suggests that far from being 'blithely democratic', English can be a source of extreme anxiety for it's 'have-nots', leading in some extreme cases to suicide (Puri 2008).

2. The efforts of pioneering publishing houses such as Katha, dedicated to bringing out translations across Indian languages, must be noted here.

3. See Mishra 2000 and Ruchir Joshi's brilliant riposte to this kind of flattening denunciation. See also Paranjape 1990, again by a scholar and novelist writing in English, which also posits rather simplistic arguments about the politics and 'ideological profile' of the class that writes in English.

4. Buford may approve of the self-styled 'St Stephen's College school of writing', comprising old boys of Delhi's elite Anglican institution with close links to Oxbridge ands its networks of influence. Not all those claimed for this 'school'—which counts Vikram Seth, Shashi Tharoor, Amitav Ghosh, I. Allan Sealy, Mukul Kesavan, Anurag Mathur, and Rukun Advani among its former pupils—may, however, acknowledge their membership. However, Buford is clearly not quite right in suggesting that anglophone writers are an entirely atomized lot. Meanwhile, in a witty, but not insincere acknowledgement, Shama Futehally thanks those who told her that 'you can write a novel without having been to St. Stephen's College'!

CHAPTER 1

1. For a full discussion of the response to Macaulay and the rise of Young Bengal, see Kopf 1969.

2. See Mukherjee 2000 for a full and insightful account and catalogue of these early works.

3. For a discussion of 'Mutiny' fiction see Chakravarty 2005.

CHAPTER 2

1. In his useful introduction to a recent translation of Fakir Mohan Senapati's *Six Acres and a Half*, Satya Mohanty points out that writing in indigenous languages such as Oriya engaged very differently with village life. There was no 'unabashed anthropological tone' as in Day's work and there is greater room for experimentation, providing a critique of both indigenous structures of oppression and colonialism. Mohanty slightly overstates his case in suggesting that *Govinda Samanta* has no political critique in it.

2. The exploitative practices of indigo planters were the subject of a play in Bengali by Dinabandhu Mitra, *Nildarpan* (*The Mirror of Indigo*, 1860).

3. See de Souza 2004 for an overview of such writings.

4. 'Motherness—excuse me if I underline the point—is a big idea in India, maybe our biggest: the land as mother, the mother as land, the ground beneath our feet' (Rushdie 1997: 137).

5. The two compendious and pioneering volumes edited by Tharu and Lalita (1991; 1993) provide a superb overview of this literature.

CHAPTER 3

1. A large body of fiction was influenced by Gandhi and Gandhism, much of it in languages other than English. A key figure in this regard is the legendary Premchand (Dhanpat Rai), some of whose works are now available in good English translations. See Das (1995: 64–80) for a comprehensive account of Gandhi's impact on literatures and a catalogue of texts across Indian languages that engage with Gandhi and Gandhism. Other English-language works include Venkataramani's *Murugan the Tiller* (1927) and *Kandan the Patriot* (1932) and K. Nagarajan's *Athavar House* (1937).

2. For a different literary perspective on the issue of caste oppression, it is useful and necessary to look at texts by Dalit writers whose understanding and analysis of their situation is often at marked variance with Anand's and, indeed, Gandhi's. Some of these texts are now available in English translation: see Sharankumar Limbale's *The Outcaste* and Dangle's anthology of modern Marathi Dalit literature, *Poisoned Bread*, Eleanor Zelliot's and Jayant Karve's translation (1982) of Namdheo Dhasal's poetry and K. Srilata's translations of women's writing from the Self-Respect movement. Meanwhile U. R. Anantha Murthy's *Samskara* offers a trenchant and powerful critique of Brahminism through its tortured Brahmin protagonist.

3. *The Guide* is a rare instance of an English novel adapted into a hugely successful Hindi film, although Narayan was said to be displeased with this cinematic rendition of his work.

CHAPTER 4

1. A notable such novel in Hindi is Kamleshwar's *Kitne Pakistan* (*How Many Pakistans?*) which, interestingly, began as a short story written in the late 1960s.

2. See Nira Yuval-Davis and Floya Anthias (1989) for a discussion of the different ways in which women are engaged with and in nationalist discourse.

CHAPTER 5

1. It is difficult to reproduce the poem's terse mood and metre; this is an approximation in the absence of other satisfactory translations.

2. Reproduced on the cover of the Penguin edition.

3. In a preface entitled 'All about', no page number.

4. For a fuller account of the novel's experiments with form and language, see Kanaganayagam 2002.

5. 'Kayasthas' were among the first Hindus to enter English educational institutions. They were also 'among the first groups in Lucknow to express their concern about their identity as "Hindus."...reformers showed a great deal of concern about what they believed to constitute "tradition"' (Joshi 2001: 104).

CHAPTER 6

1. See also Shahani 1995; Bhagwat 1995; and Kudchekar 1995.

2. Several novels are inspired by or make use of the film industry and the Bombay film, including the *Satanic Verses*, *Show Business*, and *Sacred Games*.

CHAPTER 7

1. The useful distinction between 'document' and 'monument' in approaches to the archives is made by Tharu and Lalita (1991).

2. In it, an apparently submissive maidservant subversively unveils the hypocrisy of upper-class patriarchy that indulges its own sexual proclivities but denounces the objects of their attention as 'sluts'.

3. See David's *The Book of Esther* for a more detailed biographical account of her family and its history.

4. The Arya Samaj was established with a view to reforming existing Hindu practices but with a commitment to asserting Hindu superiority, a 'dominant, pan-Hindu revivalist framework' (S. Sarkar 1983: 74).

5. It is worth pausing here briefly to consider the porous relationship between memory, personal history, and the writing of fiction that is the theme of a unique text. *Diddi*, by Ira Pande, is a daughter's and translator's memoir of her mother, Shivani, the best-known Hindi fiction writer of her time. Weaving Pande's insights together with Shivani's own writerly voice, *Diddi* highlights the fluidity of the borders between fiction and memoir, in its own writing and that of its subject: 'In this sense, I suppose, every writer becomes a character in the fictional world he or she creates. I can't say whether this is a universal truth, but I do know that Diddi bled into her plots often without knowing she was doing so' (Pande 2005: 2). Pande's English text, recreating the life of a Hindi writer, also makes visible the transactions that must take place for the writing in one language of experiences that take place in or are recounted in another, a particular challenge for Indian writers in English. Perhaps much more so than the public and the national, the domestic remained a space resistant to English or, at least, one where 'mother tongues' had at least equal sway, if not a greater hold on emotions and their expression.

6. For an account of such changes to family structures during the colonial period, see Arunima 2003.

CHAPTER 8

1. After the slave trade was abolished in 1807, Britain, France, and Holland required a supply of cheap labour to continue work on their Caribbean island colonies; this was enabled by immigration schemes from India that essentially made use of an already impoverished peasantry desperate to improve their circumstances and willing to enter into exploitative indenture schemes that would take them thousands of miles from home. Amitar Ghosh's most recent novel, *Sea of Poppies*, published after this study was completed, is set in the context of this phenomenon.

CONCLUSION

1. From the *London Review of Books* and cited on the inside cover of the 1998 edition of *Freedom Song*. Chaudhuri, like many novelists of India today, divides his time between Europe and India. His work tends, however, to

garner far more critical appreciation in Britain and America than in India, unlike Hariharan and her like for whom the opposite obtains. Family fictions that excel at evoking the inner and outer landscapes of middle-class lives, Chaudhuri's novels are light on plot and context and rich in evocative detail that, at times, turns into exoticizing as, for instance, in this description, in *Afternoon Raag*, of a magazine vendor in Bombay: 'If there had been a magazine-seller sub-caste...he would have belonged to it, so completely and immemorially did he seem to be in possession of the lineaments of his trade' (1994: 54).

BIBLIOGRAPHY

PRIMARY TEXTS

Ali, Ahmad (1966) *Twilight in Delhi*, 1st pub. 1940 (Delhi: Oxford University Press).

Anand, Mulk Raj (2001) *Untouchable*, 1st pub. 1935 (New Delhi: Penguin).

Anantha Murthy, U. R. (1989) *Samskara: A Rite for a Dead Man*, trans. A. K. Ramanujan, 1st pub. 1978 (Delhi: Oxford University Press).

Bhalla, Alok (ed.) (1994) *Stories about the Partition of India* (Delhi: Harper-Collins).

Bhattacharya, Bhabhani (1947) *So Many Hungers!* (London: Victor Gollancz).

—— (1954) *He Who Rides a Tiger* (New York: Crown).

Chandra, Vikram (1995) *Red Earth and Pouring Rain* (London: Faber & Faber).

Chatterjee, Bankim Chandra (2005) (*see also* Chattopadhyaya, Bankim Chandra) *Rajmohan's Wife*, 1st pub. 1864 (Delhi: Ravi Dayal).

—— (2006) *Anandamath, or, The Sacred Brotherhood*, 1st pub. 1882, trans. Julius J. Lipner (Oxford: Oxford University Press).

Chattopadhyaya, Bankim Chandra (2005) *The Bankimchandra Omnibus*, trans. Radha Chakravarty et al. (New Delhi: Penguin).

Chattopadhyaya, Sarat Chandra (1993) *Srikanta*, 1st pub. 1917–33, trans. Aruna Chakravarti (New Delhi: Penguin, 1993).

—— (2001) *The Final Question* [Bengali, *Shesh Prashna*], trans. Jadavpur University (Delhi: Permanent Black).

Chaudhuri, Amit (1993) *Afternoon Raag* (London: Heinemann).

—— (1998) *Freedom Song* (London: Picador).

—— (2000) *A New World* (London: Picador).

Chughtai, Ismat (1995) *The Crooked Line* [Urdu, *Terhi Lakir*], trans. Tahira Naqvi (New Delhi: Kali for Women).

Dangle, Arjun (ed.) (2004) *Poisoned Bread: An Anthology of Modern Dalit Literature*, 1st pub. 1992 (Hyderabad: Orient Longman).

Day, Lal Behari (1969) *Bengal Peasant Life* [*Govinda Samanta*], 1st pub. 1874 (Calcutta: Editions Indian).

David, Esther (1997) *The Walled City* (Madras: Manas).

—— (2003) *The Book of Esther* (New Delhi: Penguin).

Deb, Siddhartha (2003) *Point of Return*, 1st pub. 2002 (London: Picador).

Desai, Anita (1998) *Baumgartner's Bombay*, 1st pub. 1988 (London: Vintage).

—— (1999) *Fire on the Mountain*, 1st pub. 1977 (London: Vintage).

—— (2001) *Clear Light of Day*, 1st pub. 1980 (London: Vintage).

Desai, Kiran (2006) *The Inheritance of Loss* (London: Penguin).

Desani, G. V. (1998) *All about H. Hatterr*, 1st pub. 1948 (New Delhi: Penguin).

Deshpande, Shashi (1989) *That Long Silence*, 1st pub. 1988 (New Delhi: Penguin).

—— *Small Remedies* (2001) (New Delhi: Penguin).

De Souza, Eunice, and Pereira, Lindsay (eds.) (2002) *Women's Voices: Selections from Nineteenth and Early-Twentieth Century Indian Writing in English* (Delhi: Oxford University Press).

Dhondy, Farrukh (1990) *Bombay Duck* (London: Jonathan Cape).

Dutt, Soshee Chunder (1885*a*) *The Republic of Orissa: A Page from the Annals of the Twentieth Century*, 1st pub. 1845, in *Bengaliana: A Dish of Rice and Curry, and other Indigestible Ingredients* (Calcutta: Thacker, Spink, & Co.), 347–56.

—— (1885*b*) *Shunkur: A Tale of the Indian Mutiny of 1857*, 1st pub. 1845, in *Bengaliana: A Dish of Rice and Curry, and other Indigestible Ingredients* (Calcutta: Thacker, Spink, & Co.), 84–158.

—— (2005), *Selections from 'Bengaliana'*, ed. Alex Tickell (Nottingham: Trent Editions).

Dutt, Toru (2006). *Collected Prose and Poetry*, ed. Chandani Lokuge (Delhi: Oxford University Press).

—— (2005) *The Diary of Mademoiselle D'Arvers*, 1st pub. 1879, trans. N. Kamala (New Delhi: Penguin).

Faiz, Faiz Ahmad (2000) 'Subh-E-Azadi', in *Poems by Faiz*, 1st pub. 1971, trans. V. Kiernan (Delhi: Oxford University Press), 123.

Forster, E. M. (1979) *A Passage to India*, 1st pub. 1924 (London: Penguin).

Futehally, Shama (2006) *Tara Lane*, 1st pub. 1993 (New Delhi: Penguin).

—— (2006) *Reaching Bombay Central*, 1st pub. 2003 (New Delhi: Penguin).

Futehally, Zeenath (2004) *Zohra*, 1st pub. 1951 (New Delhi: Oxford University Press).

Ghosh, Amitav (1986) *The Circle of Reason* (London: H. Hamilton).

—— (1995) *The Shadow Lines*, 1st pub. 1988 (Delhi: Oxford University Press).

—— (2000) *In an Antique Land*, 1st pub. 1992 (London: Granta).

—— (2001) *The Glass Palace* (London: HarperCollins).

—— (2004) *The Hungry Tide* (Delhi: Ravi Dayal).

Hariharan, Githa (2003) *In Times of Siege* (New Delhi: Viking).

Hasan, Mushirul (ed.) (1994) *India Partitioned: The Other Face of Freedom* (New Delhi: Penguin).

Hosain, Attia (1992) *Sunlight on a Broken Column*, 1st pub. 1961 (New Delhi: Penguin).

Hossain, Rokeya Sakhawat (1988) *Sultana's Dream*, 1st pub. 1905 (New York: Feminist Press).

—— (2005) *'Sultana's Dream' and 'Padmarag': Two Feminist Utopias*, 1st pub. 1905 and 1924 respectively, trans. Barnita Bagchi (New Delhi: Penguin).

Husain, Intizar (1995) *Basti*, trans. Frances W. Pritchett (New Delhi: Harper-Collins).

—— (2002) *A Chronicle of the Peacocks: Stories of Partition, Exile and Lost Memories*, trans. Alok Bhalla and Vishwamitter Adil (Delhi: Oxford University Press).

Hussein, Abdullah (1999) *The Weary Generations* [Urdu, *Udas Naslein*], trans. by the author (London: Peter Owen).

Hyder, Qurrutulain (1998) *River of Fire* [Urdu/*Aag ka Dariya*], trans. by the author (Delhi: Kali for Women).

Joshi, Arun (1968) *The Foreigner* (Delhi: Vision/Orient).

—— (1971) *The Strange Case of Billy Biswas* (Delhi: Orient Paperbacks).

Joshi, Ruchir (2001) *The Last Jet Engine Laugh* (London: Flamingo/Harper-Collins).

Kapur, Manju (1998) *Difficult Daughters* (London: Faber).

—— (2002) *A Married Woman* (London: Faber).

—— (2007) *Home* (London: Faber).

Kesavan, Mukul (1996) *Looking Through Glass*, 1st pub. 1994 (London: Vintage).

Khan, Sorayya (2004) *Noor*, 1st pub. 2003 (New Delhi: Penguin).

Kureishi, Hanif (1990) *The Buddha of Suburbia* (London: Faber & Faber).

Lahiri, Jhumpa (2003) *The Namesake* (New York: HarperCollins).

Limbale, Sharankumar (2003) *The Outcaste* [Marathi, *Akkarmashi*], trans. Santosh Bhoomkar (Delhi: Oxford University Press).

Madhaviah, A. (2005) *Muthumeenakshi*, 1st pub. 1903, in *A. Madhaviah: A Biography and a Novella*, trans. Vasantha Surya (Delhi: Oxford University Press).

Manto, Saadat Hasan (2003) 'Cold Meat', in M. U. Memon, *Black Margins* [Urdu, *Siyah Hashiye*], trans. M Asaduddin et al. (Delhi: Katha), 204–11.

Markandaya, Kamala (2005) *Nectar in a Sieve*, 1st pub. 1954 (Delhi: Jaico).

Menon, O. Chandu (2005) *Indulekha*, trans Anitha Devasia. 1st pub. 1889 (Delhi: Oxford University Press).

Mistry, Rohinton (1987) *Tales from Firozshah Baag* (London: Faber & Faber).

—— (1991) *Such a Long Journey* (London: Faber & Faber).

—— (1997) *A Fine Balance*, 1st pub. 1995 (New York: Vintage).

—— (2002) *Family Matters* (London: Faber & Faber).

Morrison, Toni (1987) *Beloved* (New York: Knopf).

Mukherjee, Bharati (1991) *Jasmine*, 1st pub. 1989 (New York: Ballantine).

Nagarajan, Krishnaswamy (1937) *Athawar House* (Madras: Higginbothams).

Nagarkar, Kiran (1995) *Ravan and Eddie* (New Delhi: Penguin).

—— (2004) *Seven Sixes are Forty Three* (Marathi, *Saat Trekkam Trechalis*), trans. S. Subha (New Delhi: Katha).

Nahal, Chaman (2001) *Azadi*, 1st pub. 1975 (New Delhi: Penguin).

Naipaul, V. S. (1962) *The Middle Passage: The Caribbean Revisited* (London: Penguin).

—— (1987) *The Enigma of Arrival* (London: Penguin).

—— (2000) A *House for Mr Biswas*, 1st pub. 1961 (London: Penguin).

—— (2002) *The Mystic Masseur*, 1st pub. 1957 (London: Picador).

—— (2003) *Literary Occasions: Essays*, ed. Pankaj Mishra (London: Picador).

Nambisan, Kavery (1996) *The Scent of Pepper* (New Delhi: Penguin).

Narayan, R. K. (1999) *Waiting for the Mahatma*. 1st pub. 1955 (Chennai: Indian Thought Publications).

—— (2004) *The Guide*, 1st pub. 1958 (Chennai: Indian Thought Publications).

Pande, Ira (2005) *Diddi: My Mother's Voice* (New Delhi: Penguin).

Paul, Joginder (2001) *Sleepwalkers* [Urdu, *Khwabrau*], trans Sunil Trivedi and Sukrita Paul Kumar (New Delhi: Katha).

Premchand (2002) *Godaan* [Hindi, *The Gift of a Cow*], trans. Gordon C. Roadermel, 1st pub. 1968 (Delhi: Permanent Black).

—— *Karmabhumi* (2006) [Hindi/Urdu, *The Field of Action*], trans. Lalit Srivastava (Delhi: Oxford University Press).

Ramabai, Pandita (2000) *Pandita Ramabai Through Her Own Words: Selected Works*, ed. Meera Kosambi (Delhi: Oxford University Press).

Rao, Raja (2004) *Kanthapura*, 1st pub. 1938 (Delhi: Oxford University Press).

Rashsundari Debi (1999) *Amar Jiban* [Bengali, *My Life*, 1st pub. 1897] in Tanika Sarkar, *Words to Win: The Making of Amar Jiban, a Modern Autobiography* (Kali, 1999), 137–213.

Raza, Rahi Masoom (1995) *The Feuding Families of Village Gangauli* [Hindi, *Adha Gaon*], trans. Gillian Wright (New Delhi: Penguin).

Roy, Arundhati (1997) *The God of Small Things* (London: HarperCollins).

Roy, Prafulla (2002) *Set at Odds: Stories of the Partition and Beyond*, trans. John W. Hood (Delhi: Srishti).

Rushdie, Salman (1988) *The Satanic Verses* (New York: Viking).

—— (1989) *Shame*, 1st pub. 1983 (New York: Vintage).

—— (1991*a*) *Midnight's Children*, 1st pub. 1980 (London: Penguin).

—— (1991*b*) *See* Secondary Reading.

—— (1997) *The Moor's Last Sigh*, 1st pub. 1995 (New York: Vintage).

Sahgal, Nayantara (1958) *A Time to be Happy* (London: Gollancz).

—— (1985) *Rich Like Us*, 1st pub. 1985 (London: Heinemann).

Sahni, Bhisham (1988) *Tamas* [Hindi], 1st pub. 1981, trans. Jai Ratan (Delhi: Penguin).

Satthianadhan, Krupabai (1998a) *Kamala: The Story of a Hindu Life*, 1st pub. 1894, ed. Chandani Lokuge (Delhi: Oxford University Press).

—— (1998b) *Saguna: The Story of a Native Christian Life*, 1st pub. 1894, ed. Chandani Lokuge (Delhi: Oxford University Press).

Sealy, I. Allan (1990) *The Trotter-Nama* (London: Penguin).

—— (1991) *Hero: A Fable* (London: Secker & Warburg).

Senapati, Fakir Mohan (2005) *Six Acres and a Third* [Oriya, *Cha Mana Atha Guntha*], trans. Rabi Shankar Mishra et al. (Berkeley and Los Angeles: University of California Press).

Seth, Vikram (2003) *A Suitable Boy*, 1st pub. 1993 (London: Phoenix).

—— (1995) *The Collected Poems* (New Delhi: Penguin).

Shah Nawaz, Mumtaz (2004) *The Heart Divided*, 1st pub. 1957 (New Delhi: Penguin).

Sidhwa, Bapsi (1988) *Ice-Candy-Man* (Oxford: Heinemann).

Singh, Khushwant (1961) *Train to Pakistan*, 1st pub. 1956 (New York: Grove Press).

Sorabji, Cornelia (2001) *India Calling*, 1st pub. 1934 (Delhi: Oxford University Press).

—— (2003) *Love and Life Behind the Purdah*, 1st pub. 1901 (Delhi: Oxford University Press).

Srilata, K. (ed. and trans.) (2003) *The Other Half of the Coconut: Women Writing Self-Respect History* (Delhi: Kali for Women).

Suri, Manil (2001) *The Death of Vishnu* (London: Bloomsbury).

Syal, Meera (1996) *Anita and Me* (London: Flamingo).

Tagore, Rabindranath (1999) *The Home and the World* [Bengali, *Ghare Bhaire*], 1st pub. 1919, trans. Surendranath Tagore (New Delhi: Penguin).

—— (2003) *Four Chapters* [Bengali, *Char Adhyaya*], trans. Rimli Bhattacharya (New Delhi: Srishti).

—— (2005) *Home and the World* [Bengali, *Ghare Bhaire*], trans. Sreejata Guha (Delhi: Penguin).

Tharoor, Shashi (1989) *The Great Indian Novel* (New Delhi: Penguin).

—— (1992) *Show Business* (London: Arcade).

—— (2001) *Riot: A Love Story* (London: Arcade).

Vakil, Ardashir (1997) *Beach Boy* (New Delhi: Penguin).

Vassanji, M. G. (1989) *The Gunny Sack* (Oxford: Heinemann).

—— (2005) *The In-Between World of Vikram Lall*, 1st pub. 2003 (London: Canongate).

—— (2007) *The Assassin's Song* (New Delhi: Penguin/Viking).

Venkataramani, K. S. (1927) *Muragan, the Tiller* (London: Simpkin, Marshall, Hamilton, & Kent).

Venkataramani, K. S. (1934) *Kandan, the Patriot* (Madras: Svetaranya Ashrama).

Zaheer, Sajjad (ed.) (1932) *Angarey* [Urdu, *Live Coals*] (Lucknow: Nizami Press).

SECONDARY READING

Ahmad, Aijaz (1991) *In Theory: Nations, Classes, Literatures* (Delhi: Oxford University Press).

Amin, Shahid (1988) 'Gandhi as Mahatma: Gorakhpur District, Eastern UP, 1921–22' in *Selected Subaltern Studies*, ed. Ranajit Guha and Gayatri Spivak (New York: Oxford University Press), 288–350.

Anand, Mulk Raj (1995) *Conversations in Bloomsbury* (Delhi: Oxford University Press).

Anderson, Benedict (1991) *Imagined Communities: Reflections on the Origin and Spread of Nationalism*, 1st pub. 1983 (London: Verso).

Arunima, G. (2003) *There Comes Papa: Colonialism and the Transformation of Matriliny in Kerala, Malabar* (New Delhi: Orient Longman).

Bagchi, Jasodhara (1994) 'Shakespeare in Loin Cloths: English Literature and the Early Nationalist Consciousness in Bengal', in Joshi (ed.) (1994), 146–59.

Bartolovich, Crystal (2006) 'History After the End of History: Critical Counterfactualism and Revolution', *New Formations* 59: 63–80.

Bayly, C. A. (1998) *Origins of Nationality in South Asia: Patriotism and Ethical Government in the Making of Modern India* (Delhi: Oxford University Press).

Bhabha, Homi K. (ed.) (1990) *Nation and Narration* (London: Routledge).

Bhagwat, Vidyut (1995) 'Bombay in Dalit Literature', in Patel and Thorner (eds.) (1995*b*), 113–25.

Brennan, Timothy (1990) 'The National Longing for Form', in Bhabha (ed.) (1990), 44–71.

Buford, Bill (1997) 'Declarations of Independence', in *New Yorker*, 23 and 30 June.

Butalia, Urvashi (1998) *The Other Side of Silence: Voices from the Partition of India* (New Delhi: Penguin).

—— (2000) 'Community, State, and Gender: Some Reflections on the Partition of India', in Hasan (ed.), (2000), 178–207.

Chakravarty, Gautam (2005) *The Indian Mutiny and the British Imagination* (Cambridge: Cambridge University Press).

Chandra, Bipan (1971) *Modern India* (New Delhi: National Council of Educational Research and Training).

Chandra, Sudhir (1992) *The Oppressive Present: Literature and Social Consciousness in Colonial India* (Delhi: Oxford University Press).

—— (1994) *The Oppressive Present: Literature and Social Consciousness in Colonial India* (Delhi: Oxford University Press).

Chatterjee, Partha (1993) *Nationalist Thought in the Colonial World: A Derivative Discourse*, 1st pub. 1986 (Minneapolis: University of Minnesota Press).

Cohn, Bernard S. (2002) *Colonialism and its Forms of Knowledge: The British in India*, 1st pub. 1996 (Delhi: Oxford University Press).

Dalmia, Manju (1992) 'Derozio: English Teacher', in Sunder Rajan (ed.), (1992), 42–62.

Daniel, E. Valentine (1996) *Charred Lullabies: Chapters in an Anthropography of Violence* (Princeton, NJ: Princeton University Press).

Das, Sisir Kumar (1991) *A History of Indian Literature, 1810–1910* (Delhi: Sahitya Akademi).

—— (1995) *A History of Indian Literature, 1911–1956* (Delhi: Sahitya Akademi).

Das Gupta, R. K. (ed.) (1980) *Poems of H. L. V. Derozio, a Forgotten Anglo-Indian Poet* (Calcutta: Oxford University Press).

Datta, P. K. (ed.) (2003) *Rabindranath Tagore's The Home and the World: A Critical Companion* (Delhi: Permanent Black).

Desai, Anita (1992) 'Introduction', in *Sunlight on a Broken Column*, 1st pub. 1988 (New Delhi: Penguin).

De Souza, Eunice (2004) *Purdah: An Anthology* (Delhi: Oxford University Press).

Dingwaney Needham, Anuradha (2005) ' "The Small Voice of History" in *The God of Small Things*', *Interventions* 7/3: 369–91.

Edney, Matthew H. (1997) *Mapping an Empire: The Geographical Construction of British India, 1765–1843* (Chicago: University of Chicago Press).

Fanon, Frantz (1963) *The Wretched of the Earth*, trans. Constance Farrington (New York: Grove).

—— (1965) 'Medicine and Colonialism', in *A Dying Colonialism*, trans. Haakon Chevalier (New York: Grove).

Fisher, Michael H. (1996) *The First Indian Author in English: Dean Mahomed (1751–1851) in India, Ireland and England* (Delhi: Oxford University Press).

Forster, E. M. (2001) 'Preface', in Mulk Raj Anand, *Untouchable*, 1st pub. 1935 (New Delhi: Penguin).

Francisco, Jason (2000) 'In the Heat of Fratricide: The Literature of India's Partition Burning Freshly', in Hasan (ed.) (2000), 371–93.

Frankel, Francine (1978) *India's Political Economy 1947–1977: The Gradual Revolution* (Princeton, NJ: Princeton University Press).

Gandhi, M. K. (1997) *Hind Swaraj and Other Writings*, ed. Anthony J. Parel (Cambridge: Cambridge University Press).

Ghosh, Amitav (2002) *The Imam and the Indian: Prose Pieces* (New Delhi: Permanent Black).

Gopal, Priyamvada (2001) ' "Curious Ironies": Matter and Meaning in Bhabhani Bhattacharya's Novel of the 1943 Bengal Famine', *ARIEL* 32/3: 61–90.

Gorra, Michael (1997) *After Empire: Scott, Naipaul, Rushdie* (Chicago and London: University of Chicago Press).

Guha, Ranajit (1987) 'Chandra's Death', in Ranajit Guha (ed.), *Subaltern Studies*, v. *Writings on South Asian History and Society* (Delhi: Oxford University Press), 135–65.

—— (1996) 'The Small Voice of History', in Shahid Amin and Dipesh Chakrabarty (eds.), *Subaltern Studies*, ix. *Writings on South Asian History and Society* (Delhi: Oxford University Press), 1–12.

—— (2003) *History at the Limit of World History* (Delhi: Oxford University Press).

Hasan, Mushirul (ed.) (2000) *Inventing Boundaries: Gender, Politics and the Partition of India* (Delhi: Oxford University Press).

Holmstrom, Lakshmi (1983) *The Novels of R. K. Narayan* (Calcutta: Writers' Workshop).

Hutcheon, Linda (1989) *The Politics of Postmodernism* (London: Routledge).

Iyengar, K. R. Srinivasa (1985) *Indian Writing in English*, 1st pub. 1962 (New Delhi: Sterling).

Jalal, Ayesha (2001) *Self and Sovereignty: Individual and Community in South Asia Islam since 1850* (New Delhi: Oxford University Press).

Jameson, Fredric (1986) 'Third World Literature in the Era of Multinational Capitalism' in *Social Text* 15: 65–8.

Joshi, Ruchir (2000) 'The Air Beneath his Feet', on <Tehelka.com> (accessed 15 Nov. 2000).

Joshi, Sanjay (2001) *Fractured Modernities: Making of a Middle Class in Colonial North India* (Delhi: Oxford University Press).

Joshi, Svati (ed.) (1994) *Rethinking English: Essays in Literature, Language, History* (Delhi: Oxford University Press).

Kamleshwar (2000) *Kitne Pakistan?* (Delhi: Rajpal).

Kananayagam, Chelva (2002) 'H. Hatterr and Sauce Anglaise G. V. Desani', in *Counterrealism in Indo-Anglian Fiction* (Ontario: Wilfred Laurier University Press), 51–74.

Kaviraj, Sudipta (1992) 'The Imaginary Institution of India', in G. Pandey and P. Chatterjee (eds.), *Subaltern Studies*, vii. *Writings on South Asian History and Society* (Delhi: Oxford University Press).

—— (1998) 'The Culture of Representative Democracy' in Partha Chatterjee (ed.), *Wages of Freedom: Fifty Years of the Indian Nation-State* (Delhi: Oxford University Press).

Kesavan, Mukul (2001) *Secular Common Sense* (New Delhi: Penguin).

Khair, Tabish (2001) *Babu Fictions: Alienation in Contemporary Indian English Novels* (Delhi: Oxford University Press).

Khilnani, Sunil (1997) *The Idea of India* (London: Penguin).

Kopf, David (1969) *British Orientalism and the Bengal Renaissance* (Berkeley and Los Angeles: University of California Press).

Kosambi, Meera (1986) *Bombay in Transition: The Growth and Social Ecology of a Colonial City, 1880–1980* (Stockholm: Almqvist & Wicksell International).

Kudchekar, Shirin (1995) 'Poetry and the City', in Patel and Thorner (eds.) (1995*a*): 126–62.

Kumar, Krishna (2003) 'Foreword', in Shah Nawaz (2004: pp. v–vi).

Kumar, Radha (1993) *The History of Doing: An Illustrated Account of Movements for Women's Rights and Feminism in India, 1800–1990* (New Delhi: Kali for Women).

Larsen, Neil (2001) *Determinations: Essays on Theory, Narrative and Nation in the Americas* (London: Verso).

Lazarus, Neil (1990) *Resistance in Postcolonial African Fiction* (New Haven, Conn.: Yale University Press).

Lokuge, Chandani (1998*a*) 'Introduction' in Satthianadhan (1998*a*), 1–16.

—— (1998*b*) 'Introduction' in Satthianadhan (1998*b*), 1–16.

Macaulay, Thomas Babington (1995) 'Minute on Indian Education', in Bill Ashcroft et al. (eds.), *The Postcolonial Studies Reader* (London: Routledge).

Mee, Jon (2003) 'After Midnight: The Novel in the 1980s and 1990s', in A. K. Mehrotra (ed.), *A History of Indian Literature in English* (London: Hurst).

Mehrotra, A. K. (ed.) (2003) *A History of Indian Literature in English* (London: Hurst).

Menon, Ritu, and Bhasin, Kamla (1998) *Borders and Boundaries: Women in India's Partition* (New Delhi: Kali; Brunswick, NJ: Rutgers University Press).

Mill, James (1997) *A History of British India*, 10 vols. 1st pub. 1858, ed. Horace H. Wilson (London: Routledge/Thoemmes).

Mishra, Pankaj (2000) 'Little Inkling—Writing in English, the Indian Elite Discovers Nothing', *Outlook*, 17 Jan.

Mohanty, Satya P. (2005) 'Introduction', in Senapati (2005).

Mukherjee Meenakshi (1971) *The Twice Born Fiction* (New Delhi: Arnold Heinemann).

—— (1985) *Realism and Reality: The Novel and Society in India* (Delhi: Oxford University Press).

Mukherjee Meenakshi (2005) 'Afterword', in Chatterjee (2005).

—— (2000) *The Perishable Empire: Essays on Indian Writing in English* (Delhi: Oxford University Press).

Mukherji, Sajni Kripalani (2003) 'The Hindu College: Henry DeRozio and Michael Madhusudhan Dutt', in A. K. Mehrotra (ed.), *A History of Indian Literature in English* (London: Hurst), 41–52.

Mukhopadhyay, Maitrayee (1994) 'Between Community and State: The Question of Women's Rights and Personal Laws', in Zoya Hasan (ed.) *Forging Identities: Gender, Communities and the State* (New Delhi: Kali for Women).

Myers, Juliet (1996) 'Postmodernism in Rushdie's *Midnight's Children* and *The Moor's Last Sigh*'. <http://art.man.ac.uk/English/MS/rushdie/htm>. From *Manuscript* 1/2, Spring 1996; accessed January 2004.

Nandan, Satendra (2001) 'The Adventure of Indenture: a Diasporic Identity', in Makarand Paranjape (ed.), *In-Diaspora: Theories, Histories, Texts* (New Delhi: Indialog Publications).

Nehru, Jawaharlal (1983) *Jawaharlal Nehru: An Anthology*, ed. S. Gopal (Delhi: Oxford University Press).

—— (2002) *The Discovery of India*, 1st pub. 1946 (Delhi: Oxford University Press).

Paranjape, Makarand (1990) 'Politics and the New Indian English Novel', in V. Kirpal (ed.), *The New Indian Novel in English* (Bombay: Allied Publishers).

Patel, Sujata (2003) 'Bombay and Mumbai: Identities, Politics and Populism', in Patel and Masselos (eds.) (2003), 3–30.

—— and Masselos, Jim (eds.) (2003) *Bombay and Mumbai: The City in Transition* (Delhi: Oxford University Press).

—— and Thorner, Alice (eds.) (1995a) *Bombay: Mosaic of Modern Culture* (Delhi: Oxford University Press).

—— —— (1995b) *Bombay: Metaphor for Modern India* (Delhi: Oxford University Press).

Paul Kumar, Sukrita (2004) *Narrating Partition: Texts, Interpretations, Ideas* (Delhi: Indialog).

Pendse, Sandeep (1995) 'Toil, Sweat and the City', in Patel and Thorner (eds.) (1995b).

Price, D. W. (1994) 'Salman Rushdie's "Use and Abuse of History" in *Midnight's Children*', *ARIEL* 25/2.

Puri, Anjali (2008) 'English Speaking Curse', *Outlook*, 24 March.

Rai, Alok (2000) 'The Trauma of Independence: Some Aspects of Progressive Hindi Literature, 1945–7', in Hasan (ed.) (2000), 351–70.

Ramanujan, A. K. (1989) 'Afterword', in Murthy (1989), 139–47.

Rau, Santha Rama (1945) *Home to India* (London: Harper Bros.).

Ravikant and Tarun K. Saint (eds.) (2001) *Translating Partition* (New Delhi: Katha).

Rushdie, Salman (1991a) *See* Primary Texts.

—— (1991b) *Imaginary Homelands: Essays and Criticism 1981–1991* (London: Granta/Penguin).

—— (1994) *East, West* (London: Jonathan Cape).

—— (1997) 'Damme, this is the Oriental Scene for You', in The *New Yorker*, (23 and 30 June), pp. 50–61. Reprinted in Rushdie and West (1997).

—— and West, Elizabeth (eds.) (1997), *The Vintage Book of Indian Writing* (New York: Vintage Books).

—— (n.d.) 'Interview' on http://www.salon.com/06/features/interview2.html, accessed March 2008.

Said, Edward W. (1991) 'Secular Criticism', in *The World, the Text and the Critic* (New York: Vintage).

Sandhu, Sukhdev (2003) *London Calling: How Black and Asian Writers Imagined a City* (London: Harper Perennial).

Sarkar, Sumit (1983) *Modern India: 1885–1947* (New Delhi: Macmillan).

—— (1987) 'The Kalki-Avatar of Bikrampur: A Village Scandal in Early Twentieth Century Bengal', in Guha (ed.) (1987).

Sarkar, Tanika (2001) *Hindu Wife, Hindu Nation: Community, Religion and Cultural Nationalism* (New Delhi: Permanent Black).

—— (2003) 'Many Faces of Love: Country, Woman, and God in The Home and the World', in Datta (ed.) (2003), 27–45.

Seabrook, Jeremy (1987) *Life and Labour in a Bombay Slum* (London: Quartet).

Sen, Amartya (2005) *The Argumentative Indian: Writings on Indian History, Culture and Identity* (London: Allen Lane).

Shahani, Roshan G. (1995) 'Polyphonous Voices in the City: Bombay's Indian-English Fiction' in Patel and Thorner (eds.) (1995a), 99–112.

Singh, Sujala (2000) 'Secularist Faith in Salman Rushdie's Midnight's Children,' *New Formations*, 41.

Sommer, Doris (1991) *Foundational Fictions: The National Romances of Latin America* (Berkeley: University of California Press).

Spear, Percival (1965) A History of India *(Baltimore, Md.: Penguin), ii.*

Sprinker, Michael (2003) 'Homeboys: Nationalism, Colonialism and Gender in the Home and the World', in Datta (ed.) (2003), 107–26.

Sunder Rajan, Rajeswari (ed.) (1992) *The Lie of the Land: English Literary Studies in India* (Delhi: Oxford University Press).

Swami, Praveen (1997) ' "A Tiger Woodsian Debut": Arundhati Roy's Novel Goes International', *Frontline* (8 August), 100–2.

Tagore, Rabindranath (1994) *Nationalism*, 1st pub. 1917 (Delhi: Rupa Books).

Tharu, Susie, and Lalita, K. (1991) *Women Writing in India* (New York: Feminist Press).

—— (1993) *Women Writing in India*, ii. *The Twentieth Century* (New York: Feminist Press).

Viswanathan, Gauri (1989) *Masks of Conquest: Literary Study and British Rule in India* (New York: Columbia University Press).

Wainwright, Hillary (1994). *Arguments for a New Left: Answering the Free Market Right* (London: Blackwell).

Warnes, Christopher (2005) 'Naturalizing the Supernatural: Faith, Irreverence and Magical Realism', in *Literature Compass* 2: 1–16.

Waugh, Patricia (1984) *Metafiction: The Theory and Practice of Self-Conscious Fiction*, 1st pub. 2003 (London: Routledge).

Yuval-Davis, Nira, and Anthias, Floya (eds.) (1989) *Women-Nation-State* (New York: St Martin's Press).

Zelliot, Eleanor, and Karve, Jayant (1982) 'Their Eternal Pity', *Journal of South Asian Literature*, 18: 98.

INDEX

affiliation 97
afsana 73, 143
ahimsa 44, 56
Ali, Ahmad 144–5
   Twilight in Delhi 144–5
allegory 59; 68, 91, 106 (*see also*
   national allegory)
allegorical 23, 32, 33, 67, 78, 81, 95
Anand, Mulk Raj 4, 50–4, 92, 104
   Untouchable 50–4, 55
Anderson, Benedict 11, 13, 56
Angarey 145
Anglicism 15, 17
Anglicists 14
anthropology 71, 87–8, 142
anti-colonial 13, 14, 27, 32, 35, 45,
   62, 64, 74, 173

Babri mosque 131, 132, 187
Bangladesh 76, 81, 94, 103, 182
Bengal Famine 61–2
Bengal Renaissance 17–18
Bengal 12, 17, 19, 25–7, 29, 32, 33,
   35, 39, 63, 70, 78
Bengali 17, 19, 26, 27, 30, 31, 34, 36,
   38, 39–0, 181, 184
Bharatiya Janata Party (BJP) 178, 185
bhasha literature 2
Bhattacharya, Bhabhani 61–3
   He Who Rides a Tiger 61–3
   So Many Hungers 61
Bombay 12, 94, 116–38, 139, 165, 167,
   168–9, 173

Booker Prize 1, 4, 91, 106, 155, 183
brahmin 62, 63, 137

Calcutta 17, 32, 62, 82, 107, 116, 128,
   145, 186
caste 44, 47, 48, 50, 52, 54, 62, 63, 109,
   110, 111, 117, 121, 122, 124, 137, 158,
   see also Dalits
Chatterjee, Bankim Chandra 29–33,
   140
   Anandamath 30–3
   Rajmohan's Wife 29–30
Chatterjee, Partha 11, 44
Chaudhuri, Amit 186–7
   Freedom Song 186–7
chauvinism 83, 118, 133, 137, 150, 173,
   178, *see also* Hindutva
child(ren) 22, 32, 75–6, 77–8, 91, 96,
   97, 99, 100, 101, 105, 116, 124, 129,
   134, 148, 149, 153, 156, 158, 165,
   166, 172, 173
Christianity 41
Christian(s) 28, 40, 41–2, 117, 131
Chughtai, Ismat 104, 141, 142
cinematic 59, 122, 126, *see also* Hindi
   film
citizen(s) 56, 66, 103, 119
Citizenship 119
city 17, 29, 48, 61 62, 116–18, 121–5,
   129–30, 132, 135, 136, 137, 144, 145,
   146, 147, 150, 154, 165, 168, 169,
   173, *see also* Bombay, Calcutta
   and Delhi

class 4, 16, 17, 27, 55, 64, 66, 96, 107,
111, 117, 121, 124, 143; middle- 6,
17, 35, 36, 105, 108–11, 123–24,
151–2, 183, 186; upper- 72, 76,
130, 140, 141, 142
Cohn, Bernard 15
colonialism 16, 19, 28, 33, 35, 38, 83,
87, 92, 165, 183
colonial discourse 14, 16, 28, 92
communal tensions 118, 126, 177, 185
communal violence 35, 69, 122, 126,
147, 181
critical realism 98

Dalits 50
Dalit literature 124
David, Esther 146
The Walled City 145–8
Day, Lal Behari 25–8
*Govinda Samanta, or Bengal
Peasant Life* 25–8, 29
Deb, Siddharta 181–2
Point of Return 181–2
Delhi 65, 94, 144–5, 153–5, 169, 181
Derozio, Henry Vivian 18
Desai, Anita 1, 140–3, 126–7, 151–5
Baumgartner's Bombay 126–8
Clear Light of Day 153–5
Fire on the Mountain 152–3
Desai, Kiran 183
The Inheritance of Loss 183–4
Desani, G. V. 92–3
All about H Hatterr 92–3
de Souza, Eunice 145–8
The Walled City 145–8
Deshpande, Shashi 141, 151
domesticity 74, 139, 153, 175
domestic sphere 28–9, 40, 111, 144
Dutt, Michael Madhusudhan 18,
19, 31
Dutt, K. C. 21
Dutt, Soshee Chunder 20–4

Republic of Orissa 21
Shunkur 21–4, 32
Dutt, Toru 40

East India company 12, 15, 17, 117
Emergency 65–8, 94, 99, 119, 123
empire 6, 7, 21, 22, 66, 87
English in India 2, 3, 4–5, 13, 15,
16, 26, 27, 45, 46, 48, 114, 118,
186, 187
English literature 15, 18, 64
epic 67, 70, 82, 90, 91, 99, 104, 106,
121, 122, 124, 134, 139, 155, 156,
160, 169
ethnography 21, 25, 26, 52, 71, 92
exile 30, 127, 152, 165, 173, 180, 181, 182

Faiz, Faiz Ahmad 70, 90
family 42, 65, 77, 82, 85, 91, 93, 94, 97,
100, 106, 109, 111, 119, 125, 130,
131, 139–59, 164, 173, 177
family saga 91, 94, 97, 106, 111
Fanon, Frantz 113, 169
filiation 97
food 59, 62, 81, 99–100, 153
freedom 13, 21, 39, 42, 44, 45, 53, 55,
56, 61, 63, 64, 65, 66, 68, 73, 74,
75, 90, 106, 132, 137, 148–9, 172,
173, 175, 179, 185
Futehally, Shama 118, 185
Tara Lane 129–30
Reaching Bombay Central 185–6

Gandhi, Indira 65, 94, 97, 103, 119,
120, 122
Gandhi, M. K. 43–68, 78, 80, 83, 84,
134, 163, 180
gender 7, 29, 31, 34, 40, 72, 140
Ghosh, Amitav
In an Antique Land 86–9
The Hungry Tide 184–5
The Shadow Lines 81–2, 181

girmit diaspora 162
Guha, Ranajit 13, 14, 19–20, 123, 157

Hariharan, Gita 177–9
    In Times of Siege 177–9
Hegel, G. W. F. 13–14, 37, 47
heterodoxy 88, 120
Hindi 3, 70, 74, 114, 184
Hindi film 91, 105, 117, 122, 135, 136
Hindu College 17–19
Hindu 14, 17, 18, 19, 29, 32, 33, 41, 42,
        48, 49, 50, 52, 73, 74, 75, 83,
        85, 88, 109–15, 131, 132, 136,
        137, 143, 147, 148, 165, 172,
        177, 179, 180, 186
    legend 14, 47
    mythology 91, 125, 126
    nationalism 35, 37
    reformers 34
    tradition 18
    women 28, 137, 175
historiography 86, 101, 157
Hosain, Attia 140–5
    *Sunlight on a Broken
        Column* 140–4

indenture 161–5, 173
Independence 44, 45, 47, 55, 57, 63,
        64, 65, 68, 69, 70, 72, 84, 85, 90,
        91, 94, 95, 103, 106, 108, 111, 112,
        113, 116, 117, 119, 122, 129, 141, 148,
        172, 173, 180, 181
Indian English 92, 133, 137, 152
Indian National Congress (INC) 31,
        70, 83, 85, 114
Indian People's Theatre Association
        (IPTA) 104
Islam 18, 33, 85, 86, 167, *see also*
        Muslims

Jews 66, 117, 134, 146, 147
Jewishness 127, 146, 147

Jones, Sir William 14, 15
Judaism 88

Kapur, Manju 148–9
    Difficult Daughters 148–9
Kashmir 94
Kesavan, Mukul 83–5, 186
    Looking through Glass 83–6
Khan, Sorayya 75–7
    Noor 75–8
Kureishi, Hanif 170–1
    The Buddha of Suburbia 170–2

London 50, 110, 166, 168–70, 173, 174

Macaulay, Thomas Babington 15–16,
        18, 45
magical realism 20, 100, 156
The Mahabharata 19, 67, 91, 125, 169
majoritarianism 84, 133, 137, 178
Malgudi 54–8
Manto, Saadat Hasan 70, 76, 80, 88,
        91, 104
masculinity 38
memory 76, 79, 80, 99, 102, 157, 158,
        180, 182
metafiction 101; historiographic 101
Migration 29, 90, 122, 160–76, 184
migrants 79, 80, 117, 166, 168, 170, 183
Mill, J. S. 14, 19, 20, 25, 47
minorities 115, 119. 120, 121, 131, 133,
        136, 140
'Minute on Indian Education' 16
Mistry, Rohinton 118–21, 123–5,
        149–51
    Family Matters 149–1
    A Fine Balance 121–5
    Such a Long Journey 119–21
modernity 5, 11, 13, 17, 18–19, 44,
        47, 53, 107–10, 111, 114, 116,
        140, 148
Mother India 32, 35, 120, 134

Mukherjee, Bharati 174–6
 Jasmine 124–6
Muslim League 69, 72, 74, 85, 86
Muslims 18, 32, 33, 34, 48, 69, 72–4,
  75, 83–6, 88, 110, 112, 114, 118, 129,
  131, 139, 140–6, 171, 180, 185

Nagarkar, Kiran 2, 135–7
 Ravan and Eddie 135–7
Naipaul, V. S. 1, 162–5, 172
 A House for Mr Biswas 162–5, 172
Narayan, R. K. 46, 54–60
 The Guide 57–60
 Waiting for the Mahatma 54–7
'national allegory' 96, 112
nationalism 6, 11, 12, 18, 19, 31–4,
  35–9, 44, 45, 55, 61, 74, 84, 85, 90,
  103, 173, 178, 180, see also Hindu
  nationalism
nationalitarians 74
Nehru, Jawarharlal 5, 43, 85, 90, 92,
  94, 97, 112, 132, 134, 163, 180
non-violence 44, 47, 55–6, 68, 69

Orientalists 14–15, 26

Pakistan 7, 12, 69, 71, 72–4, 77,
  78–80, 81, 84, 86, 94, 128, 141,
  143, 182
Parsi(s) 75, 110, 118, 119, 121, 147,
  149–51
Partition 43, 68, 69–89, 90, 104, 106,
  110, 122, 128, 141, 143, 150, 154, 181
A Passage to India 51, 127
pastoral 129–30
poetry 3, 14, 18, 20, 37, 106, 114, 119,
  145, 179, 180, 184; Romantic 30,
  41
poverty 116, 117, 119, 123, 124, 132
Progressive Writers Association
  (PWA) 4, 50, 52, 53, 142, 145

prose 1, 3, 4, 7, 13, 14, 17, 20, 25, 26,
  27, 30, 31, 33, 45, 70, 91

The Ramayana 19, 91
Rao, Raja 27, 46–9
 Kanthapura 27, 46–9
Debi, Rassundari 40, 153
realism 20, 26, 52, 79, 92, 105, 106,
  122, 156, see also critical realism
  and magical realism
religion 34, 41, 44, 49, 50, 58, 88, 90,
  94, 142, 150, 151, 178
religiosity 49, 53, 55, 59
romance 22, 29, 30, 72–4, 109, 129,
  143, 145
Roy, Arundhati 1, 155–9
 The God of Small Things 155–9
Rushdie, Salman 1–5, 29, 78–81,
  90–105, 113, 116, 117, 118, 119,
  131–5, 146, 156, 161, 165–70,
  186
 Midnight's Children 6, 78, 82, 83,
  90–105, 116, 119, 131–2, 135, 180
 Shame 77, 78–81, 89, 134
 The Moor's Last Sigh 130–5,
 The Satanic Verses 165–70, 180

Sahgal, Nayantara 63–7
 Rich Like Us 63–4
 A Time to be Happy 64–7
Said, Edward W. 97
Sanskrit 15, 26, 27, 92, 137
satire 22, 91, 97, 104, 135, 136, 165,
  167, 171
Satthianadhan, Krupabai 40–2
 Kamala 40–2
 Saguna 40–1
Sealy, I.Allan 6, 93–4
 The Trotter Nama 6, 93
secularism 33, 72, 83–5, 97, 108, 109,
  120, 133, 135, 136, 150, 151, 177, 180

self-fashioning 17, 57, 59, 60, 105–11
sex 30, 35, 38, 158, 170
    sexual politics 34
Shah Nawaz, Mumtaz 72–4
    The Heart Divided 72–4
Shakespeare 12, 134
Sidhwa, Bapsi 75–6, 119
    Ice-Candy Man 75–6
Sikhs 69, 72, 176, 122
Singh, Khushwant 70–2
    Train to Pakistan 70–2
slums 65, 96, 104, 121, 129, 150
socialism 66–7, 94, 97, 119,
    130, 186
socialists 50, 114
Sorabji, Cornelia 40
South Asia 12
subalterns 63, 125, 126, 152, 157, 184,
    185; subaltern history 114, 123
Suri, Manil 125–6
    The Death of Vishnu 125–6
Swadeshi 34

Tagore, Rabindranath 31, 33, 34–9,
    74, 127, 139, 140, 162
    The Home and the World 34–9
Tharoor, Shashi 67–8, 91

The Great Indian Novel 67–8
    translation 4, 26, 36, 134, 184–5

United States of America 119,
    174–6, 183
'untouchables' 44 47, 50, 52, 53, 137,
    158
Urdu 70, 73, 80, 106, 139, 141, 142, 145

Vassanji, M. G. 172–4, 176,
    179–81, 182
    The Assassin's Song 179–81
    *The In-Between World of Vikram
    Lall* 172–4
villages 26–9, 46, 47–9, 55–7, 59, 61,
    64, 71, 107, 124, 153, 182 and
    'Indian Village Time' 47
violence 37, 71, 76, 77, 78, 80, 83, 103,
    121, 123, 126, 128 147, 168, 169
    communal 68, 69, 70, 122, 179, 181
    'pornography of' 71, 75
    sexual 75, 79, 81

Young Bengal 18

zamindars 27, 35
zamindari 27, 108